Praise for *Learning Personalized*

"Everyone talks about personalization as a goal but few people have visualized what it can realistically mean. Allison Zmuda, Diane Ullman, and Greg Curtis have done a masterful job of helping us move beyond platitudes toward schooling that really honors learners' right to a personalized education."

—Grant Wiggins, president, Authentic Education

"This important book helps educators go beyond 'personalized learning' as a buzzword to make it a reality in every classroom. An essential tool for every teacher."

—Tony Wagner, author of *The Global Achievement Gap* and *Creating Innovators*

"What a timely book! Educators are struggling with how to make a jump from the more traditional curriculum to one that fosters innovation, collaboration, and rigorous thinking. The authors offer practical strategies, case studies, and numerous charts to help teachers make that transition."

—Bena Kallick, educational consultant; cofounder and director, Institute for Habits of Mind

"In the 21st Century, every student needs to be self-directed and self-managed. That's why the time for 'personalized learning' has finally come. Unfortunately, people use the phrase 'personalized learning' without having a common understanding of its elements and milestones. My suggestion: Do not use this term again until you read this book!"

—Ken Kay, chief executive officer, EdLeader21; founding president, Partnership for 21st Century Skills; coauthor, with Valerie Greenhill, of *The Leader's Guide to 21st Century Education: 7 Steps for Schools and*

"For educators who want to invest in personalized learning to more deeply engage and challenge students, this book offers a balanced overview of the terrain, as well as clear and helpful definitions, structures, and strategies. It rejects the all-or-nothing dichotomy of individualized versus collaborative learning and shares multiple pathways for personalized learning to be woven into the fabric of schools."

—Ron Berger, chief academic officer, Expeditionary Learning

LEARNING
PERSONALIZED

LEARNING PERSONALIZED

The Evolution of the Contemporary Classroom

Allison Zmuda
Greg Curtis
Diane Ullman

Foreword by Heidi Hayes Jacobs

A Wiley Brand

Published by Jossey-Bass
A Wiley Brand
One Montgomery Street, Suite 1200, San Francisco, CA 94104-4594—www.josseybass.com

Jossey-Bass books and products are available through most bookstores. To contact Jossey-Bass directly call our Customer Care Department within the U.S. at 800-956-7739, outside the U.S. at 317-572-3986, or fax 317-572-4002.

Wiley publishes in a variety of print and electronic formats and by print-on-demand. Some material included with standard print versions of this book may not be included in e-books or in print-on-demand. If this book refers to media such as a CD or DVD that is not included in the version you purchased, you may download this material at http://booksupport.wiley.com. For more information about Wiley products, visit www.wiley.com.

Library of Congress Cataloging-in-Publication Data is on file.

ISBN 978-1-118-90479-4 (pbk.)
ISBN 978-1-118-90481-7 (ebk.)
ISBN 978-1-118-90483-1 (ebk.)

Printed in the United States of America

FIRST EDITION

PB Printing   10 9 8 7 6 5 4 3

Contents

Foreword   xi

Acknowledgments   xv

About the Authors   xvii

Introduction   1

1 Making the Case for Personalized Learning   **5**

Disconnect between Traditional School and Preparation for a
     Postsecondary World   6

The Power of a Student-Driven Model   7

Contemporary Issues of Control   12

Personalized Learning Evolution   15

Conclusion and Reflective Questions   21

Works Cited   21

2 The Aims of Contemporary Schooling   **23**

Element 1: Disciplinary Outcomes   25

Element 2: Cross-Disciplinary Outcomes   30

Element 3: Mindsets   47

Conclusion and Reflective Questions   55

Works Cited   56

3 The Design of a Student-Driven Learning Experience   **59**

Element 4: Task   60

Element 5: Audience   63

Element 6: Feedback   67

Element 7: Evaluation   70

Conclusion and Reflective Questions   72

Works Cited   73

4 Tasks That Demonstrate Personalized Learning Evolution in Practice   **75**

Inspiration for Task Designs   76

How the Role of the Teacher Shifts   95

How the Role of the Student Shifts   103

Needed Systems and Supports beyond the Classroom   104

Conclusion and Reflective Questions   107

Work Cited   108

5 What Personalized Learning Looks Like at the Instructional Level   **109**

Element 8: Process   110

Element 9: Environment   119

A Day-in-the-Life Narrative   124

Conclusion and Reflective Questions   128

Work Cited   129

6 What Personalized Learning Looks Like at the Systems Level   **131**

Element 10: Demonstration of Learning   132

Element 11: Time   143

Element 12: Advancement   145

Conclusion and Reflective Questions   147

Works Cited   147

7 Leading the Change for Personalized Learning   **149**

Clearly Articulating and Creating Urgency for Personalized Learning
(the "Why")   150

Giving Back the Work to Teachers (the "How")   152

Managing Change as It Is Occurring (the "What")   155

Conclusion and Reflective Questions   160

Works Cited   161

The Conclusion of the Era of "One-Size-Fits-All Schooling"   **163**

Appendix A: Additional Resources for Chapters 1–3   **165**

Appendix B: Additional Resources for Chapter 4   **181**

Appendix C: Additional Resources for Chapters 5 and 6   **193**

Appendix D: Additional Resources for Chapter 7   **203**

Index   209

To Jay McTighe — a connector of people and ideas. You open the door and show the vision of what schools can be and welcome people to join you in that pursuit.

Foreword

A learning rush of digital media and global access is seeping into our classrooms, bringing remarkable possibilities and genuine challenges. Certainly most teachers and school leadership are attempting to adjust to the reality that this is a new time requiring new approaches. Yet, without doubt, it is our learners who have already made the transition and in many ways are actually waiting for school to catch up with them.

It seems reasonable to assume that educators throughout the world acknowledge that our teaching approaches are in need of an upgrade. Curriculum and assessment design must reflect contemporary choices if they are to be relevant; otherwise, our students are mired in the past. The question is, How do we make a shift that is responsive to new kinds of learning?

Personalized learning is a viable and dynamic answer. As a burgeoning field of practice, personalized learning has also been in need of operational definition. The term *personalized learning* has been used perhaps too broadly to cover a whole host of strategies and values. You have in your hands a book providing the very definition we need. *Learning Personalized: The Evolution of a Contemporary Classroom* provides clarity, insight, and direction for educators committed to implementing programs that engage students in directing their own learning. Three exceptionally talented and experienced educators, Allison Zmuda, Greg Curtis, and Diane Ullman, have collaborated brilliantly in generating new concepts that can inform our actions.

They begin the book with a logical and provocative case for employing personalized learning as an antidote to the inherent boredom of disengaged learners. What is more, they have generated a genuine breakthrough in their detailed analysis of differentiated instruction, individualized instruction, and personalized learning. By extracting the distinctions between these three concepts and the significant implications for implementation of each, the authors have contributed to program decision making. As readers, we see what is possible when learners become self-navigators in determining problems for investigation and projects.

With the potential of becoming a curriculum classic, the authors' design model is based on six elements: disciplinary outcomes, cross-disciplinary outcomes, mindsets, task design, audience, and feedback. They detail how each of these elements "evolves" from the old-style teacher determined and controlled to student-driven direction with the thoughtful guidance of teachers. Strategies and essential questions to garner creative input and involvement are laced throughout the chapters. It is here that we see a genuine revolution afoot.

The questions the authors ask us to pose when designing tasks will directly engage learners in determining demonstrations of their own learning: *What is the challenge? Who is the audience? How does that affect communication? How do students use feedback?* What is more, they lay out how the implementation of this design model can and should shift the roles of teacher and student. There is emerging and refreshed pedagogy on these pages.

Grounded in the reality of school life, the authors have provided abundant examples of effective personalized learning. Whether it is a unit on the laws of motion in a physics class or primary-level children researching different types of insects, the revision to personalization is clearly illustrated with specificity. The implications for instructional strategies and delivery are examined through the elements of environment and process with insightful "day-in-the-life" narratives. Not only in the curriculum and instruction chapters of the book but throughout is the extensive use of accessible tables to quickly inform the reader about the critical points regarding practice. These charts are anchors in particular as the authors ask us to consider the big picture of implementing on the school and district levels.

In a very real sense, the authors are asking institutions to shift significantly to sustain personalized learning beyond the initial euphoria and excitement of a genuinely new direction for education. Central to the examination of the challenges of this new movement is the critical chapter of the book focused on personalized learning on the systems level. The issues of how to liberate teachers and support their roles in shaping learning are akin to the issues raised about our students. In a very real way, a school needs to undertake its own form of personalized learning as an institution. It is why the concluding section resonates as "the end of one-size-fits-all schooling." Inspired and insightful, *Learning Personalized: The Evolution of a Contemporary Classroom* supports the evolution of the individual educator and the learning organization committed to breaking new ground for now and the future.

January, 2015   Heidi Hayes Jacobs

Heidi Hayes Jacobs *has served as an education consultant to thousands of schools nationally and internationally. She works with a wide range of educational organizations, schools, and districts K–12 on issues and practices pertaining to curriculum mapping, digital media learning, vertical alignment, and modernizing school programs.*

Acknowledgments

This work not only represented the collaboration of the three authors but also was greatly informed by our friends and colleagues who took the time to provide feedback and offer contributions. Our heartfelt thanks to

Marie Alcock

Mary Kay Babyak

Kate Bean

Peyton Brick

Sebastian Cognetta

Linda Croushore

Kathleen Cushman

Susan Epstein

Michael Fisher

Edward Fuhrman

Lorena Kelly

Robert Kuklis

David Loertscher

Christine Loughlin

Tom March

Janelle McGann

Erin McMahon

Allison Rodman

Donna Rusack

Jill Thompson

Grant Wiggins

Chris Winters

Paul Wright

Cuda Zmuda

Zoe Zmuda

Special thanks to our thought partners who were a sounding board throughout the development of the manuscript: Jay McTighe, Grant Wiggins, Michael Fisher, Marie Alcock, Lorena Kelly, and Jill Thompson. Larry Schaefer, Janet Garagliano, and the Connecticut Association of Public School Superintendents collaborated with two of the authors to propose state policy in support of personalized learning. We also had the good fortune of working as thought partners with staff who tested out key elements in the book and refined our thinking as well as offered quality examples: Avon Public Schools, Connecticut; Charlotte-Mecklenberg School District, North Carolina; Learn4Life Charter Schools, California; Newport News Public Schools, Virginia; Prosper Independent School District, Texas; and ThunderRidge High School, Colorado. Aveson Charter School students and staff, who are already doing so much of what we described here, opened their doors to one of the authors to see what daily work can look like in a student-centered model; they continue to evolve based on ideas in the book.

We also want to acknowledge Susan Epstein and Donna Rusack for their attention to detail in service to the bigger picture.

Thank you to Heidi Hayes Jacobs for writing our foreword; you have been an education visionary for decades, and we are grateful that you see the promise of this book as a clear framework for personalized learning.

We appreciate the expertise of the staff at Jossey-Bass/Wiley, most notably Kate Gagnon, Tracy Gallagher, and Robin Lloyd. Your direction and helpful feedback kept us on schedule and added tremendous value to the collaborative process.

Finally, thanks to our families, who endured and supported countless hours of crafting, tweaking, and agitating: Tom, Cuda, and Zoe Zmuda; Cindy, Ethan, and Max Curtis; Peter, Rebecca, Steve, and Sarah Ullman.

About the Authors

Allison Zmuda is an author and independent consultant based in Virginia who works with schools and districts to create dynamic learning environments for like-minded educators, parents, and kids. Allison received her undergraduate degree at Yale University and graduated with her teaching certification. She then became a public high school social studies teacher for eight years and earned National Board Teaching Certification during that time. Allison went directly from the classroom to being a consultant and author. She collaborates with school staff on curriculum assessment and instructional practices to make learning more purposeful, relevant, and engaging for students. She has written seven books, most notably *The Competent Classroom* (2001), *Transforming Schools* (2004), and *Breaking Free from Myths about Teaching and Learning* (2010). Her latest project is the founding and curating of a website, learningpersonalized.com—a community where students, parents, and educators can view blog posts, share stories, contribute resources, and pose questions for further discussion. Allison can be reached at zmuda@competentclassroom.com. Her Twitter handle is compclass.

Greg Curtis is an author and independent consultant. He is currently based in Beijing and has spent much of his career working with international schools around the world. He began his teaching career in Canada, receiving his teaching degree at Queen's University (Kingston, Ontario) and his postgraduate degree at the Ontario Institute for Studies in Education (University of Toronto). Greg has been a technology director, a curriculum and professional learning director, and a strategic planner for schools in Europe and Asia. He currently works with such organizations as EdLeader21 and New England Association of Schools and Colleges, and with several schools around the world. The focus of this work is on long-term, systems-based change in schools and districts, starting with futures visioning and the alignment of all systems with a forward-looking mission focused on powerful impacts for students. He is currently cowriting a book with Jay McTighe on this process for education reform. He can be reached at http://gregcurtis-consulting.ca.

Diane Ullman, PhD, has been an educator for forty years, as a classroom teacher, principal, and superintendent. She served as chief talent officer at the Connecticut State Department of Education and as director of the principal preparation program at the Neag School of Education at the University of Connecticut. Diane is now senior director at the District Management Council, a Boston-based consulting firm that partners with public school district leaders to improve student outcomes. Diane loves to travel and has worked with schools and organizations abroad (China, Nepal, Africa, Germany, Italy, Japan, and Guatemala) to improve principal preparation, teacher effectiveness, and student learning, and she is currently working with the Queen Rania Teacher Academy in Amman, Jordan. She is vice chair of the NEASC Commission on American and International Schools Abroad. Diane earned her PhD at the University of Colorado in Boulder, her MA at Northeastern University in Boston, and her undergraduate degree at Regis College in Weston, Massachusetts.

LEARNING PERSONALIZED

Introduction

Learning between grown-ups and kids should be reciprocal. The reality, unfortunately, is a little different, and it has a lot to do with trust, or a lack of it . . . . Kids need opportunities to lead and succeed. Are you ready to make the match? Because the world's problems shouldn't be the human family's heirloom.

— Adora Svitack, age twelve (excerpt from her TED Talk)

Imagine a student you know and care about. Imagine that student bubbling over with excitement about what she is doing in school. How she can't wait to tell you the latest details of how she spent her day. Notice how she buries herself in her work, which spills over into every aspect of her life. Notice how it becomes the lens through which she sees the world, how it brings urgent questions, wonderings, and insights into her thinking.

Imagine a teacher who walks into the classroom filled with energy for the day ahead, a teacher who can't wait for students to walk through the door so that they can resume the learning journey, a teacher who moves from group to group, individual to individual eager to hear the latest in her students' thinking and see their progress. This is a classroom where learning is personalized; where students learn that they are powerful forces in their environment and where teachers see their work as a fascinating collaboration with students; where students learn to become competent, knowledgeable, and compassionate individuals and where teachers rediscover the excitement that comes from unleashing human potential.

Learning Personalized: The Evolution of a Contemporary Classroom offers guidance for educators eager to begin the evolution to personalized learning. Certainly personalized learning is not a new idea, but many contemporary leaders are embracing this model in conjunction with technology purchases and policies that render "anytime, anywhere learning" an attainable reality. The power of personalized learning stems from the integrated approach and commitment to disciplinary, cross-disciplinary, and mindset development for our students. These are not separate goals, nor do they represent a hierarchy. None are simply "nice to haves": they are integrally tied to achievement in the twenty-first century, and each contributes to a richer notion of success in learning and in life. They are not just connected; they are inseparable.

In chapter 1 of this book, we make the case for personalized learning by discussing the disconnect between traditional school and postsecondary life and the level of customization that our children have grown up with and expect from the organizations they frequent. We then define and clarify our conception of personalized learning in relation to other design models and debates on what personalized learning is and isn't. Finally, we introduce a framework for the design of a student-centered learning experience that is the organizing structure for the remainder of the book.

In chapter 2, we describe the goals of contemporary schooling: disciplinary outcomes (based on established local, state, or national standards) as well as key cross-disciplinary outcomes and academic and behavioral mindsets.

In chapter 3, we focus on the task design elements: task, audience, feedback, and evaluation to produce work worthy of accomplishment.

In chapter 4, we share illustrative examples and ideas to make a shift to greater student-driven learning an accessible idea with the resources you have on hand. We also describe how the roles of teachers and students shift with personalized learning. When we expect students to move from a passive to an active role, teaching, too, needs to adapt, such that student-teacher partnerships cocreate learning experiences through the design of authentic problems, projects, and possibilities that can impact the broader community.

In chapters 5 and 6, we explore key elements on the classroom and system levels that also evolve to support a student-driven model: process, environment, assessment of learning, time, and advancement. A *personalized learning system* transforms schooling by providing voice and choice on what, where, and how students learn in relation to disciplinary and cross-disciplinary outcomes.

In chapter 7, we talk about personalized learning as an adaptive change, fraught with conflict, uncertainty, excitement, possibility, or some combination of these—depending on your perspective and your vision of the broader aim of schooling. For leaders to navigate through this change, we encourage collectively articulating a vision for a better school and giving the work back to teachers to figure out how to realize that vision.

The text, illustrative examples, and reflective questions throughout this book are designed with you, the reader, in mind *regardless* of your level of familiarity or experience with personalized learning. We want to create a guiding set of elements to initiate collective conversations in which students are no longer bystanders in their own education. As a reader, all you need to do is start—the evolution and implications may seem daunting at times, but we believe that the successes you and your students will experience will also make it an exciting and rewarding journey.

Chapter 1

Making the Case for Personalized Learning

> I'm constantly going through the motions down a path that has been chosen for me by others. When is it going to be my turn?
>
> —Grade 7 student

From a typical student's point of view, schooling is a series of required experiences. Students move from one topic to another, one classroom to another, one grade to another as part of a larger design to accomplish ... what, exactly? As educators, we typically spend most of our time focusing on what is covered and how it is delivered. We, and the systems that guide us, tend to reduce and compartmentalize learning into a linear, step-by-step process. We break standards or topics down into small parts and hope that if we simply move through the components of our design, students will master the material. The result? Students experience sanitized assignments designed more for efficiency than for deep learning. Students move through the pacing guide we establish for them, despite the reality that different people learn at different rates and in different ways. They grow accustomed to their role as compliant, "direction-following" learners who arrive at a predictable response rather than confront messy problems fraught with ambiguity, complexity, and unknown answers. Rather than simply moving through school as consumers of a lockstep system of lessons, units, courses, and grades, *every* student needs to be invested in his learning—to see school and learning as a way of acting on his interests and passions.

DISCONNECT BETWEEN TRADITIONAL SCHOOL AND PREPARATION FOR A POSTSECONDARY WORLD

There is a disconnect between the traditional school model and the challenges and opportunities of today's world. How do we reconceptualize *learning* to move beyond passive student roles of recording and recalling, because the world beyond the school walls demands adaptive, creative problem solvers? How do we reconceptualize *teaching* to move beyond a "sage on the stage" mentality, because knowledge is no longer scarce? Heidi Hayes Jacobs frames the problem this way in her book, *Leading the New Literacies*: "Breaking through the barriers of a 19th century schedule with a 20th century curriculum designed for 21st century learners will be inherently uncomfortable. Just because we are used to something does not mean we should be comfortable with it. Education is disruptive" (5). We can reconceptualize learning if we move from a compliance-oriented structure to a passion-filled learning structure; if learners are intrinsically committed to a given topic, problem, or profession, *they will learn*. Many educators talk about the bigger picture, but they do it in the language of "someday" rather than "right now." Students deserve clarity on the long-term aims of school—*Why do I have to do this?*—and *how* those aims are connected to challenges in the world. When we defer their dreams to a couple of years down the road, most students (and adults) struggle to stay engaged. We have a structural design problem that can be ameliorated by empowering ourselves and our students to navigate problems, discern truth, create texts, contribute knowledge, and become invested in community and global problems. We can do this by

- Designing customized learning experiences around what learner(s) are fascinated by, rather than marching through predetermined topics and texts

- Creating a collaborative classroom and school culture where students *own* the learning process because they set a goal, do the work, seek out feedback, improve their performance, and document their accomplishments

- Breaking down traditional classroom walls to connect learners to experts and audiences far beyond the schoolhouse door

- Increasing our focus on contemporary literacies (digital, media, and global) and ways to work (social production, social networks, media grids, semantic web, nonlinear learning), integrating them into our design and instructional practices

- Persisting when obstacles interfere with progress and providing additional time to produce quality work

THE POWER OF A STUDENT-DRIVEN MODEL

We propose the following as a definition of personalized learning:

Personalized learning is a progressively student-driven model in which students deeply engage in meaningful, authentic, and rigorous challenges to demonstrate desired outcomes.

Our major premise is twofold, and it guides the structure of this book: personalized learning is a better way to attain current learning outcomes, and personalized learning is a better way to grow children.

Personalized learning is a better way to attain current learning outcomes. We're well aware that teachers and schools are surrounded by a host of expectations focused on attaining content. This is reality; we can't wish it away. We simply start with the premise that personalized learning is a sound and effective way to learn. Compared to the outdated approaches of transmission, retention, and recall, personalized learning allows for deeper, more lasting learning in an engaging and relevant environment. But personalization is not just a better mousetrap to achieve the same goals as past models of teaching and learning, nor is it simply a new delivery vehicle that achieves the same goals.

Personalized learning is a better way to grow children. We believe that education must strive to achieve more transformational outcomes *alongside* the achievement of existing or more traditional ones. We don't teach subjects—we teach children and young adults. Personalized learning is the best way we know to grow these people into the best versions of themselves, with all of the skills and mindsets needed to succeed and contribute to our shared future.

Personalized learning has deep roots in education. Susan Yonezawa, Larry McClure, and Makeba Jones trace the concept back to the 1700s, when Jean-Jacques Rousseau advocated for schools that "built on individual capacities and choices to capitalize on inherent motivations" (4). In the early 1900s, John Dewey "promoted the idea of building on students' interests and incorporating outside experiences to meet students' individual needs" (Yonezawa et al. 4). In 1919, inspired by the progressive ideology of John Dewey and Maria Montessori, Helen Parkhurst developed the Dalton Plan, a new model of schooling designed to tailor each student's program to her needs, interests, and abilities; to promote both independence and dependability; and to enhance the student's social skills and sense of responsibility toward others. She published *Education on the Dalton Plan* to describe her idea to address significant structural and policy school challenges: "Not until school machinery is reorganized and the energies of the pupils released from the time-table and the class-tent will they begin to develop that initiative, resourcefulness, and concentration which are the indispensable preliminaries to the process of learning." This model became the basis of the Dalton School and was embraced by many Montessori schools around the world. In the 1980s, Theodore Sizer launched the Coalition of Essential Schools predicated on nine common principles: learn to use one's mind well; less is more, depth over coverage; goals apply to all students through personalization (creating smaller classrooms); student-as-worker, teacher-as-coach; demonstration of mastery through performance on real tasks; a tone of decency and trust; commitment to the entire school; resources dedicated to teaching and learning; and democracy and equity. In an issue of *Education Leadership* devoted to the theme of personalized learning, Sizer promotes his vision of a very different secondary education grounded in freedom and cooperation: "At its heart, 'personalization' implies a profoundly different way of defining formal education. What is here is not the delivery of standard instructional services. Rather, it is the insistent coaxing out of each child on his or her best terms of profoundly important intellectual habits and tools for enriching a democratic society, habits and tools that provide each individual with the substance and skills to survive well in a rapidly changing culture and economy ... It can be done. It is being done, however against the traditional grain." As educators, we cannot design instructional experiences *regardless* of who the students are; they are vital and relevant to the creation process.

Personalized learning has become popularized of late for many reasons, most notably proliferation of technology to create shared networking platforms, a documented and pervasive lack of student engagement, significant changes in the global economy, an abundance of information, and an increased desire to care about something much larger than oneself. In 2010, a national symposium was hosted by the Software & Information Industry Association, ASCD, and CCSSO on "the need for the systemic redesign of our K–12 education system to one that is centered on the personalized learning needs of each student" (Wolf 5). Three assumptions were confirmed in the report (6):

- Today's industrial-age, assembly-line educational model—based on fixed time, place, curriculum, and pace—is insufficient in today's society and knowledge-based economy. Our education system must be fundamentally reengineered from a mass production, teaching model to a student-centered, customized learning model to address both the diversity of students' backgrounds and needs as well as our higher expectations for all students.

- Educational equity is not simply about equal access and inputs, but ensuring that a student's educational path, curriculum, instruction, and schedule be personalized to meet her unique needs, inside and outside school. Educational equity meets each child where she is and helps her achieve her potential through a wide range of resources and strategies appropriate for her learning style, abilities, and interests, as well as her social, emotional, and physical situation.

- Personalized learning requires not only a shift in the design of schooling but also a leveraging of modern technologies. Personalization cannot take place at scale without technology. Personalized learning is enabled by smart e-learning systems, which help dynamically track and manage the learning needs of all students, and provide a platform to access myriad engaging learning content, resources and learning opportunities needed to meet each student's needs everywhere at anytime, but which are not all available within the four walls of the traditional classroom.

What remains timeless is meeting students where they are and growing their capacities in a way that is respectful and inclusive of their voices, aspirations, and interests. That also is why personalized learning is a bit amorphous—it sounds very similar to other delivery models that tailor or customize for the student.

See table 1.1 to compare personalized learning with other delivery models that you may be more familiar with: individualization and differentiation.

Individualization. The student is in charge of the *pacing* rather than the content or product. Students can replay videos, take practice problems or questions, and receive instant feedback on their work. Individualization typically uses technology to provide a self-paced instructional path for a given topic. Personalized learning, in contrast, requires students to take charge of not only the pace but also the nature of the challenge itself and the active direction they take. Engagement does not come from how quickly a student races through the material; it comes from how relevant, interesting, and worthy the topic is.

Differentiation. Differentiation requires teachers to tailor content, process, product, and/or the learning environment for individual students in the classroom to make it more likely that each student will succeed. Carol Tomlinson describes the hallmark of differentiated classrooms: "teachers begin where students are, not the front of a curriculum guide. They accept and build upon the premise that learners differ in

Table 1.1 Distinctions between Personalized Learning, Individualization, and Differentiation

Delivery Model	How Student Owns the Learning Experience	Teacher's Role	Illustrative Examples
Personalized Learning	Student actively pursues authentic, complex problems that inspire cocreation in the inquiry, analysis, and final product.	Teacher facilitates learning through questions, conferences, and feedback.	• Student develops and uses playlists (e.g., curation of texts, experiences) to inform. • Student leads teacher-parent conferences to evaluate performance and determine next steps. • Student moves through learning experiences at his own pace to demonstrate desired outcomes or competencies in ways designed by him.
Individualization	Student controls the pace of the topic as well as when to demonstrate mastery.	Teacher drives instruction through teacher-created tasks and related lesson plans.	• Teacher develops playlists. • Teacher assigns or student independently uses a digital tool to focus on fluency (e.g., Khan Academy). • Teacher assigns online independent study or intervention program (e.g., Dreambox or Compass Learning).

Table 1.1 *(continued)*

Delivery Model	How Student Owns the Learning Experience	Teacher's Role	Illustrative Examples
Differentiation	Student assesses and chooses instruction around content, process, product, and learning environment.	Teacher tailors instruction based on individual student need and preference	• Teacher creates literature circles around different texts but same theme. • Student develops a learning contract with the teacher. • Teacher develops choice board or menu to provide student choice.

important ways" (2). Personalized learning has students envision the investigation, idea, or challenge, and allows them to have a significant influence on the "what" and the "how." The larger aims of a given course or program are fixed, but the content of the exploration is shaped by the individual tasks.

Many secondary and postsecondary schools are designing *blended learning* experiences. The Clayton Christensen Institute for Disruptive Education ("Blended Learning Model Definitions") describes blended learning by referring to its three core attributes: "(1) at least in part through online learning, with some element of student control over time, place, path, and/or pace; (2) at least in part in a supervised brick-and-mortar location away from home; (3) and the modalities along each student's learning path within a course or subject are connected to provide an integrated learning experience." Typically, blended learning is implemented through a rotation model (regular combination of online learning, small-group teaching, and individual conferences); a flex model (individually customized to the student, where online learning is the primary delivery structure); an à la carte model (online courses that students can take to supplement a traditional course model); or an enriched virtual model (primarily an online learning model, where students appear infrequently on campus). Although blended learning can be a component of any of the three delivery models we've explored here, it does not, in itself, equal personalized learning. This is a classic example of confusing *ends* and *means*. Blended learning is a vehicle. It is an approach that can help us achieve something. It can liberate us from using the classroom as a delivery platform and allow us to engage in other, deeper learning enterprises. But, by itself, blended learning is *not* personalized. In fact, it can be a delivery platform for very standardized "box sets" of learning content and assessments. This is true whether we're speaking of Khan Academy modules or the growing sources of massive open online courses (MOOCs). These are very standardized content packages delivered to a crowd of largely faceless consumers via the web. It is in *how* students and teachers use blended learning as a contributor to (and not synonymous with) a personalized learning approach that is important.

If blended learning allows us, in its simplest form, to remove a certain amount of content transmission and skills practice from the classroom, how can it change our face-to-face interaction to support personalized learning? This idea is much bigger than education technology products and platforms, which are marketed promising "customization." Although we agree that technology is a powerful tool to aid in the consumption and production of knowledge, it is not a substitute for the deep thinking, problem solving, and reflection that are at the heart of every powerful learning environment.

CONTEMPORARY ISSUES OF CONTROL

In the effort to improve student achievement, we have pushed the existing system of schools into hyperdrive, asking students and staff to work at a speed that negatively affects learning in the long run. Despite intentions to ensure that all learners can be successful, educators seem to be working harder than ever but accomplishing less, while students seem to be more disengaged than ever but longing for more. Peter Greene, self-proclaimed "grumpy old teacher trying to keep up the good classroom fight in the new age of reformy stuff," surmised: "Every educated person needs—and deserves—an education that is built around the student. Everything else must be open to discussion." The real issue centers around control: who sets the parameters (for example, inquiry, pace, process, product, quality) of the learning experience. Figure 1.1 offers a simple continuum: the far left side represents a teacher-directed, wholly

Figure 1.1 Who Controls the Experience?

| Teacher-driven | | Student-driven |
| learning experience | | learning experience |

prescribed learning experience; the far right side is a student-initiated and designed experience that is not bound by established standards and outcomes.

On one end of the personalized learning spectrum is the power of the student to shape the learning experience. Education journalist Valerie Strauss of the *Washington Post* featured Sam Levin, the founder of the Independent Project at a public high school in western Massachusetts where eight students experimented with full autonomy to design their school experience. Levin advocates for "a blank sheet that says curriculum at the top." Will Richardson pushes the conversation to be more in line with other institutions that have been revolutionized by the role of the consumer and citizen who demands responsiveness. In a blog post titled "'Our' Curriculum vs. 'Their' Curriculum," he rails against an "institutional curriculum [that] almost necessarily denies students agency over their own learning. And this is especially damaging when most kids now have the ability to create a personal curriculum around the things they truly care about learning out of the abundance of information, people, and tools they now have access to." On the other end of the personalized learning spectrum is the power of teacher-led instruction to deliver and assess content. In response to Richardson's blog post, Dan Meyer questions,

> A blank sheet of paper seems very much like "throwing all curriculum out." If you'd like to keep /some/ curriculum, I'm sure you've anticipated my next questions and maybe already written about them:
>
> 1. What curriculum should we keep?
> 2. Should /every/ student learn that curriculum?
> 3. How would you assess whether or not they learned it?
> 4. How are we not now in the realm of nationalized curriculum and assessment?

On his own blog post titled "Don't Personalize Learning," Meyer cites Benjamin Riley's argument that by giving control over to students to determine path and pace, that level of autonomy will lead to "large knowledge deficits" in many students, especially those that are at risk. According to Riley, "The only way to prevent this slow downward spiral for these students is to push them harder and faster. But they *need to be pushed,* which means we should not cede to them control of the pace of their learning." Riley concludes, "the problem is not the seating arrangement or lack of smartphones, it's the pedagogy." Daniel Willingham, an academic mentor of Riley, participated in another blog where he referred to his 2012 article, "Teaching to

What Students Have in Common," in which Willingham and David Daniel contend that every student must have factual (domain-specific) knowledge, practice (a focus on automaticity or immediate recall), and feedback from a knowledgeable source (to improve thinking or performance). "Pointing out cognitive needs (*must haves*) does not dictate pedagogical methods or lesson plans (*could dos*)—just as listing protein as essential to maintain health, for example, does not prescribe which protein-rich foods to prepare, much less specific recipes." The research clearly is much stronger in the area of the teacher-driven learning experience, but contemporary personalized learning is appealing to students and their families who want to have a curriculum that is designed or at the very least responsive to them, one that opens up space in the schedule, the topic, the audience, and the development of meaningful work.

What are we advocating for? *A balanced approach through which the teacher and student collaborate in the design of the learning experience.* Figure 1.2 indicates how personalized learning is situated between the two endpoints on the continuum.

As with many educational models, personalized learning exists along a continuum or as part of a spectrum of approaches, environments, and relationships. As is the case with most polarities, the ideal state lies somewhere in between. Neither end of the spectrum is really a desirable place to be. Our contention is that we must deal with a segment of the spectrum that challenges us to meet the needs of the future yet is still achievable. We must articulate a desired future state, focus on achieving it, and work backwards to plan to do so.

Personalized learning requires a series of pedagogical and policy shifts that are rooted in classic ideas, but with a modern twist. In 1922, Parkhurst proposed that the beacon lights of schooling should be making students "industrious, sincere, open-minded, and independent" through the establishment of student freedom and responsibility to tackle real problems. This nearly hundred-year-old sentiment has resonance today. Students develop capacities in setting goals, designing tasks, persevering through challenges, providing feedback and encouragement to others, and creating and using knowledge that go beyond the classroom walls. The teacher is more relevant than ever to build trusted relationships, demonstrate steadfast belief in students' potential competency,

Figure 1.2 Who Controls the Experience? Where We Are

Teacher-driven learning experience — Where we are — Student-driven learning experience

provide timely and high-quality feedback, and approach new learning with a proactive and reflective attitude.

PERSONALIZED LEARNING EVOLUTION

In this section, we identify twelve elements in our Personalized Learning Evolution (see table 1.2) to advance the design of learning experiences that invite students to expand their ownership of what they learn, how they learn, and how they demonstrate learning. Before we unveil these elements, consider the following examples that illustrate the reason we are doing this in the first place and demonstrate the gray area between the extremes of a fully teacher-driven or student-driven environment.

- Imagine two kindergarten girls at work. They are extending an investigation the class did on buoyancy, testing new objects that visitors to the class website suggested to see whether each one will sink or float. They will make predictions, record findings, and post the results on the class website.

- Imagine a fourth-grade student at work. He carefully examines personal writing samples produced during the past four weeks to look for patterns of performance in relation to objectives that were mutually agreed on by the teacher and himself. This is in preparation for his student-led conference, in which he will present his goals, performance patterns, and selected artifacts and create consensus on next steps with conference participants (teacher, parent).

- Imagine a room of sixth graders at work. They are collaborating with another classroom at a school in Madrid to create a virtual art gallery to honor the work of Picasso. Currently, they are on a video call, where the students from Madrid are describing the emotions and ideas they experienced when they saw Picasso's paintings at the local museum that week. The students in both classrooms will continue to work together on both the creation of the pieces and critiques of one another's work.

- Imagine two groups of ninth graders at work. They are designing a solution in response to an IDEO (an innovation and design firm) challenge to make low-income urban areas safer for women and girls. One group focuses on how to make the pathways from school to local transit safer through the design of an inexpensive streetlight. Another group researches neighborhood policing, both locally and globally, to propose guidelines on how to look out for one another based on accepted cultural practices.

Table 1.2 Personalized Learning Evolution

	Elements	Minimal Student Input	Some Student Input	Student Driven
Chapter 2	**Disciplinary Outcomes** *What are the subject-specific goals of learning?*	Established standards dictate the content and skills to be learned.	Student has some choice to focus on particular topics, concepts, or skills within established standards.	Student determines the content and skills he or she wishes to learn within established standards.
	Cross-Disciplinary Outcomes *What learning goals cut across subject areas?*	Cross-disciplinary outcomes have been established.	Student has opportunities to develop based on explicit teaching and assessment.	Student identifies cross-disciplinary outcomes from a common set.
	Mindsets *What mindsets are necessary for success?*	Teacher creates a classroom culture that uses the four mindsets (relevance, growth mindset, self-efficacy, sense of belonging).	Teacher guides students to use the four mindsets to strengthen performance and development.	Student uses mindsets to work harder, engage in more productive behaviors, and persevere to overcome obstacles to success.
Chapter 3	**Task** *What is the challenge?*	Teacher, curriculum, or computer generates the problem, idea, design, or investigation.	Teacher guides definition and articulation of the problem, idea, design, or investigation.	Student independently defines and articulates the problem, idea, design, or investigation.
	Audience *Who is the audience? How does that shape communication?*	Teacher is primary audience for student product or performance.	Student has input into or choice of audience.	Student engages with authentic audience to demonstrate learning and to add value through contribution.

Table 1.2 (*continued*)

	Elements	Minimal Student Input	Some Student Input	Student Driven
Chapter 3 (continued)	**Feedback** *How is feedback provided, and how is it used?*	Teacher provides formal and informal feedback on the task to help student revise and refine the task.	Teacher and others (e.g., peers, experts in the field) provide feedback to help student revise and refine the task.	Student seeks and uses feedback from teacher and others to guide performance.
	Evaluation *How is performance evaluated on a given task?*	Teacher generates a score and provides explanation of performance.	Student rates performance based on given outcomes to inform teacher evaluation.	Student and teacher interpret evidence of achievement in relation to key outcomes and goals.
Chapter 5	**Process** *Who controls the sequence and pace of learning?*	Learning sequence and pace are specified by the curriculum, teacher, and/or resource.	Learning sequence and pace are specified but somewhat flexible based on student interest and need.	Learning sequence and pace are developed based on student interest and need and flexible based on assessment of progress.
	Environment *Where does the learning take place?*	There is a top-down environment in which teacher instructs and assesses disciplinary and cross-disciplinary outcomes.	The environment is more collaborative; teacher considers student voice and choice in the instruction and assessment of disciplinary and cross-disciplinary outcomes.	Teacher and student work together as learning partners to design and assess learning for disciplinary and cross-disciplinary outcomes.

(continued)

Table 1.2 (*continued*)

	Elements	Minimal Student Input	Some Student Input	Student Driven
Chapter 6	**Demonstration of Learning** *What constitutes evidence of learning?*	Teacher and district assessments specify the way(s) in which disciplinary and cross-disciplinary outcomes will be demonstrated.	Student chooses among a set of options to determine how disciplinary and cross-disciplinary outcomes will be demonstrated.	Student proposes or shapes way(s) that both disciplinary and cross-disciplinary outcomes will be demonstrated and will provide evidence of learning (e.g., personalized portfolio).
	Time *When can/does learning occur?*	Schooling is defined by "seat time"— prescribed number of school days (e.g., 180 days, Carnegie units)	Schooling is a more variable blend of time-based and outcome-based measures.	Schooling can take place 24/7, 365 days a year and be determined by outcome-based measures.
	Advancement *How does a student progress through the system?*	Student is advanced based on age, irrespective of achievement.	Promotion or retention at the end of the year is based on achievement in the course or grade level.	Advancement is based on demonstrated competency whenever that is achieved.

- Imagine a group of tenth graders at work. They are predicting how long the potable water supply will last for their town given the cost, population density, and existing water infrastructure (the age of treatment plants, the projected need for repair, and so on). Their local data are part of a larger project, with five other schools from around the world, to identify what government policies may need to change in response to water scarcity.

These scenarios can exist within current structural parameters (in terms of how we group students, organize courses, indicate mastery, and report progress) or innovative ones. For example, the tenth graders in the last example could be in an Algebra II class; a multidisciplinary course that involves environmental science, public policy, and mathematics; or an independent project where students collaborate once a week for two hours. As educators, we sometimes get stuck in trying to change school structures (for example, block scheduling, competency-based systems, 1:1 technology) instead of focusing on change in instruction (for example, student-driven inquiry, progress monitoring, focus on revision for authentic audiences). In *Five Levers to Improve Student Learning*, Tony Frontier and James Rickabaugh contend that the key to education reform is doing the right work and making the right changes: "Education is littered with well-intended transactional solutions to problems that, in reality, require transformational changes in practice. Too often, the surface-level changes that were implemented resulted in neither improved organizational capacity nor improved student learning" (17).

There are four noteworthy points to provide context to the evolution:

1. There is a column to the left of Minimal Student Input that has intentionally been left off of the Personalized Learning Evolution chart. The descriptors in the Minimal Student Input column represent a traditionally hierarchical model, but a nonetheless effective professional practice. These descriptors represent good schools where the common expectation is that the job of a teacher is to design, develop, and deliver instruction and the job of a student is to receive and then recall or represent learning. In this column, the teacher is positioned in the active role, and the student is relegated to a passive role. To the left of this column (again, which does not exist) are descriptors of the absence of an element—for example, "Cross-disciplinary outcomes have not been identified" or "Feedback is only given in the form of a grade or on summative assessments." For many teachers and leaders, the aspiration is the achievement of the descriptors in the Minimal Student Input column. The power of the evolution is in describing how each element becomes more personalized so that you can use the tool to reflect on where you are, where you want to be, and how you intend to grow there.

2. We are *not* advocating that the goal is always to be in the Student Driven column for every element. (Many innovative or democratic schools would struggle to classify themselves this way.) We are suggesting, however, that educators ask themselves the question "How can we create and sustain an environment where students believe they have a substantive role in the development of their own learning?" Yes, there are times when minimal student input has a role, but if we live only in this column, how are students going to be self-driven, independent learners outside school? There must be a better balance in how we design school if we are serious about ensuring that students are truly prepared for college, careers, and global citizenship. As you start looking at the Some Student Input descriptors, are you seeing missed opportunities to grow student-teacher partnerships?

3. Personalized learning shifts the role of the teacher but in no way makes the teacher an "endangered species." Diane facilitated a Connecticut task force charged with creating a policy paper to support and encourage personalized learning (PL) in school districts across the state (Connecticut Association of Public School Superintendents). In the paper, the authors described six essential roles that teachers play in a PL model (3) (references in brackets are connected to the twelve elements in Table 2.1):

- *Curriculum planner:* What is essential for students to learn? [1, 2]
- *Classroom facilitator and coach:* How can I structure learning so that students can explore interests, pose questions, and discover their own answers? [1, 2, 3, 8, 9]
- *Assessor:* How do I collect evidence of learning as an ongoing process? [4, 6, 7, 10, 12]
- *Advisor:* How do I ensure that students are on track in relation to the goals? [1, 2, 7, 10, 12]
- *Communicator:* How do I ensure that students have clarity about their progress as learners? [3, 6, 8, 12]
- *Connector:* How can I use my professional network to create opportunities for students? [4, 5, 6, 11]

The underlying theme among the six roles is the vision of a learning partnership between teacher and student where both play an active role in the design and development of the experience.

4. There may be a huge "Yes, but" in your head after reading the descriptions of the twelve elements and anticipating what they ask of you. In a profession where burnout is rampant, where teachers feel as though their opinions don't count (Hargreaves and Fullan 2012), this is not only one more change but an adaptive, messy change that requires considerable investment of time, effort, and resources. Many educators are resigned about what schooling has to be because they cannot see it for what it is: a set of habits that feel permanent but do not have permanence. We were not predestined for a system of Carnegie units, standardized tests, and grade-level expectations. For just a little while, turn your back on your certainty and instead make space for the possibility that there must be a better way to "do" school, a way that requires—but also creates—tremendous energy.

CONCLUSION AND REFLECTIVE QUESTIONS

Most educators, parents, community leaders, and students are deeply concerned with what schooling has become. Although many insist that the "one-size-fits-all" model is ineffective, there is limited consensus on what school can be. In this book, we have made a conscious effort not to delineate how schools are failing our children, but rather to focus on a reimagined vision of schooling based on timeless and contemporary elements. Every educator can pursue a learning partnership with students to develop tasks around problems, challenges, texts, and ideas that are both meaningful to the student and aligned with expected outcomes. Students become entrusted with greater responsibility and freedom in shaping the "what" and the "how" of learning. Yet this is a balanced approach, shaped by the needs of the school community, by local and state/ministry policy, and by collective conversations about contemporary schooling. In chapters 2 through 6, we will explore each element of the Personalized Learning Evolution—describe what it is, provide illustrative examples, and offer recommendations for growth in this particular element.

Before we leave this chapter, consider the following reflective questions:

1. To what extent does your school have a "one-size-fits-all" curriculum with little space for students to pursue ideas and inquiries of their own choosing?

2. To what extent do teachers in your school have latitude to pursue "interesting" in the classroom—space with students to explore questions, events, and ideas that arise from diverse student backgrounds, news events, and experts in the field?

3. To what extent do state, ministry, and national assessments help and hurt the case for personalized learning?

4. To what extent are technological platforms and devices being viewed or used as a replacement for teaching rather than as powerful enhancements?

WORKS CITED

"Blended Learning Model Definitions." *Clayton Christensen Institute for Disruptive Education*, 2012. Web. 14 Apr. 2014. <http://www.christenseninstitute.org/blended-learning-definitions-and-models/>.

Connecticut Association of Public School Superintendents. *A Look to the Future: Personalized Learning in Connecticut*. West Hartford, CT: CAPSS, 2014. Print.

Frontier, T., and Rickabaugh, J. *Five Levers to Improve Learning: How to Prioritize for Powerful Results in Your School*. Alexandria, VA: Association for Supervision and Curriculum Development, 2013. Print.

Greene, P. "An Educated Person." *Curmudgucation*, 5 May 2014. Web. 1 July 2014. <http:// curmudgucation.blogspot.com/2014/05/an-educated-person.html>.

Hargreaves, A., and Fullen, M. *Professional Capital: Transforming Teaching in Every School*. New York: Teachers College Press, 2012. Print.

Jacobs, H. H. "Curricular Intersections of the New Literacies." *Leading the New Literacies*. Ed., Heidi Hayes Jacobs. Bloomington, IN: Solution Tree, 2014. Print.

Meyer, D. "Don't Personalize Curriculum." *dy/dan*, 23 June 2014. Web. 1 July 2014. <http:// blog.mrmeyer.com/2014/dont-personalize-learning/>.

Parkhurst, H. *Education on the Dalton Plan*. n.pag. Boston: Dutton, 1922. E-book.

Richardson, W. "'Our' Curriculum vs. 'Their' Curriculum." *Will Richardson*, 19 April 2014. Web. 1 July 2014. <http://willrichardson.com/post/83198278855/our-curriculum-vs-their -curriculum>.

Riley, B. "Don't Personalize Learning." *Kuranga*, 20 June 2014. Web. 1 July 2014. <http:// kuranga.tumblr.com/post/89290487631/dont-personalize-learning>.

Sizer, T. "No Two Are Quite Alike." *Education Leadership* 57.1 (1999): 6–11. Web. 10 Jan. 2014. <http://www.ascd.org/publications/educational-leadership/sept99/vol57/num01/No-Two -Are-Quite-Alike.aspx>.

Strauss, V. "Students Don't Need a 'Voice.' Here's What They Really Need." *Answer Sheet* (blog). *Washington Post,* 13 April 2013. Web. 15 July 2014. <http://www.washingtonpost.com /blogs/answer-sheet/wp/2014/04/16/students-dont-need-a-voice-heres-what-they-really -need/>.

Tomlinson, C. *The Differentiated Classroom: Responding to the Needs of All Learners*. Alexandria, VA: Association for Supervision and Curriculum Development, 1999. Print.

Willingham, D., and Daniel, D. "Teaching to What Students Have in Common." *For Each to Excel* 69.5 (2012): 6–21. Web. 10 July 2014. <http://www.ascd.org/publications/educational -leadership/feb12/vol69/num05/Teaching-to-What-Students-Have-in-Common.aspx>.

Wolf, M. A. *Innovate to Educate: System [Re]Design for Personalized Learning; A Report from the 2010 Symposium*. Washington, DC: Software & Information Industry Association, 2010. Web. <http://siia.net/pli/presentations/PerLearnPaper.pdf>.

Yonezawa, S., McClure, L., and Jones, M. *Personalization in Schools*. Jobs for the Future and Nellie Mae Education Foundation: Students at the Center Series, 2014. Web. <http://www .studentsatthecenter.org/topics/personalization-schools>.

Chapter 2

The Aims of Contemporary Schooling

I think the reason why is because they actually had some connection to their own learning. They weren't just learning facts. They were learning the facts for a reason. They had a goal. A mission, or however you want to say it. An objective. And, I think that helped. I think that helped a lot.

—Teacher quoted in Pederson and Liu (70)

As a society, we want our children to use their knowledge to investigate, analyze, and create in a thoughtful manner. We want them to attend to details: laboring over language, numbers, evidence, and techniques to ensure the veracity of their statements. We want them to not give up, to have faith in themselves, and to access the abundant resources around them. The first three elements of the Personalized Learning Evolution—disciplinary outcomes, cross-disciplinary outcomes, and mindsets—are aims of contemporary schooling. Disciplinary outcomes delineate the broader goals of a subject area (for example, mathematics, history, art). Cross-disciplinary outcomes indicate skills that are essential to be successful, but are not bound by one subject area (for example, critical thinking, problem solving, communication). Mindsets describe academic and behavioral dispositions (relevance, growth mindset, self-efficacy, and sense of belonging) that impact how students feel about the possibility of success given the environment and the assignment. Personalized learning is a means to achieve those ends: a way to grow our children so that they are better equipped to handle the uncertainty, complexity, and excitement of the world.

Before we explore each element individually, it is important to establish how the cross-disciplinary and mindset aims of schooling differ from the disciplinary aims.

- *They are not acquired in the same ways.* Acquiring content knowledge is something we are very familiar with. However, we can't treat the acquisition of cross-disciplinary outcomes and mindsets in the same way. For example, on entrance to school, students already have a "starter set" of skills and aptitudes related to cross-disciplinary outcomes (such as creative thinking) and mindsets (such as a growth mindset). We do not "transmit" these to students in the same way that we transmit new knowledge—nor will they acquire these by simply being exposed to them. The impact of this is that we need to consciously attend to these goals in ways that differ from how we attend to the acquisition of disciplinary outcomes.

- *They are not developed in the same ways.* Cross-disciplinary outcomes and mindsets are developed through experience, awareness, reflection, and conscious attention to the roles they play in our success. Although some of the related subskills can be practiced (for example, one can practice strategies for more effective collaboration), this process is much more experiential than practicing solving mathematics problems. The impact of this is that learning experiences must also be designed with an opportunity for students to make use of these cross-disciplinary elements and mindsets and reflect on their own related performance.

- *They are not demonstrated in the same ways.* Cross-disciplinary outcomes and mindsets are demonstrated in the "doing" of something. A student, or anyone for that matter, brings them to the fore in a variety of situations as needed and as the student decides is appropriate to succeed at a task or in a situation. They are not demonstrated on demand, but *in situ*. The impact of this is that we need to design experiences that explicitly *require* students to access these skills and aptitudes as part of the process and in overt ways.

- *They cannot be assessed in the same ways.* We cannot assess cross-disciplinary goals and mindsets in the same way as we can assess more cognitively discrete disciplinary outcomes. For example, we cannot assess a student's critical thinking abilities by asking her to list six different types of critical thinking and reasoning approaches (for example, comparison and contrast, inductive, deductive). This is not an authentic way to assess the level to which a student can bring her critical thinking skills into the process of successful learning or achievement of a goal. The impact of this is that we need to design assessments and interpret performance based on a very different set of criteria (such as performance indicators) than we would apply to assessing the attainment of disciplinary outcomes.

Personalized learning allows us to intentionally attend to these different types of learning together. But it is important that we consciously design the learning environment, learning experiences, and performance tasks to deal with each in an appropriate and authentic way.

ELEMENT 1: DISCIPLINARY OUTCOMES

The first element is perhaps the most familiar one: articulation of disciplinary outcomes specified in national, state, and provincial content standards (see table 2.1). Many new and revised standards articulate disciplinary goals that are compatible with personalized learning. However, we can get a bit lost in how we use standards to design and evaluate student learning experiences. If we see the value of broader goals, how do we stay true to the purpose of schooling in our daily work?

Standards are *not* curriculum. Standards delineate what students are expected to know, be able to do, and understand; curriculum is a path to the achievement of those standards. Essentially, curriculum is a design issue that can and should evolve. In his blog, *Granted, and …*, Grant Wiggins made the case: "Suppose knowledge is not the goal of education. Rather, suppose today's content knowledge is an *offshoot* of successful *ongoing* learning in a changing world—in which 'learning' means 'learning to perform in the world.' Only blind habit keeps us from exploring this obvious logic. The point is to do new things with content, not simply know what others know—in any field." To that end, key stakeholders in any education system can ignite conversations and pursue actions to describe the "what" (goals of schooling and disciplinary outcomes) and the "how" (organization and delivery of curriculum).

Table 2.1 Personalized Learning Evolution: Disciplinary Outcomes

Elements	Minimal Student Input	Some Student Input	Student Driven
Disciplinary Outcomes *What are the subject-specific goals of learning?*	Established standards dictate the content and skills to be learned.	Student has some choice to focus on particular topics, concepts, or skills within established standards.	Student determines the content and skills he or she wishes to learn within established standards.

Let's pause for a moment and engage in a thought exercise. Imagine a roomful of elementary school classroom teachers trying to make sense of reading content standards and how they impact daily instruction. The teachers are immersed in specific learning objectives, comprehension strategies, and consideration of multiple texts. In the midst of this analysis, someone raises the question "What are we after, anyway? What does a good reader do?" This question sends people into a tailspin for a moment: some become disgruntled because they see this as a tangent, outside of what they were asked to do, rather than the heart of the matter. But after a robust conversation, they settle in on the larger goal: *we want students to* independently *comprehend and engage with any text to analyze how what is being said impacts thinking*. This is an example of a long-term transfer goal that gets to the heart of the demonstration of learning desired, regardless of grade level or teacher personality. There is a coherent focus now from a student's point of view:

- I can read and understand *any* text by using appropriate strategies.
- I can figure out the author's purpose.
- I can make meaning and draw conclusions from *any* text by using evidence.

In any given subject area, disciplinary outcomes provide the reason we care deeply about certain skills, concepts, or topics—how a particular area of focus connects to student capacity. Jay McTighe and Grant Wiggins (9) assert, "In the real world, no teacher is there to direct and remind you about which lesson to plug in here or there: transfer is about intelligently and effectively drawing from your repertoire, independently, to handle particular contexts on your own." Long-term disciplinary outcomes have the following characteristics:

- They emphasize independent application when the student faces new challenges both in and outside of school.
- They establish purpose and relevance for students (that is, they answer common student questions: "Why should I learn this?" or "How/where/when will I use this?").
- They create coherence across grade levels within the subject-area program.

Disciplinary outcomes are generated from the wisdom and expertise of the teaching staff in grades PreK–12. The starting question is as simple as *What are the handful of priorities that I want students to learn?* After the list is delineated, pose a follow-up question: *How is that grounded in the core tenets of my subject area?* These questions are essential to answer as standards are viewed and revised and aligned to the larger aims of the school; they are not seen in isolation, which results in disciplinary outcomes that are either loosely coupled or a forced fit.

Let's look at three illustrative examples: the first in mathematics, the second in science, and the third in English (for English as a Second Language).

Seven mathematics high school teachers/curriculum writers from Learn4Life worked with Allison to articulate disciplinary outcomes that appropriately encompass a range of courses.

Disciplinary Outcomes for Mathematics: Content

- Use functions or equations to model relationships among quantities.
- Compose, transform, and decompose mathematical objects to establish relationships through properties and laws.
- Represent, summarize, and interpret data.
- Infer properties of graphed functions and objects from their shape, location, and measurements.

Disciplinary Outcomes for Mathematics: Process and Communication

- Make sense of a problem, initiate a plan, execute it, and evaluate the reasonableness of the solution.
- Apply a variety of methods to accurately and efficiently solve problems.
- Use appropriate tools to make mathematical concepts more concrete and visible.
- Recognize how mathematical concepts relate to one another in the context of a problem or abstract relationships.
- Represent mathematical objects and data verbally, symbolically, numerically, and graphically.
- Communicate effectively based on purpose, task, and audience using appropriate academic vocabulary and medium.

The second example comes from Avon Public Schools in Connecticut. As part of a multiyear effort to revise all curricula to make them more powerful and coherent from a student's point of view, leaders assembled a vertical team to establish disciplinary outcomes and related understandings, essential questions, and performance tasks to anchor the subject-area K–12 curriculum.

Disciplinary Outcomes for Science

- Integrate knowledge from a variety of disciplines and apply it to new situations to make sense of information, formulate insightful questions, and/or solve problems.

- Design an investigation or model using appropriate scientific tools, resources, and methods.

- Collect, analyze, and evaluate the quality of evidence in relation to a question.

- Develop a valid scientific conclusion, assess its validity and limitations, and determine a future course of actions to inspire further questions.

- Communicate scientific information clearly, thoroughly, and accurately.

The third example comes from Newport News, Virginia, where English as a Second Language curriculum designers framed disciplinary outcomes specifically for audiences of students and teachers. Here is an excerpt from their work on comprehension of text (encompassing reading, viewing, and listening).

Disciplinary Outcomes for English as a Second Language

- Student outcome: *I can read any text on my own with confidence because I have the necessary strategies.*

  o Teacher outcome: Comprehend *any* text by inferring and tracing the main idea, critically appraising use of language and imagery, and making connections (text to text, text to self, text to world).

  o Teacher outcome: Analyze an author's/speaker's/artist's theme(s) through examination of figurative language, sentence structure, and tone.

  o Teacher outcome: Analyze textual evidence to make predictions, draw conclusions, or establish generalizations.

- Student outcome: *I can find information that is trustworthy.*

  o Teacher outcome: Evaluate claims and analyze motivations to verify the credibility of that point of view.

- Student outcome: *I can see how culture influences the texts I experience.*

  o Teacher outcome: Develop insight into the nature of language and the concept of culture and realize there are multiple ways of viewing the world.

For more information on how to create disciplinary outcomes and to see more examples, see appendix A.

When learning experiences are anchored to such larger learning goals, teachers and students have a wide range of choices of content and methods for personalizing the learning experience. Even when specific content or topics are prescribed, the larger learning goals serve as a North Star for each student's learning path. Imagine what the student's experience is like when not only one teacher but the whole school takes this approach. You create what Ron Berger (*An Ethic of Excellence*) coined an "ethic of excellence": "students whose work is strong, accurate, and beautiful" (1). The challenge that educators face today is not the quality of the national, state, or provincial standards we have, but how to leverage them to design meaningful, personalized experiences for our students while still preparing them for standardized assessments.

In fact, a number of education boards and ministries are encouraging personalized learning innovations. The Ministry of Education in British Columbia has been actively pursuing personalization of learning to achieve rigorous standards. In a report titled *Enabling Innovation: Transforming Curriculum and Assessment,* the ministry commits to focusing on a clear goal: a more "flexible curriculum that prescribes less and enables more." One of many notable highlights of the report: "Going forward, the task for the Ministry as it develops new curriculum and assessment guidelines is to remove barriers to personalizing instruction so that the curriculum is optimally manageable for teachers and allows them more freedom to find approaches that work for schools and students alike." In the United States, an increasing number of legislatures and departments of education have created pilot programs or full-blown initiatives to move beyond Carnegie units or seat time to certify credit- and classroom-based assignments as the sole indicator of mastery. To date, a total of thirty-six states have policies that provide school districts and schools with some flexibility for awarding credit to students based on mastery of content and skills as opposed to seat time. As policy continues to open up space for personalized learning, the challenge may lie in opening up local practices where educators conceive of their job as teaching and testing discrete knowledge and skills. This is understandable, given the narrowing effect of textbooks and high-stakes tests, but to support personalized learning, teachers need to conceive of curriculum more broadly and appreciate that retention of desired knowledge and skills improves when students actively use and apply them, rather than being "taught them" and soon forgetting.

ELEMENT 2: CROSS-DISCIPLINARY OUTCOMES

The second element is cross-disciplinary outcomes: broader skills (for example, collaboration, problem solving) that are essential to postsecondary success (see table 2.2). Demographer Richard Florida (104) described how the labor market has fundamentally changed: "People don't stay tied to companies anymore. Instead of moving up through the ranks of one organization, they move laterally from company to company in search of what they want ... Americans now change jobs on average every 3.5 years—a figure

Table 2.2 Personalized Learning Evolution: Cross-Disciplinary Outcomes

Elements	Minimal Student Input	Some Student Input	Student Driven
Cross-Disciplinary Outcomes *What learning goals cut across subject areas?*	Cross-disciplinary outcomes have been established.	Student has opportunities to develop based on explicit teaching and assessment.	Student identifies cross-disciplinary outcomes from a common set.

that has been declining steadily for every age group; and workers in their twenties switch jobs on average every 1.1 years, according to 2001 figures from the Bureau of Labor Statistics." In addition, the rise of freelancers indicates that people want to exercise more control of their own paths, but with that comes more pressure to be continuous learners (Florida; Godin; Pink; Richardson). Although there is significant uncertainty about what postsecondary futures will hold, there are several seminal quotations that make the case for why cross-disciplinary outcomes must also be aims of contemporary schooling.

> The illiterate of the 21st century will not be those who cannot read and write. The illiterate will be those who cannot learn, unlearn, and relearn.
> **—Herbert Gerjoy (as cited in Richardson)**

> There's no competitive advantage today in knowing more than the person next to you. The world doesn't care what you know. What the world cares about is what you can do with what you know.
> **—Tony Wagner (video, unknown title)**

> People have to learn to adapt. I can guarantee that the job I hire someone to do will change or may not exist in the future, so this is why adaptability and learning skills are more important than technical skills.
> **—Clay Parker (as cited in Wagner, *Global Achievement Gap* [30])**

To train students to be truly "college and career ready" requires regular opportunities for students to apply learning wisely and strategically in novel situations. The Council of Chief State School Officers (6) offered states and local municipalities the following definition of what college and career readiness requires: "Students must graduate having mastered rigorous content knowledge and demonstrated their ability to apply that knowledge through higher-order skills including but not limited to critical thinking and complex problem solving, working collaboratively, communicating effectively, and learning how to learn. Students must also be prepared to navigate the pathways and systems that will allow them to gain access to positive postsecondary opportunities." Therefore, students need to experience problems with no clear solution paths, questions that require an investigation rather than a straightforward answer, and tasks that inspire students to collaborate and persist because they see the larger contribution to a community.

The set of cross-disciplinary outcomes shown in table 2.3 is based on our analysis of several twenty-first-century learning frameworks (most notably Tony Wagner's

Table 2.3 Illustrative Examples of Cross-Disciplinary Outcomes

Cross-Disciplinary Outcomes	Related Skills
Creative Thinking	• Assemble raw material and let the collection define the purpose and intent • Take a different perspective on the same problem, topic, idea, or object • Sample, mix, and repurpose information into new forms
Critical Thinking	• Apply a questioning eye • Make predictions, articulate patterns, and draw conclusions • Examine messages and stories presented
Problem Solving	• Frame a question to identify what you don't know • Pursue knowledge and conduct research to find a viable solution • Manage information effectively and ethically • Draw conclusions and define next steps
Communication	• Use mode(s) of communication to share information and ideas for a specific purpose, task, and audience • Frame and present a point of view in a way that is compelling and engaging • Listen to a point of view to verify, deepen, or disagree
Collaboration	• Build consensus around a shared goal and approach • Take individual responsibility for a shared goal and common task • Attend to the cohesiveness and quality of the common task
Metacognition	• Know what you don't know and use mechanisms (tools, strategies, context) to figure it out • Think about your thought process • Analyze performance along the way • Seek and use feedback

Seven Survival Skills, Bena Kallick and Art Costa's Habits of Mind, Partnership for 21st Century Skills' 4 C's, and Michael Fullan's 6 C's). Before you become immersed in the descriptions and examples, a couple of key points. First, the intention of this set is to model what a draft *could* look like. Each cross-disciplinary outcome is broken down into a small set of related skills or performance indicators. The intent is to make these manageable to integrate into the classroom. Second, this set demonstrates the expansive nature of the cross-disciplinary outcomes and related skills. To emphasize this point, we provide illustrative examples from a range of content areas and grade levels to inspire new ideas or to aid you in identifying them within your current practice.

Creative Thinking

Assemble raw material and let the collection define the purpose and intent.

Although many have mythologized creative thinkers as being eccentric, with little connection to the real world, this is rarely the case. Creative thinkers do not simply chase an idea that came to them like a bolt from the blue. They find excitement in capturing raw material (ideas, artifacts, sketches, and the like) and allow their collection to shape an investigation, performance, text, or design. To develop this skill, creative thinkers periodically step back from collection to

- Separate themselves from ideas and view them dispassionately, critically, and deeply
- Determine how to move forward (for example, continue the search for more material, focus on an intriguing set of ideas, develop a prototype)
- Seek out applications that would allow their ideas to add value to the world

Example: In a second-grade classroom, each student is given a shoe box to collect and document objects found outside (for example, in a playground, park, or apartment building) for two weeks. The only limitations are that the objects must fit inside the box and may not be stinky, dangerous, gross, or alive. Every few days, the teacher prompts students to review their individual collections and reflect on "what they noticed" and "what they wondered about" as part of a running log. One student drew a picture of cigarette butts scattered outside his front door (putting a cigarette butt in the box would have violated the dangerous or gross limitation), several weeds that he pulled out of the sidewalk, and an empty can that was tossed aside. The student "notices" that this is typical of where he lives and "wonders" about how to get people to be more respectful of the natural world. Another student fills her box with every autumn leaf she can find because she loves the color. Yet over the course of the two weeks, she "notices" that the color has faded and the leaves are more brittle, and "wonders" if there is a way to capture the beauty of the leaves when she first found them. At the end of the two weeks, students are given an opportunity to create based on their collection. The first student spends an afternoon cleaning up the area in front of his home and writes a poem about how the natural world that surrounds the neighborhood affects the people who live there. Working with her art teacher, the second student experiments using different techniques to preserve the color and avoid the brittleness of autumn leaves.

Take a different perspective on the same problem, topic, idea, or object.

Creative thinking is not about grabbing ideas from thin air, but is typically inspired by seeing a problem or situation from a different vantage point. To do that, this skill requires creative thinkers to

- Examine the problem to determine current issues from current practice or design

- Develop a prototype, design, or idea to address identified issues

Example: To prevent the spread of malaria, students from the Denver Montessori School reached out to students in Zambia to discuss fundraising efforts to provide mosquito netting. The students in Zambia told them that the mosquito nets they had received didn't work well for them because they took up a lot of space in their small homes, were less effective at preventing mosquito bites in children, and were difficult and time consuming to put up and take down. The Montessori students raised funds to design and test a collapsible mosquito spring net that was based on a child's toy or a collapsible laundry basket. (For more information on this project, visit http://www.connectallschools.org/node/132163.)

Sample, mix, and repurpose information into new forms.

Remixing is a viable creative thinking skill: a compilation that builds on the great ideas that have come before you. Contemporary students have been remixing content they find online into their own artistic creations, informational reports, and design ideas. In *Remix Culture,* Erin Reilly asserts, "By remixing texts, teens re-create and redefine them to share with others. In the process, they are acquiring new habits of expectation, meaning, and credibility; new ways of acting, interacting, and doing; and gaining the competencies to become part of this digital world" (144). But this is nothing new—inventors, musicians, scientists, and authors have been doing it for centuries. Henry Ford once said, "I created nothing new. I simply assembled the discoveries of other men behind whom were centuries of work ... Progress happens when all the factors that made for it are ready and then it is inevitable" (quoted in Ferguson). In a 1996 interview, Steve Jobs matter-of-factly described what Apple does: "Picasso had a saying: Good artists copy, great artists steal. And we have always been shameless about stealing great ideas" (quoted in Ferguson). This skill requires creative thinkers to

- Repurpose or remix content through copying, transforming, and combining to design, produce, and/or communicate a perspective, idea, relationship, or narrative

Examples: Common Sense Media (https://www.commonsensemedia.org/educators /lesson/rework-reuse-remix-6-8) offers lesson materials to create an original text through remixing and reusing other texts. A no-tech option is to have students make a new image using a collage of other images from magazines. A higher-tech option is to have students take excerpts from various film clips to make a new piece (or to take musical beats/lyrics and remake them into a new song).

Critical Thinking

Apply a questioning eye.

Critical thinkers suspend judgment and resist the desire to jump to simple conclusions. This skill requires critical thinkers to

- Label information and ideas by category (for example, fact from truth, main idea from supporting detail, relevant from irrelevant data)
- Examine claims of others and the evidence supporting those claims
- Question existing assumptions
- Review their reasoning and conclusions for bias

Example: Students in Paul Wright and Carl Rosin's eleventh-grade Viewpoints on Modern America class engage in at least seven Socratic seminars throughout the year. These are structured, student-led conversations during which multiple groups of six or seven students take on different aspects of a similar topic, such as a specific novel or historical event. The expectation is that students will engage in collaborative discussion driven not only by the question but also by their research into the novel or event. They demonstrate this by making connections and using multiple quotations, and submitting their prep notes afterwards. Because the expectations for the seminars increase in rigor (but do not technically change from the beginning of the year), students show their skills as they develop. Quiet kids say more, talkative kids learn to share the spotlight, and research becomes more extensive. Students also learn to offer constructive criticism, knowing they'll be receiving it in their own seminar. Group members are never the same, so they are constantly in front of a different audience, both in their group and the larger class.

Make predictions, articulate patterns, and draw conclusions.

The nature of "critical thinking" changes depending on the discipline; each involves different content, levels of "objectivity," and lines of inquiry. These differences require students to be agile in the ways they think and act. The ability to bring all that one has learned into a cohesive and accessible "end" helps provide value for others from the process. This skill requires critical thinkers to

- Make predictions based on data and understanding of context

- Recognize patterns in nature, objects, and systems

- Determine which of several possible conclusions is most strongly supported by evidence or which should be rejected

- Draw conclusions that reflect clear and logical links between the information or observations and the interpretations

Example: An Algebra II teacher designed the following problem for students to analyze: "Starbucks opened its first store in Seattle's Pike Place Market in 1971. It seems as though there's one on almost every corner these days. You have to wonder what effect, if any, the economic changes over the past forty-plus years have had on their retail presence. If you were offered the opportunity to invest in a brand new Starbucks store, would you? Justify your response using data."

The main jumping-off point for this problem was a study of regression analysis, particularly linear. The choice of Starbucks may seem random, and, in fact, any company could have been used. Past experience indicated, however, that the years from 1971 to 2005 present a relatively good linear pattern. The students are not presented with any specific instruction or algorithm to execute. They must create their own set of algorithms (or describe the process behind the regression analysis done with a calculator or Excel) and present their findings graphically and numerically. The inclusion of the line "You have to wonder what effect, if any, the economic changes over the past forty-plus years have had on their retail presence" is an intentional red herring, as the changes may, in truth, not have had any effect. The other intent of that line is to encourage students to look at smaller increments of time, where appropriate, and to comment on why that particular point or set of points may be either above or below the best-fit line. (This allows for a discussion of residuals.) The question posed about whether or not to invest may not be able to be answered conclusively from just the data.

Examine messages and stories presented.

Reading, viewing, and listening to texts can be quite powerful if students are trained to evaluate the literal and figurative messages. This skill requires critical thinkers to

- Seek to make sense of messages, not just passively absorb them

- Evaluate a communication product based on aesthetic knowledge and sensibilities

- Identify their own reactions and interpretations to images and the reasons behind these responses

Example: In a Film Studies class, every student selects a favorite film and isolates a memorable moment or sequence. The student then needs to dissect that moment through the lens of special effects, color, lighting, symbolism, music, and set design to understand that moment's communicative power. Each student shows the featured clip and the related explanation at a local film festival.

Problem Solving

Frame a question to identify what you don't know.

Problems are not always self-evident; we are often presented with symptoms of a problem rather than the root cause. Effective problem solvers do not target the symptoms, but dig down to find the real cause(s) of a problem. This skill requires problem solvers to

- Clearly define a problem and what it will take to resolve it
- Formulate question(s) to drive inquiry or investigation

Example: Philadelphia high school students worked to design a system that could identify the most efficient and safest travel route to and from school. Personal safety when traveling through Philadelphia was a concern for students at the Academy at Palumbo, particularly those who came early or stayed late for extracurricular activities. Due to recent budget cuts in Philadelphia, a number of schools were closed. This displaced students and resulted in longer walks to school. Students sought to design a system that could evaluate travel routes for relative safety, and thereby enable students (and community members) to identify the most efficient and safest travel route. Students worked with their Algebra II and Physics teachers to collect data from students on their current travel routes, develop an algorithm, and communicate the results to the student body. (For more information, please see table 4.7.)

Pursue knowledge and conduct research to find a viable solution.

A powerful problem solver can dig deep into the heart of a problem through research, investigation, and analysis. In his book *Personalized Learning,* John Clarke advocates, "Because solving problems may be the defining activity in adult life, students have to learn to see the term essential to gaining control over their lives" (99). Throughout their schooling, students should wrestle regularly with asking open-ended questions, investigating sources or materials, and developing workable answers, and should view trial and error as part of the problem-solving process. Frequently, these open-ended questions lead to more focused questions, which in turn lead to the heart of the issue(s) and parameters involved. This skill requires problem solvers to

- Formulate and refine a range of questions to frame the investigation
- Design and conduct an investigation based on a defined strategy
- Explore new topics/questions as inquiry or investigation progresses

Example: A sixth-grade student desperately wants to play football, but his father refuses to sign the release form because he is worried about his son getting concussions. The sixth grader tries to persuade him by explaining that the football rules have changed, which should keep people safer. But is that true? How do rule changes at the professional level affect how youth football games are played? And to what extent have those rule changes reduced the number and seriousness of concussions? The sixth grader tackles this personalized inquiry as part of a multidisciplinary research project (Math, Science, ELA) and presents the findings to his father.

Manage information effectively and ethically.

Problem solvers work to evaluate every source to verify whether the information, ideas, and images are relevant and whether the author and content can be trusted. If the source passes the test, problem solvers use appropriate formatting to cite it. This skill requires problem solvers to

- Make basic determinations of source reliability
- Identify evidence and judge its merits and strength for providing an explanation
- Apply ethical judgment to the use and citation of resources and information

Example: A fifth-grade project asks students to consider scooter safety: Whose job is it to protect the child? According to the National SAFE KIDS Campaign and US Consumer Product Safety Commission, approximately 217,000 children are treated at hospital emergency rooms for toy-related injuries, and riding toys, such as tricycles and nonpowered scooters, are the leading cause of toy-related injuries.

Students locate and sift through injury statistics, news reports, manufacturer warnings, and parent advice blogs to figure out reliable and relevant scooter safety information to draft a reasonable set of guidelines from a child's point of view. Students then communicate their guidelines to a broader audience (for example, in a response to a parent blog on the subject, an email to the consumer division of a particular manufacturer, a starting point to a dialogue with a parent at home, a school news report).

Draw conclusions and define next steps.

A rich problem-solving process should require a student to present to an audience everything she has learned, the solution she has devised, and the conclusions she has drawn. Good solutions, and the thinking that leads to them, should be communicated in an accessible and compelling manner. This skill closes the circle for a student in the problem-solving process and helps elevate the value of her work. This skill requires problem solvers to

- Connect the solution or conclusion directly with the original problem

- Articulate how the conclusion adequately addresses the problem or issue

- Document and justify a position through appropriate inferences, generalizations, and opinions

- Identify (and perhaps take action on) the next steps or growth applications

Example: As a Health, ELA, and Foods project, students redesigned meals in the school cafeteria to make them nutritionally balanced, cost-effective to produce, and attractive to kids. One student wondered whether students were dependent on cafeteria meals as a primary source of nutrition, because that made the stakes for improving the quality of cafeteria food even higher. Her next step was to write a letter both to the cafeteria manager and to the principal to advocate for the experience to become a permanent project whereby students could be involved in collecting data on food preferences, offering suggestions for new recipes, and writing customer reviews to provide feedback.

Communication

Use mode(s) of communication to share information and ideas for a specific purpose, task, and audience.

These modes of communication are intended to go beyond a focus on the teacher as audience. This skill requires communicators to

- Communicate beyond the boundaries of a normal classroom

- Add effectiveness and impact to communication through the inclusion of graphics and multiple media

Example: The *Journal of Emerging Investigators* (http://www.emerginginvestigators .org/) is run by a nonprofit group established by graduate students at Harvard University to inspire middle and high school students to conduct research, submit scientific papers based on a clearly stated scientific question, and receive critical feedback from Harvard-trained scientists. The group's mission is "to engage students in inquiry-based science with the intent to publish their high-quality work in a prestigious national journal." Papers for submission must comprise an abstract, introduction, results, discussion, methods, references, and acknowledgments. Recently published articles include

- "Friend or Foe: Investigating the Relationship between a Corn Crop and a Native Ragweed Population"
- "Is Cloud Cover One of the Effects of Climate Change?"
- "What Can You See in the Dark? The Effects of Contrast, Light and Age on Contrast Sensitivity in Low Light"
- "Development of Two New Efficient Means of Wastewater Treatment"
- "A Simple Printing Solution to Aid Deficit Reduction" (This article made national headlines this past year; students projected that by switching to the Garamond typeface, US federal agencies would lower printing costs by a minimum of $62 million and a maximum of $394 million.)

Frame and present a point of view in a way that is compelling and engaging.
Narrative provides a context and relevance to ideas and allows us to engage with them in a social-emotional context. Many of the most popular digital games involve complex and engaging narratives. The TV programs that younger learners love (such as *The Simpsons, South Park,* and *Sesame Street*) last for years because we become engaged with the characters. Narrative involves more than enjoying a story; it's also about creating one. Those who can create a compelling narrative out of ideas, issues, dilemmas, and choices can entertain, call attention to important causes, and mobilize people to create a better world. This skill requires communicators to

- Sequence ideas and events to move the audience smoothly through the communication from beginning to end
- Use images and other media elements to tell a story effectively
- Communicate with empathy and caring that connect to audiences

Example: High school students in the greater Pittsburgh area in Pennsylvania had an opportunity to be the reporters for the One Young World Summit. They were first trained and mentored by professionals through a "reporter boot camp" and then had the opportunity to pitch an idea; once it was approved, they worked in small teams to produce the story from beginning to end. Students shared their reporting through social media, open-source blogging, and the group's website. Evan, a boot camp alumnus from Northgate High School, said, "It gave us very interesting insight into the process media undertake to organize coverage of a major event. We watch the news every day, but to learn what it takes to put something like this together, how you need to work together and what you need to be looking for to produce a news story is really fascinating." (For more information, please see table 4.8.)

Listen to a point of view and respond to verify, deepen, or disagree.

Students are confronted with carefully constructed messages when they engage in real-world issues and sources. Their ability to extract meaning from them and to find the meaning behind the meaning supports independent thought. This skill requires communicators to

- Use features, conventions, and etiquette appropriate for the mode of communication

- Use open, probing, and clarifying questions to heighten understanding

- Observe and interpret multiple modes of information to draw logical inferences and conclusions

Example: In a humanities class, students are paired with senior citizens to gain insight into how technology has fundamentally changed the seniors' lives. They develop questions and elicit stories from the senior citizens about technological advancements, personal impact, and societal change. Segments of the interview inspire the research and collection of photographs to paint a picture of the change. These are paired in a photo essay capturing the experience, and presented to the senior citizens as a gift.

Collaboration

Build consensus around a shared goal and approach.

Productive groups, and the individuals within them, formulate a unified set of goals, determine what is required to achieve each goal, and assess the existing knowledge within the group as a whole. This skill requires collaborators to

- Brainstorm and sift through ideas to approach the task/problem

- Ask questions to clarify their understanding of others' ideas

- Engage in back-and-forth dialogue

- Act on others' perspectives to broaden their understanding and approach

Example: In a Materials and Design course in Wesley College, Australia, students spend half the year making projects to donate to various community organizations. The class splits itself into groups of three or four students, researches a variety of community organizations, and contacts them directly to negotiate a project that the group makes and then delivers to the organization. Each individual researches organizations and produces an object (or part of an object) that fits the agreed-on design. Examples of delivered products include toy boxes for the Foster Care Association and raised garden beds for a community house. (For more information, please see table 4.6.)

Take individual responsibility for a shared goal and common task.

Teams are made up of individuals, and the skill of being a good team member must be nurtured. This skill requires collaborators to

- Work independently on a given task in relation to the shared goals of the group
- Explain their own thinking and ideas clearly
- Listen to someone's view on a problem, challenge, and idea
- Offer feedback and guidance to others on the team
- Demonstrate respect and recognize the feelings of others

Example: Elementary school students and teachers work together to create "edible gardens," participating in "a complete seed-to-table experience." Students become more connected to the food they eat through cultivating, harvesting, and preparing their plantings. Each individual has a job to do to make the edible garden thrive—planting, composting, recycling water, and creating recipes. The students (as well as community experts and staff) also offer support to others on the team, such as feedback on the health of the plants and the flavor of the dishes.

Attend to the cohesiveness and quality of a common task.

Collaboration is not just a way to complete a task; it is also an increasingly common way to learn in the world outside of school. Yet most groups don't start as a naturally cohesive unit; no one can reasonably enter a team environment without bringing "themselves" along. Productive teams discover and harness the talent that exists within the group, develop norms to help navigate the process, and use tools to break down the task at hand into smaller chunks. These are not difficult challenges for experienced collaborators, but students need to learn how to use specific tools and processes to maximize the talent and efficiency within the team. This skill requires collaborators to

- Structure tasks to maximize the talents and experience of individual team members
- Adjust plans as needs arise
- Use tools and processes to aid work (for example, norms, use of a timekeeper and project planner)

Example: At the International School of Beijing, grade 7 students worked in small groups to devise best-case scenarios for their city around certain essential areas, such as education, infrastructure, health, and employment. Before they started this task, students engaged in a series of activities to strengthen teamwork and created group norms to help guide their collaboration. They also developed team member talent and skill profiles to better understand how to maximize their group's division of tasks and to take advantage of their group's makeup. Students self-assessed collaborative skills throughout the project and reported their processes and experiences as part of their final presentations.

Metacognition

Know what you don't know and use mechanisms (tools, strategies, context) to figure it out.

At the heart of metacognition is identifying what you don't know and then leveraging resources to work through the related problem. Metacognitive learners regularly ask, "What don't I know? How do I figure it out?" as a natural part of any robust learning experience. This skill requires metacognitive learners to

- Ask questions or identify areas where more information or development is needed
- Identify needs and context for a new learning challenge
- Develop a plan to help solve the problem or answer the question

Example: Students in a world language class visit a cultural marketplace in a city (for example, Little Havana in Miami, Chinatown in San Francisco) to produce descriptive writing that makes the marketplace compelling to tourists. Students must determine the size of the market and the cultural food items and wares that can be found there, and identify common cultural practices (for example, bartering, slurping soup with a spoon). The descriptive writing is submitted to the local Chamber of Commerce so that it can use excerpts from student writings on its website.

Think about your thought process.

Students' beliefs about themselves as learners have a direct impact on their attitudes and achievement. If students believe that learning should be easy, they are more likely to shut down when they face a difficult challenge. If students feel that they are overcome by stress or anxiety, they are more likely to go through the motions of the assignment rather than striving to become more skillful. Educators can make a significant difference if they ask students to reveal their beliefs about learning, teach them about mindsets, and loosen their ingrained restrictions on "what I can and can't do" as a learner. This skill requires metacognitive learners to

- Understand their own learning style and effective modes of learning
- Advocate for what they need to feel more confident and capable

Example: While coming to terms with the realities of her Asperger's syndrome diagnosis, a fifth grader at Aveson Charter Elementary School saw a project on developing a philanthropic business model as a unique opportunity to help children with similar diagnoses. Ten years old at the time, and increasingly aware of what worked to regulate herself when experiencing some of the complications of Asperger's, such as anxiety attacks, she set out to change the lives of students grappling with the similar issues. Frequent "Bugsy breaks" helped significantly lower the rate and severity of the anxiety attacks that would all too often disrupt her learning. Bugsy was the class pet rabbit she would visit and hold in order to calm herself and reintegrate into the classroom. Bugsy breaks were overwhelmingly effective. Her philanthropic entrepreneurial vision was clear. She was going to help put class pets like Bugsy into classrooms all over the world. In such classrooms, students like her didn't just like the idea of Bugsy breaks; their academic and social well-being depended on them. (For more information on this project, see table 4.3.)

Analyze performance along the way.

When students have increased responsibility and choice in their learning, they need to apply their growing sense of self-awareness to the task at hand. In a lesson titled "Thinking about Thinking" Linda Darling-Hammond and her coauthors describe metacognition as "becoming an audience for your own performance ... Typically, we do not know what we are doing when we do it, but it is very hard to improve a process that we are engaged in if we do not have a sense of what we are doing in the moment." Metacognitive learners regularly ask themselves, "What strategies do

I need to apply? Am I skilled in those strategies, or do I need to develop them? When and where might I need help or feedback?" This skill requires metacognitive learners to

- Step back to evaluate the task (for example, design, text, solution)
- Determine the next step(s) and make adjustments based on goals

Example: Eighth-grade math and science teacher Bryan Harms from High Tech High School designed the following project for his students:

> What is Motion and how do we create and control it? ...
>
> Working in teams, you will design and build rockets powered by water and pressurized air. Using what you learn about the fundamentals of force and motion, you will design and build a fully functional rocket including: payload compartment, propulsion system, recovery system and guidance system ...
>
> You will compete and be assessed on how high your rocket goes, the effectiveness of guidance and recovery systems of your rocket, and overall creativity, aesthetic and thoughtful design of the final product.

Seek and use feedback.

Metacognitive learners seek and provide perspective on their skills and performance and that of their peers. These students learn how to critique work to delineate areas of strength and improvement and to offer concrete suggestions. Students also should be able to "hear" the critiques and determine how to make appropriate revisions given those suggestions, without disassociating from the task (trying to do what the teacher wants, not thinking about how the suggestions may impact other criteria the task measures, and the like). This skill requires metacognitive learners to

- Discuss potential plans and strategies with others
- Adjust thinking, development, or performance based on feedback

Example: Grade 1 students provide a recorded set of directions that school visitors can access to find their desired location. Employing their geography, math, and communication skills, they work in pairs to create a set of directions that explain how visitors go from the main office to a specific location within the school. The students record the directions, seek feedback from other students and staff, and rerecord until they are satisfied that the directions are clear. Each recording is then uploaded on the school's website and linked to a QR code (Quick Response bar code to provide easy access to information). Visitors are encouraged to give feedback on the directions so that students can continue to make improvements.

Personalized Learning Recommendations

Many schools and districts have talked about "21st century skills" at some point over the past decade, but did not identify what each skill meant, how to incorporate it in assessment and instruction, and what counts as evidence.

Here are some practical suggestions when developing a set of cross-disciplinary outcomes.

1. **Look at existing cross-disciplinary outcomes rather than starting from scratch.** Cull from your school or district website, examine philosophy statements within subject areas, and revisit accreditation reports to identify the outcomes. By doing so, you demonstrate respect for the work that has already been done, especially for those educators who experience déjà vu because they have done similar exercises before.

2. **Articulate the "why" first.** We want students to become skillful at key processes that define and transcend subject-area silos. For example, to effectively collaborate requires a common vision of what collaboration looks like (why we need related skills) as well as regular opportunities to engage in the experience. This cannot be relegated to a particular subject area (for example, collaboration is the job of the Physical Education and Career and Technology Education programs; critical thinking is the job of the English Language Arts program); share powerful examples of how it can live in multiple or all subjects.

3. **Get the right people in the room.** A "heavyweight team" is one that is assembled for a deliberate purpose and once that purpose is accomplished, the team is disbanded (Christensen). Ideally, representatives from the local community as well as from school staff will be included. The easy part is the creation of the list of skills. Where it becomes difficult is crafting cross-disciplinary definitions. Parent and community representatives should take a leadership role in defining the skills because they are employed outside of the school walls. Their life and work experience is great fodder for developing not only the definitions but also ideas of what "proficient" and "exemplary" look like. Ideally, the heavyweight team can draft this set of outcomes in one to two days for full school-community review.

4. **Make it matter.** Once the cross-disciplinary outcomes are established, the work moves to more permanent "middleweight" teams (that is, departments, grade-level teams, long-standing leadership committees) to clarify the descriptors for staff and students. Steps of the problem-solving process can be written in the form of student-friendly reflective questions as a resource to guide students. A set of examples of creative thinking assembled by a range of experts can be posted (physically or virtually) and analyzed to determine what made the examples original, innovative, or insightful. A list of observable classroom indicators can be developed for critical thinking to determine the rigor of internal dialogue and external discussions.

ELEMENT 3: MINDSETS

We turn our attention to the third element, mindsets (see table 2.4), and focus on how we use what we know about the nature of learning and infuse that in our classroom practices. Academic mindsets are psychosocial attitudes or beliefs one has about oneself in relation to academic work. In other words, how students *feel* about the work has an impact on their effort. The four mindsets are **relevance, growth mindset, self-efficacy, and sense of belonging.** These mindsets are pivotal to students' success, both during and beyond the school day, to handle the complexity of challenges, problems, and tasks they will face.

Psychological research substantiates how academic mindsets impact performance. In their educational research review titled "Social-Psychological Interventions in Education: They Are Not Magic," David Yeager and Gregory Walton explain: "Social-psychological interventions are not magic. They are not inputs that go into a black box and automatically yield positive results. Instead, they are tools to target important psychological processes in schools that can unleash the potential of students and of the educational environments in which they learn." Let's take a look at the mindsets in more detail (see table 2.5), clarified by Eduardo Briceño of Mindset Works and research from the University of Chicago Consortium on the Chicago Schools (Farrington et al.).

Although we may not be able to "teach" these mindsets the same way that we teach content, we can construct the experience intentionally to reinforce the need for these attributes and their development over time.

Relevance

Relevance describes the thinking and doing that is expected in a given environment: why the problem, idea, or inquiry matters. For decades, Kathleen Cushman has studied

Table 2.4 Personalized Learning Evolution: Mindsets

Element	Minimal Student Input	Some Student Input	Student Driven
Mindsets *What mindsets are necessary for success?*	Teacher creates a classroom culture that uses the four mindsets (relevance, growth mindset, self-efficacy, sense of belonging).	Teacher guides students to use four mindsets to strengthen performance and development.	Student uses mindsets to work harder, engage in more productive behaviors, and persevere to overcome obstacles to success.

Table 2.5 Four Academic and Behavioral Mindsets

Mindsets	Explanation	What the Research Says
Relevance "This work has value for me."	Students engage in learning much more energetically and deeply when they value the knowledge and skills that they're working to acquire, or find them relevant or interesting. That leads them to think deeply, question, pursue, and put their full selves into their work.	The degree to which students value an academic task strongly influences their choice, persistence, and performance at the task.
Growth Mindset "My ability and confidence grow with my effort."	Students with a growth mindset realize that their abilities to think and do are a result of their past behaviors. They see effort as what makes people smart, they are motivated to focus on continued growth, and they persist in the face of setbacks.	Beliefs about intelligence and attributions for academic success or failure are more strongly associated with school performance than is one's actual measured ability.
Self-Efficacy "I can succeed at this."	Students must believe that they can achieve their goals, however they define those goals. If students think they need help or resources, they must see a path they can take in order to obtain the required help or resources. The stronger their growth mindset, the more students will seek ways to overcome adversities and search for alternate strategies to achieve their goals.	Individuals tend to engage in activities that they feel confident in their ability to complete and to avoid those in which they lack such confidence.
Sense of Belonging "I belong in this academic community."	When students feel they belong to a community of peers that values going beyond one's comfort zone and learning about the world, students connect learning activities and objectives with social rewards they value.	Learning is a social activity, and understanding is constructed through interaction with others; students need to feel as though they belong to a community of learners and that their academic self is a "true" self.

Sources: Excerpted from Briceño (Explanation column) and Farrington et al. (What the Research Says column)

motivation and mastery through the lens of the student. In her most recent book, *The Motivation Equation,* she offers a simple algorithm to conceptualize motivation:

$$v \text{ (value)} \times e \text{ (expectation of success)} = m \text{ (motivation)}$$

Relevance is connected to the first part of the equation: the perceived value of the learning activity. Cushman elaborates:

- It is worth my time, attention, and enthusiasm
- It asks me to make connections based on my personal experience, the world around me, and my peers
- It invites me to "put my own stamp on it"—encourages creation of content, process, and product

Student perception of "worthiness" can be amplified by the design and scope of the assignment: authentic problems, rich tasks, real audiences, and regular feedback are pivotal and will be explored further later in this chapter.

Growth Mindset

We want students to be willing to get messy, agonize over details, and persist until they accomplish their goal. In her seminal book *Mindset,* Carol Dweck articulates two opposing mindsets that affect how people respond to struggle and challenge, which in turn affects their feelings toward learning. Those students with a fixed mindset have decided that what comes easily is a sign of intelligence, and that what is a struggle, or where they fail, is a sign of stupidity. They become comfortable with those subject areas (and with certain tasks within those subject areas) where they have a track record of success. Students with a growth mindset, in contrast, believe that they can always improve regardless of whether success comes easily or proves to be more elusive. Let's compare these two mindsets side by side (see table 2.6).

A growth mindset can be nurtured, but it requires explicit conversations and cues. The stories that learners conjure up about themselves do matter, and the quality of their thinking affects the quality of the experience. When a student struggles in spite of exerting a significant amount of effort or when a student flounders and asks for help, the goal is to intervene through prompts or questions rather than swoop in and save them from the assignment. For more information on how to do this, see the recommendations at the end of the "Mindsets" section.

Table 2.6 Essential Characteristics of Fixed and Growth Mindsets

Fixed Mindset	Growth Mindset
Intelligence is static.	Intelligence can be developed.
Challenges and obstacles are to be avoided.	Challenges and obstacles are to be embraced; failure is a learning opportunity.
Effort is unnecessary if you are talented or "naturally gifted."	Effort is necessary for growth.
Criticism of capabilities is a criticism of the individual.	Criticism (feedback) is about current performance rather than future potential.
Others' success is threatening.	I'm inspired by my own success and that of others.

Self-Efficacy

From the student's point of view, learning goals should clarify what he is aiming for and provide an opportunity to check progress along the way. These goals help the student articulate "a reasonable dream"—a challenge that motivates him but is still doable. As educators, we work with students to articulate and then navigate learning goals. A goal may be a vague abstraction ("I want to get an A in math"), a long-term task ("I want to figure out my science fair project"), or an area of concern ("I want to get better at reading"). The translation of a goal into tangible actions helps students feel that the goal is achievable, and allows them to take ownership, monitor their own progress, and make appropriate course corrections as they move toward their desired end.

Framing goals in this way aligns with recent findings in neuroscience and cognitive psychology. These findings dovetail nicely with the second part of Cushman's equation: expectation of success—*Am I likely to be successful if I put in a reasonable amount of effort?* Cushman describes how it feels when students are doing challenging work while still being independent.

- It "opens new doors"
- It pushes my thinking because it is hard but not *too* hard
- It "stretches" me to improve my academic and personal skills

Noted neuroscientist, educator, and author Judy Willis wrote a blog post for *Edutopia* in which she describes how dopamine, a powerful pleasure chemical, is released when a student focuses on a challenging but doable goal and is successful. Dopamine is not produced, however, if the work is perceived by the student as too easy or too difficult. The challenge is to work together with students to articulate goals that are "just right," to support them as they determine the steps to achieve their goals, and to provide them with the tools and the encouragement to persevere, become more skillful, and seek out even more difficult challenges. Willis makes a connection to the instructional model of video games and how we can use that to reconsider how we design instruction.

> Games insert players at *their achievable challenge level* and reward player effort and practice with acknowledgement of *incremental goal progress,* not just final product ... It may seem counter intuitive to think that children would consider harder work a reward for doing well on a homework problem, test, or physical skill to which they devoted considerable physical or mental energy. Yet, that is just what the video playing brain seeks after experiencing the pleasure of reaching a higher level in the game. A computer game doesn't hand out cash, toys, or even hugs. The motivation to persevere is the brain seeking another surge of dopamine — the fuel of *intrinsic reinforcement.*

Fortunately for teachers, the central elements that make computer games intrinsically rewarding can be applied without software or gaming consoles. Decades of studies conducted by eminent research psychologist Mihalyi Csikszentmihalyi have enabled him to enumerate "the conditions of flow." In their simplest rendering, the conditions are a clear set of goals; a balance between perceived challenges and perceived skills; and clear, immediate feedback. Empowering students through personalized learning takes them most of the way to dopamine-releasing experiences: the goals are clear and students self-select appropriate challenge levels; if teachers develop simple formative assessments, students can receive the immediate feedback that fuels the flow cycle.

Some schools, districts, and states/provinces are already working on the design of competency-based curricula through which students pursue each learning hurdle when they are ready for it. Until those curricula are in place, transitional methods can help students start to articulate their learning goals. Many educators are familiar with SMART (**s**pecific, **m**easurable, **a**chievable, **r**elevant, **t**ime-bound) goals as part of a larger classroom, schoolwide, or district-wide initiative. This model also can serve as a frame to aid students in creating a personalized learning plan. The connection between SMART goals and the video game model are delineated more fully in table 2.7. In both

Table 2.7 Empowering Students to Take Action on Their Goals

SMART Goals	Video Game Model *Adapted from Judy Willis*	Student Brainstorm #1	Student Brainstorm #2
Strategic and Specific *What do I want to accomplish?*	Short-term goals that require significant exertion of physical or mental energy	Conduct research on the Arab Spring to identify the tipping point toward a more free society.	Change school policy to end Internet filters in my school.
Measurable *How will I know whether or not my goal has been reached?*	Clarity as to what progress and accomplishment look like	Write a blog post on tipping point based on my research.	Whether the policy changes.
Attainable *Is the goal achievable with my available resources?*	Achievable challenge level—reasonable possibility of success	Figure out where to post and how to elicit feedback from a global audience, and revise based on feedback.	The presentations, yes. The policy, no.
Realistic and Relevant *How does it relate to the larger learning goals? What's the reason, purpose, or benefit of accomplishing the goal?*		Demonstrate research, communication, and critical analysis in my class based on a problem that fascinates me.	Demonstrate persuasive communication skills, become an agent of change, document the extent of a problem that frustrates me and many of the students and teachers I know.
Time-Bound *When will the goal be accomplished?*	Time parameters established by the game itself	This will be a multiple-week project to seek out other points of view, evaluate research, look for pattern to form conclusion. I'll probably need 2–3 days to write the blog once investigation is done.	My first target audience is the principal. I want to pitch it to him first (60-second elevator speech) and then see what the appropriate channels are to do a more formal presentation for the board of education.

cases, the goal is phrased in student-friendly language and developed collaboratively between teacher and student. The tasks are clear, measurable, and time-bound, and they push the student out of her comfort zone.

Self-efficacy is truly student driven: each individual is the only determinant of what is "too easy" or "too hard," of where it is necessary to slow down or move more quickly if she has a clear goal of what "success" looks like. To get good information from the student about her perceived level of challenge and focus, educators must include her as an integral part of planning and reflection.

Sense of Belonging

Sense of belonging is about relationships: a collaborative culture where everyone actively participates in the discourse and where students are citizens, not subjects, in the world of schooling. Berger ("Fostering an Ethic of Excellence") explains, "Students adjust their attitudes and efforts in order to fit into the culture. If the peer culture ridicules academic effort and achievement—it isn't cool to care openly about school—this is a powerful force. If the peer culture celebrates investment in school, this is just as powerful. Schools need to consciously shape their cultures to be places where it's safe to care, cool to care." Students' perceived sense of belonging has a powerful effect on emotional, motivational, and academic functioning; when they are not connected, students are more likely to suffer anxiety, distress, disengagement, and thoughts of dropping out. Goodenow described a sense of belonging as "students' sense of being accepted, valued, included, and encouraged by others (teacher and peers) in the academic classroom setting and of feeling oneself to be an important part of the life and activity of the class. More than simple perceived liking or warmth, it also involves support and respect for personal autonomy and for the student as an individual" (25).

To cultivate those attributes, as educators we have to create safe and respectful spaces where we talk openly, learn from failure, grow from feedback, and celebrate accomplishments. Gone are the days when the teacher is the sole purveyor of knowledge; students contribute their own ideas to a shared body of work. Many personalized learning tasks provide students the opportunity to collaborate in small or large teams to produce something of value. These experiences engender a sense of kinship with peers, staff, community members, and experts, allowing students to feel that lots of people are pulling for their success.

Personalized Learning Recommendations

1. ***Teach students about the brain.*** Judy Willis and Kathleen Cushman both explain that every brain can grow like a muscle with deliberate effort and immediate feedback. This may not align with how students see intelligence ("I'm bad at reading," "I will never get science"). These erroneous assumptions stymie many well-intentioned efforts to improve student achievement because students don't believe they can improve. Both authors have developed resources, accessible for students, parents, and educators, that describe how the brain works and shatter many misconceptions of what it means to be "smart."

2. ***Use explicit prompts with students to support a growth mindset.*** Have students look at the progress they have made so far. Reframe "I can't do it" with "I can't do it *yet*." Encourage them to reflect back on the problem or failure in order to learn from what went wrong and consider next steps. For more strategies like this, visit Carol Dweck's Mindset Works organization at www.mindsetworks.com.

3. ***Use (or create an adapted version of) SMART goals with students.*** Share with students that SMART goals are used in many professional, personal, and academic lives to turn larger aims into tangible realities. For example, if a student says, "I want to end poverty because there is enough food to feed everyone," have the student take that idea and translate it into a goal that can be acted on: "I want to take the untouched food items in the cafeteria and donate them to a local food pantry." The student would then investigate the logistics entailed (for example, transportation, legal issues, personnel requirements) to see if the goal is viable. A precautionary note: when implemented badly, SMART goals can become one more top-down task. To guard against that, we propose the use of a student-developed pathway plan, illustrated in table 4.13 in chapter 4. (A blank version can be found in appendix B.)

4. ***Communicate and uphold a policy that freedom and responsibility go hand in hand.*** Students may crave and ask for autonomy, but that opportunity should be earned. The gradual release of responsibility is based on how each student navigates a given assignment, not on a classwide decision. A student's readiness is best ascertained by regular check-ins with the student about progress, needs, and suggestions for modified action.

5. ***Ask your students, "Where in school do you feel important?"*** This question opens up dialogue that reveals the extent to which students believe that "student-centered learning" is at the heart of schooling. For more questions to gain insight into students—how they see themselves, their teachers, their job as learners—take a look at the teacher's guide published by What Kids Can Do, "First Ask, Then Listen How to Get Your Students to Help You Teach Them Better" (http://whatkidscando.org/pdf/FirstAsk,ThenListen.pdf).

6. ***Incorporate mindsets in classroom structures and conversations.*** Mindsets are manufactured by the learner based on his perception of experience, and therefore can be changed as experiences with learning change.

   o Focus praise on students' efforts and not on their abilities or intelligence.

- Provide feedback about effort or strategies—how every individual can improve.
- Teach and model the value of taking on a challenge.
- Provide methods to track learning rather than using only grades and test scores as the sole indicators.
- Engage students to set clear and attainable goals, reflect on their progress, and make necessary adjustments toward those goals.

7. **Cocreate a student's bill of rights.** Students and staff articulate and verify a "bill of rights" that is an agreed-on set of parameters a teacher will uphold. Allison worked with staff at Henry Street School for International Studies to draft a schoolwide set for their students in grades 6–12. Here we have added parenthetical references indicating the four related mindsets.

- I have a right to learn in a safe environment. (Sense of belonging)
- I have a right to be treated with respect. (Sense of belonging)
- I have a right to understand the purpose of an assignment. (Relevance)
- I have a right to clear expectations about what is expected from me. (Self-efficacy)
- I have a right to get assistance in a timely manner when I have a question or problem. (Self-efficacy)
- I have a right to get feedback on my work so I can improve it. (Growth mindset)
- I have a right to make mistakes and learn from them. (Growth mindset)
- I have a right to advocate for myself and others. (Sense of belonging)

CONCLUSION AND REFLECTIVE QUESTIONS

The contemporary aims of school must evolve to align with what we know to be true about how we learn and with the deep thinking and creativity that employers desire and students crave. The next chapter focuses on the elements of task, audience, feedback, and evaluation. Before we move on, consider the following questions:

1. What are the goals of your school or district?

2. How are those goals communicated to teachers, students, parents, and community members?

3. To what extent do those goals have an impact on what happens in the classroom?

4. How do you "grow" people (students and staff) in your school? What opportunities or experiences can you identify? How do you know that they are working as intended?

WORKS CITED

Berger, R. *An Ethic of Excellence: Building a Culture of Craftsmanship with Students.* Portsmouth, NH: Heinemann, 2003. Print.

Berger, R. "Fostering an Ethic of Excellence." *Fourth and Fifth Rs: Respect and Responsibility* 12.1 (Winter/Spring 2006): 1–4. Print.

Briceño, E. "Mindsets and Human Agency." *UnBoxed*, no. 10. Spring 2013. Web. 15 July 2014. <http://www.hightechhigh.org/unboxed/issue10/mindsets_and_student_agency_contributors/>.

Christensen, C., and Horn, M. *Disrupting Class.* New York: McGraw-Hill, 2008. Print.

Clarke, J. *Personalized Learning: Student Pathways to High School Graduation.* Thousand Oaks, CA: Corwin, 2013. Print.

Council of Chief State School Officers. "Knowledge, Skills, and Dispositions: The Innovation Lab Network State Framework for College, Career, and Citizenship Readiness, and Implications for State Policy." *Resources.* Council of Chief State School Officers, Feb. 2013. Web. 10 July 2014. <http://www.ccsso.org/Resources/Publications/ILN_CCR_Framework.html>.

Cushman, K. *The Motivation Equation.* Providence, RI: Next Generation Press, 2013. Print.

Darling-Hammond, L., Austin, K., Cheung, M., and Martin, D. "Lesson 9: Thinking about Thinking: Metacognition." *The Learning Classroom: Theory into Practice.* Annenberg Learner. n.d. Web. 12 July 2014. <www.learner.org/courses/learningclassroom/support/09_metacog.pdf>.

Dweck, C. *Mindset: The New Psychology of Success.* New York: Ballantine Books, 2006.

Farrington, C. A., Roderick, M., Allensworth, E., Nagaoka, J., Keyes, T. S., Johnson, D. W., and Beechum, N. O. "Teaching Adolescents to Become Learners: The Role of Noncognitive Factors in Shaping School Performance." Chicago: University of Chicago Consortium on Chicago School Research, June 2012. Web. 15 July 2014. <https://ccsr.uchicago.edu/publications/teaching-adolescents-become-learners-role-noncognitive-factors-shaping-school>.

Ferguson, K. "Embrace the Remix." *TedGlobal*, 2012. Web. 4 May 2014. <http://www.ted.com/talks/kirby_ferguson_embrace_the_remix>.

Florida, R. *The Rise of the Creative Class … and How It's Transforming Work, Leisure, Community, and Everyday Life.* New York: Basic Books, 2003. Print.

Godin, S. *Stop Stealing Dreams.* 2012. Web (self-published book). 1 Aug. 2014. <http://www.squidoo.com/stop-stealing-dreams>.

Goodenow, C. "The Psychological Sense of School Membership Among Adolescents: Scale Development and Educational Correlates." *Psychology in the Schools* 30 (1993): 70–90.

Harms, B. "Actually, It Is Rocket Science" [math and science project]. 2014. Web. 1 Nov. 2014. <http://www.hightechhigh.org/projects/?name=Actually,%20it%20is%20Rocket%20Science&uid=ab6e6e0f7c8714c2706dc61637259093>.

McTighe, J., and Wiggins, G. *From Common Core Standards to Curriculum: Five Big Ideas.* Sept. 2012. Web. 15 May 2014. <http://grantwiggins.files.wordpress.com/2012/09/mctighe _wiggins_final_common_core_standards.pdf>.

Ministry of Education in British Columbia. *Enabling Innovation: Transforming Curriculum and Assessment.* Aug. 2012. Web. 10 July 2014. <www.bced.gov.bc.ca/irp/docs/ca _transformation.pdf>.

Pederson, S., and Liu, M. "Teachers' Beliefs about Issues in the Implementation of a Student-Centered Learning Environment." *Educational Technology Research and Development* 51.2 (2003): 57–76.

Pink, D. *Drive: The Surprising Truth About What Motivates Us.* New York: Riverhead Books, 2011. Print.

Reilly, E (2010). "Remix Culture: Digital Music and Video Remix Opportunities for Creative Production." *Teaching Tech-Savvy Kids.* Ed., Jessica Parker. slideshare. 2010. 143–166. Web. 4 May 2014. <http://www.slideshare.net/ebreilly/remix-culture-digital-music-and-video -remix-opportunities-for-creative-production>.

Richardson, W. *Why School? How Education Must Change When Learning and Information Are Everywhere.* New York: TED Conferences, 2012. Web.

Wagner, T. (2010). *Global Achievement Gap: Why Even Our Best Schools Don't Teach the New Survival Skills Our Children Need—and What We Can Do About It.* New York: Basic Books.

Wagner, T. Video, Speech for "A Collaborative Leadership Summit." 2013. Web. 28 Apr. 2014. <http://colabsummit.com/speakers/tony-wagner/>.

Wiggins, G. "Everything You Know About Curriculum May Be Wrong. Really." *Granted, and …* Grant Wiggins, 13 Mar. 2012. Web. 28 Apr. 2014. <http://grantwiggins.wordpress.com/2012 /03/13/everything-you-know-about-curriculum-may-be-wrong-really/>

Willis, J. "A Neurologist Makes the Case for the Video Game Model as a Learning Tool." *Edutopia,* 14 Apr. 2011. Web. 10 Feb. 2014. <http://www.edutopia.org/blog/video-games -learning-student-engagement-judy-willis>.

Yeager, D., and Walton, M. "Social-Psychological Interventions in Education: They Are Not Magic." *Review of Educational Research* 81.2 (June 2011): 267–301. Available at <http:// rer.sagepub.com/content/81/2/267>.

Chapter 3

The Design of a Student-Driven Learning Experience

Students today want to be actively engaged, they want to determine the path of their own learning, chart their own learning journeys. Technology tools have exploded the way they interact with the world around them, and it's changed how they want to be in the classroom.

— Fifth- and sixth-grade teacher (as cited in Fullan and Langworthy 11)

Students are much more likely to be invested in work that engages them intellectually if they see the value in the assignment. The focus of a valuable assignment has moved away from a grade to a perception of worth: Is it worth a student's time, attention, and effort? Students want to do work that is challenging (but not impossible), to see evidence of improvement, and to make an impact on others.

This chapter focuses on the design of a student-driven learning experience through the elements of task, audience, feedback, and evaluation. The underlying shift described in this chapter is one toward cocreation: an opportunity for students to work with educators as learning partners to have an increasing stake in the "what" and "how" of schooling. Such an opportunity is far from a "free-for-all" or independent study with no parameters. Rather, we begin to invite students to the design table to define problems that are worth solving, share ideas that are worth pursuing, and develop action plans that are worth accomplishing.

ELEMENT 4: TASK

The fourth element is task: the design of a challenge that is authentic, relevant, and meaningful (see table 3.1) to the student. When we as teachers attempt to design a performance task (one that makes students apply their learning to novel situations), it can still feel as if it is our creation and the students are simply playing in our sandbox. As we examine the evolution of task from left to right in table 3.1, we see that students increasingly cocreate with us.

In much of the literature on personalized learning to date, proponents talk about the importance of tasks that involve "voice and choice." We want to move from this as a sentiment or a catchphrase to a way to solidify the teacher-student partnership. Here, *voice* represents active participation in the discourse; it makes students citizens, not subjects, in the world of schooling. This requires that students feel valued and known by the teacher and other students; it also requires a school that is a safe place to collaborate, take risks, and share ideas. *Choice* represents students' freedom to pursue what they find fascinating. The task is much more robust because it is not a teacher-controlled decision around content, product, and process. Instead, it comes from the questions students ask, the ideas they seek to capture, and the paths they take. Students want to experience more than the predictable tasks that a canned program offers; they want to believe that because they are in the room—asking questions, making sense of data, challenging assumptions—the learning and the performance look different.

Australian education consultant Tom March developed a framework to assist educators in moving students from indoctrinated passive roles to actively managing their learning. Based on research from Ryan and Deci, Csikszentmihalyi, Seligman, Duckworth, and Pirsig, the student self-managed framework aligns nicely with the mindsets in the previous chapter. To access the framework, visit http://tommarch.com/strategies/ceqall/.

Table 3.1 Personalized Learning Evolution: Task

Element	Minimal Student Input	Some Student Input	Student Driven
Task *What is the challenge?*	Teacher, curriculum, or computer generates the problem, idea, design, or investigation.	Teacher guides definition and articulation of the problem, idea, design, or investigation.	Student independently defines and articulates the problem, idea, design, or investigation.

Figure 3.1 The Design Process

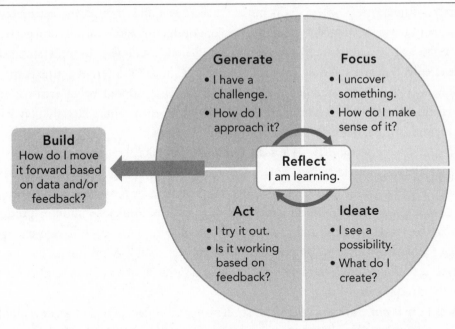

Developed by Allison Zmuda with Charlotte-Mecklenburg Schools in North Carolina

For students to become more instrumental in the learning experience, it is helpful to establish a project design cycle to focus their work process. Most project design cycles identify similar stages, with some variation in the sequence, characteristics of the stages, and the dynamic nature of the design process. Although there are many takes on the design cycle, we offer our own here (see figure 3.1), inspired by Alex Osborne and Sydney Parnes's Creative Problem Solving structured process from the 1970s and the internationally recognized IDEO design firm. This model was designed in partnership with Charlotte-Mecklenburg Schools, and the intended audience comprises students and teachers.

Generate: *I have a challenge. How do I approach it?* In this phase, the student identifies a problem, dilemma, or issue that ignites her passion. The teacher can offer ideas, or the student can generate her own questions about a topic or issue, but the overarching focus in this stage of cocreation is to formulate a question or dilemma that will drive learning forward. Often, the dilemma can be a driving question that highlights its inherent challenges. For example, "How can we ensure safe access to public spaces in our town when the budget doesn't allow for their upkeep?" or "How can we encourage young children to eat healthy foods?"

Focus: *I uncover something. How do I make sense of it?* In this phase, the student actively considers the problem or dilemma. Once a question is framed, there is much to learn about the issues that surround the problem or dilemma, the various perspectives that exist, and its context and root causes. Students should seek to understand the issue deeply. Designers should look for similar dilemmas in different contexts to see what was tried, what succeeded, and what failed. They should bring creative and critical thinking to bear, make inferences, think divergently, and generally *play* with the dilemma by looking at it from unconventional angles.

Ideate: *I see a possibility. What do I create?* This phase requires the student to generate, develop, and test ideas. This creation consolidates the generative thought the student has engaged in thus far into a focused prototype. A prototype, an important device to engage with real-world issues and dilemmas, is a quick solution or product that can be tested multiple ways to gain insights that support rapid design changes without expecting a perfect implementation "off the shelf." A prototype can be as complex as a functioning model or as simple as a preview of an idea to audiences to elicit their responses.

Act: *I try it out. Is it working?* The student needs to decide what "success" looks like to evaluate her observations of the prototype in action. Her observations allow her to tune a solution or response so that she can learn from early design stages and refine her ideas so as to increase the potential for success.

Build: *How do I move it forward based on data and/or feedback?* In this phase, the student not only needs to "fix" things that came up in the prior stage but also needs to consider how to explain and expand the idea, design, or solution. How would I convey this idea to people? How would it work in the real world? What about the production and/or sustainability of the design or solution? The design process can end here or can repeat until the task is completed or the student wants to pursue a new idea.

Personalized Learning Recommendations

1. ***Encourage students to take action on original ideas as part of an established task.*** This task can be directly connected to your coursework and may merit a personalized, cocreated assignment that the student or a group of interested students pursues. Another option is to mentor the student: become a sounding board for ideas, goals, and timeline; use your own network to find opportunities for students to participate; and provide critiques mindful of the purpose, task, and audience.

2. ***Encourage students to question or wonder through journaling.*** When an idea surfaces in a student's thoughts, train him to capture it in the moment, before it is replaced by a new one. Have the student enter those ideas in a journal, an index card that is then posted on a bulletin board, or with a virtual tool (for example, Padlet, ePads). Then have students regularly review their ideas to evaluate which ones are worthy of pursuit.

3. ***Create an environment where it is a safe to try and to fail forward.*** We want students to swing for the fences rather than regurgitate existing answers. Students need to make sense of the data, evidence, and ideas to determine what is possible, valuable, and necessary. In this way, they can experience growth in all three areas of contemporary learning: disciplinary outcomes, cross-disciplinary outcomes, and mindsets.

4. ***Provide tools to frame the work.*** Most students have never tackled a complex problem, inquiry, or idea that takes weeks, months, or years of planning and effort to solve. The tools should establish a set of parameters from which they can be creative, rather than a set of instructions that they must follow.

ELEMENT 5: AUDIENCE

The fifth element is audience—how that shapes effort, attention to detail, and language to ensure that one is understood (see table 3.2). Relevant, authentic, and meaningful learning experiences typically happen when learners have the opportunity to work on a problem, project, or challenge that adds value to a broader audience outside the classroom. The evolution moves from having the teacher as an assessment audience to engaging with a community that not only serves as an audience but also informs the work.

Shawn Cornally's powerful blog post reminisced on a conversation that transformed his perspective on the teacher as primary audience for assessment.

Table 3.2 Personalized Learning Evolution: Audience

Element	Minimal Student Input	Some Student Input	Student Driven
Audience *Who is the audience? How does that shape communication?*	Teacher is primary audience for student product or performance.	Student has input into or choice of audience.	Student engages with authentic audience to demonstrate learning and to add value through contribution.

In a conversation with a veteran educator—a man with years of experience teaching English and acting as a headmaster—I was confronted with a prejudice so ingrained in my teaching that I was almost embarrassed to admit it. He said, "You know, when I ask a student to write a paper and turn it in to me, that's ridiculous; I'm the worst audience they could have." I was intrigued. He went on, "Who am I to assume that someone will want to write their best work, something truly personal and creative, for me? A single-person audience is a pretty lame audience, let alone the fact that I'm a middle-aged white guy." That hit me like a rolled-up newspaper. As I absorbed this veteran educator's words, I realized that … I [was] wrong in my assumption that I (or any teacher) is a meaningful audience … Over the years I've come to believe that the use of single-shot, for-point assessments is one of the worst possible things we can do to students. If students don't recognize assessments as a chance to show their learning, then these things aren't even assessments; they're something altogether alien to real learning.

Cornally then shared an interaction he had with a chemistry class working to ferment an exotic species of switchgrass: "The fervor in the room was contagious, and I jumped in to help. I asked the students why they were so excited, and one turned to me and said, 'This is for a town in the Philippines. We Skyped with them last week, and we found some of the same grass they have. We want to help them make ethanol. Regular gasoline is a really high cost of farming for them, and they have *a lot* of switchgrass.'" The students were taking action on an authentic problem and were trying to add value through experimentation.

Creation that engages with an authentic audience motivates students to invest themselves in the work because what they do has a tangible impact on others. When David Mitchell, deputy headmaster at Heathfield Community Primary School in Bolton, England, first introduced his sixth-grade students to blogging, the students wrote that they spent more time and attention on their writing because someone else was listening. Suzie Boss reported, "The first year he introduced blogging to his Grade 6 students, the number who earned top writing scores on British achievement tests increased from 9 percent to 60 percent."

Elena Aguilar shared an assignment for which students were asked to select and research a public health concern about which people needed quality information. Students produced brief informational brochures, which were translated into several languages that were spoken in the community. These brochures were then distributed throughout the community. Aguilar remarked, "After they got responses, they were even more motivated to write long, detailed letters full of explanation and description—and without a single grammar, spelling, or convention error."

Another remarkable illustration of authentic audience was a project to test water quality for a town in western Massachusetts. Ron Berger's sixth-grade class partnered with a Hampshire College professor to do a sample study on lead and sodium pollution. The sixth graders led an assembly for the full school to instruct every student on how to draw an appropriate water sample as well as outfit every student with sample kits. This yearlong project included analyses on the gathered water samples, search for patterns in the data, drawing conclusions, and presentation to a watchful audience (which included local health department employees, community reporters, and anxious community members). At the end of the project, Berger declared, "Our student scientists felt on top of the world. The work they had accomplished was not only accurate, clear, and elegantly portrayed, but it was important. Not important school work, but important work in the real world. To this day, I'm not sure that any community in the state has more accurate data on possible road salt contamination of wells than these studies prepared by elementary students for the town of Shutesbury" (125).

In all of these examples, students felt useful and valuable—because their work mattered. Creating rich tasks with authentic audiences is a design problem that stretches teachers to seek assistance outside their classroom and school walls. In Mark Miller's blog post on audiences for assessment, he explains the power of authenticity: "When you make a piece of work real, you change the role of students in the class … The work has to be good enough to present to that audience. If it isn't, it has to be improved … Having a real audience in mind helps students to focus on the minutiae of improvement but also makes them more receptive to critique."

Yet every educator has lived through public presentations that were obligatory demonstrations of learning (for example, science fairs, poetry readings). Even though the information and ideas presented may have been solid, the enthusiasm, the attention to detail, and the effort to make it come alive for the audience were sorely lacking. How can we increase the likelihood that public presentations are assessments that students truly own? Students should become accustomed to reaching out to others to exchange information and ideas. As a student, to know that "you are on to something" or to be asked "tell me more" informs the next iteration of the work. Students grow more comfortable and confident in their ability to be taken seriously, and expect the learning to become deeper because of audience feedback.

Personalized Learning Recommendations

1. *Seek out local experts.* Consult with organizations that do research, tackle thorny problems, pursue a question with no known answer, or create a performance or work of art. Ask them to share their ideas, process, and challenges. See if you can create a collaborative partnership in which students contribute to part of the process.

2. *Conduct a needs assessment of your community.* Canvas neighbors to determine what problems they face and how students can make an impact on those problems. Creation of a community garden, cleanup of a dilapidated space, and reimagining traffic flow for a school parking lot are responses to concrete problems that can be connected to particular content topics and standards.

3. *Focus on audience as well as media.* Andrea Hernandez states, "There are only so many people 'out there' who want to read poorly written, lacking-in-passion posts with titles like 'Journal #5.' Posting to a blog does not guarantee either student motivation or high quality work." What is it that you are trying to say? What type of response do you hope to elicit from the reader? Hernandez cautions that much of online behavior is attention seeking. "We post something on Facebook because we hope it will be liked. We are excited for the 'success' of a video gone viral. Is this the right measuring stick for work of meaning and depth, work that shows quality and growth? Therefore, engage students in conversation about instant response versus thoughtful response. What do you hope your post communicates … about you, your ideas, your stance on an issue, your view of the world."

4. *Have students take the lead.* Provide students a set of parameters for leading conferences about their learning: each student identifies evidence of key goals in the course or subject, shares areas of strength and difficulty that the selected piece(s) demonstrate, and facilitates a conversation with participants (for example, teacher, parent, counselor) about future actions.

5. *Give students the opportunity to select panelists for their presentations.* In Mt. Abraham High School in Vermont, John Clarke reports that every student assembles a panel, including two teachers, two students, and two adults, who will listen, take notes, and comment on what they have seen and heard.

6. *Invite school-community members to listen and engage in the work.* Jim Moulton describes his experience as an audience member in middle school presentations: "What I saw was a uniform desire to do their best, and a willingness to engage not only with content but also with their audience in a mature and thoughtful way. I am confident that the presence of a few extra caring adults in the room made a difference … The audience applauded at the end of each presentation, and, once the students were all done presenting, asked serious questions about the research—not simply out of politeness but because we had been engaged."

7. *Design opportunities for feedback as part of the presentation.* Whether the presentation is physical or virtual, encourage students not only to solicit questions or comments but also to use that feedback to give the work more impact. In-the-moment responses as well as follow-up revisions and commentary deepen the learning for the student and show the audience that their participation was valued.

8. ***Design opportunities for students to provide feedback to presentations of information and ideas.*** Hernandez wonders, "How many bloggers leave regular comments for others?" Part of a dynamic conversation is challenging our students (and ourselves) to craft an appropriate response.

9. ***Create a global/online partnership with other classrooms for ongoing collaboration.*** In a conversation with Allison, educator Tom March suggested developing virtually linked classroom partnerships in which "We read yours, you read ours" is part of the daily routine of learning and producing. These partnerships can be challenging to establish, but once they are, each side enjoys an authentic audience, a short feedback loop, and means for crowdsourcing information that can be used for specific projects. Like all great partnerships, these probably start with the sparks and chemistry arising between two like-minded teachers. March suggests pursuing such partnerships by reaching out and connecting with people in your personal learning networks; you may soon find yourself enjoying virtual team teaching.

10. ***Talk with students about selection and use of media (for example, films, data displays, models, demonstrations) to highlight the learning.*** What is the best way to showcase the accomplishment? Every student should have a mental picture of what quality work looks like for a particular medium, so that her revisions focus on that high level of quality.

11. ***Provide assignments where there is an established audience already.*** Social media sites, consumer reviews, and active blogs are places where students can describe their experience or evidence-based point of view. In addition, students can examine and respond to others' critiques, ideas, or findings to broaden their knowledge base, appreciate viewpoints much different from their own, and reflect on new ideas or questions worthy of pursuit.

ELEMENT 6: FEEDBACK

The next element discussed in this chapter is feedback, its role and key characteristics (see table 3.3). Regular feedback loops inform students of the effectiveness of their efforts in relation to the goal they are attempting to achieve. Grant Wiggins elaborates: "Feedback is information about how we are doing in our efforts to reach a goal. I hit a tennis ball with the goal of keeping it in the court, and I see where it lands—in or out. I tell a joke with the goal of making people laugh, and I observe the audience's reaction—they laugh loudly or barely snicker. I teach a lesson with the goal of engaging students, and I see that some students have their eyes riveted on me while others are nodding off" (8).

With only a handful of goals, students are more likely to believe that success is attainable and more likely to self-navigate toward that success. Although it is customary for students to receive comments on their work, the question is whether or not the comments compel them to action. John Hattie and Helen Timperley make a case that

Table 3.3 Personalized Learning Evolution: Feedback

Element	Minimal Student Input	Some Student Input	Student Driven
Feedback *How is feedback provided, and how is it used?*	Teacher provides formal and informal feedback on the task to help student revise and refine the task.	Teacher and others (e.g., peers, experts in the field) provide feedback to help student revise and refine the task.	Student seeks and uses feedback from teacher and others to guide performance.

"teachers and parents often assume that students share a commitment to academic goals, whereas the reality is that developing this shared commitment to learning needs to be nurtured and built" (89). To build this shared commitment requires regular, student-friendly, action-oriented feedback.

- **Regular.** Students need to be updated on the impact of their performance, and the feedback should be incremental. When students understand that the goal is improved autonomous performance, then the evaluator's job (teacher, peer, expert, self) is to engage immediately: ask the student to describe and analyze what happened. In turn, the student's job is to focus on what to do next in light of that information. The more time that elapses between the performance and the feedback, the less likely that the feedback will have an impact on future performance.

- **Student friendly.** The student should be able to comprehend the feedback in terms of the accessibility of language and clarity of the descriptors. Many rubrics and criteria fail this test. For example, the use of vague terms such as *none, some, many,* and *most* implies that what is important is the quantity of information and ideas, not the quality. Another concern is the length and sophistication of the description, which, depending on the student's age and comprehension level, can make the feedback difficult to understand.

- **Action oriented.** Students should focus on one or a handful of improvements rather than be overwhelmed by errors. In the design stage, acting on feedback is how the student improves. When students review feedback, they should get clear information: How do I proceed? Where do I make adjustments? Do I need a new idea? Action-oriented feedback should propel prototyping, so that the product can be tested as a part of its development. Action-oriented and regular (or immediate) feedback go hand in hand.

Another obstacle that may keep students from action has to do with their concerns as to how they might be perceived in the culture of the classroom. Hattie and Timperley explain, "Student engagement in learning is likely to be constrained by the evaluative dimensions of classroom lessons because there is personal risk involved in responding publicly and failing" (100). In other words, if students do not feel that their teacher and/or their peers value risk taking, they usually respond only when they are fairly confident of their answer, interpretation, or solution. Further support for this comes from the findings of Ryan and Deci, whose work shows that when students see themselves as competent and experience a positive sense of "relatedness" with their teachers, they experience greater intrinsic motivation, which then leads to greater outright achievement. Thus such informed and sensitive feedback begins a positive self-fulfilling cycle.

Personalized Learning Recommendations

1. *Provide every student with an authentic challenge.* Students deserve to be pushed to tackle challenges, problems, texts, and performances that are initially daunting but still doable. Regularly doing work that is "too easy" makes students less inclined to struggle, pay attention to details, or focus on the task at hand. Regularly doing work that is "too hard" sends a message to students that this topic, subject, or skill is "not for them," or they decide they are "bad at it." When students are expected to participate in learning that is outside the zone of proximal development, they are more inclined to feel that school is either boring or overwhelming—both promote chronic stress and make it more likely that students will shut down.

2. *Focus on a handful of specific goals.* This shift in practice means that every student can work on a few high-leverage goals in consultation with the teacher rather than engage in a "one-size-fits-all" revision process.

3. *During the process, praise the effort, not the performance.* This shift in practice means that every student can improve based on where he is—a focus on continuing to get better rather than being satisfied with current performance.

4. *Figure out a way to get feedback to students as quickly as possible.* Wiggins said, "Although the universal teacher lament that there's no time for such feedback is understandable, remember that 'no time to give and use feedback' actually means 'no time to cause learning.' As we have seen, research shows that *less* teaching plus *more* feedback is the key to achieving greater learning" (11). Design predictable routines and use technology to free yourself to observe and confer; create student-friendly rubrics; and have students revise the language as needed.

5. *"Feedback causes thinking"* (Dylan Wiliam). Students should be expected to do something rather than casually glance at the commentary and make superficial (if any) changes. Thinking and growing from feedback are as important for a second grader as they are for a proficient adult. Wiggins offers, "The problem is not in making errors; you

will all miss many balls in the field, and that's part of learning. The problem is when you don't learn from the errors." Make students *think* before taking the next step.

6. ***Model the need for revision through regular student reviews of your own work.*** More teachers are asking students to provide information about delivery, instruction, and classroom climate. However, this feedback typically comes at the end of the grade or course, meaning that any action taken does not immediately benefit that group of students. Exit tickets are an example of immediate feedback; they can provide insight into how well students understand content, the level of challenge they confronted, the comfort level in the classroom, and their ability to collaborate with the teacher and other students.

7. ***Separate feedback from grades as much as possible.*** Through feedback, focus students' attention on the quality of their current work and how they can improve it. Do not distract them from the learning and improvement process with a grade.

8. ***Once the process is over, praise the performance.*** We all must have a "delivery point" or a performance that represents the realization of our goals. Articulate the specific, overall strengths exhibited in the design, investigation, and communication.

ELEMENT 7: EVALUATION

The final element in this chapter is evaluation: how we score student performance. Grading is not something "done" to the students; it is an informed judgment based on an analysis of work measured against a set of criteria. In a more traditional classroom environment, we evaluate what is easily measurable (for example, accuracy of response, inclusion of information, completeness of the assignment). Given a more expansive view of outcomes (disciplinary, cross-disciplinary, and mindsets), evaluation shifts in a personalized learning model (see table 3.4).

Table 3.4 Personalized Learning Evolution: Evaluation

Element	Minimal Student Input	Some Student Input	Student Driven
Evaluation *How is performance evaluated on a given task?*	Teacher generates a score and provides explanation of performance.	Student rates performance based on given outcomes to inform teacher evaluation.	Student and teacher interpret evidence of achievement in relation to key outcomes and goals.

To interpret student performance consistently and fairly, we need common expectations against which to interpret performance, even when one student's type of performance can differ greatly from another's. The articulation of each of our types of outcomes into appropriate indicators of performance and proficiency is central, providing common elements to measure personalized learning and development *against*. In short,

- *Disciplinary outcomes* require delineation of the subject-area expectations as informed by the cognitive demand of the standards. This requires a qualitative scale or rubric for more sophisticated or complex tasks.

- *Cross-disciplinary outcomes* require a qualitative scale or rubric that is integrated with or parallel to that for disciplinary outcomes.

- *Mindsets as outcomes* require a set of observable traits that students can demonstrate, enabling teachers to provide useful feedback or to encourage and look for growth over time. Observing and interpreting performance related to mindsets is difficult for teachers; these attributes are tricky to "spot." In the case of mindsets, students must be enlisted to identify instances when they have demonstrated these mindsets and the qualitative level to which they called on them to assist in achieving success.

Evaluation will have an impact on current grading practices and systems: what we score, how we score, and how we report learning may need to be substantially revised. An individual educator can undertake some of the revision by

- Developing rubrics that measure disciplinary and cross-disciplinary outcomes

- Engaging students in the analysis and clarification of rubrics to build a collective understanding of the descriptors as well as how to become more skillful and sophisticated over time

- Using rubrics consistently (for example, descriptors for a powerful argument don't change even when the topic or issue does)

There are many policies and practices that are beyond a teacher's control, however. Although it is important to acknowledge that grading and reporting student work in a personalized learning model represent a significant challenge, we wanted to stay focused on design elements, not scoring. Therefore, when you read through the illustrative examples in the next chapter, you will not see how the work was "graded."

1. ***Develop rubrics that measure desired outcomes.*** This challenge can (and ideally should) involve a range of teachers to articulate descriptors based on the cognitive demand of standards and a shared commitment to the cross-disciplinary outcomes and mindsets.

2. ***Begin conversations about shifts in grading policies and practices.*** Many education leaders have entertained and perhaps implemented significant shifts in how learning is reported. This challenge requires all key stakeholders (that is, parents, students, and staff) to be included from the very beginning to ask fundamental questions around the purpose of the reporting. Then people may be open to considering more radical questions, such as:

   o What if we no longer reported out in predictable increments, because there is a continuous assessment of learning?

   o What if we expected students to play a greater role in the scoring and revising of their work?

   o What if we developed rubrics that can be used across grade levels to clarify what quality work looks like in a given subject area?

CONCLUSION AND REFLECTIVE QUESTIONS

The explanation, examples, and recommendations in chapters 2 and 3 paint a picture of what personalized learning is and how it can be designed at the classroom level. The next chapter puts the elements together and shares tangible examples from a range of schools, nonprofit organizations, and families. Before we move on, consider the following questions:

1. What task idea(s) in your classroom or school are in the Some Student Input or Student Driven category?

2. What tasks in your classroom are not well suited to become personalized? For those tasks, can you identify why not?

3. What are the barriers to treating students as design partners? Which barriers could you reduce or eliminate, and how?

4. How can you move beyond teacher as audience for student work? Where do you find willing audience members outside the classroom?

5. How can you figure out how to provide regular, action-oriented, student-friendly feedback so that students can continue to refine or revise their work?

WORKS CITED

Aguilar, E. "Motivating Students: Writing for an Audience." *Edutopia*, 18 February 2011. Web. 15 May 2014. <http://www.edutopia.org/blog/motivating-student-writers-audience-elena-aguilar>.

Berger, R. "Water: A Whole School Expedition." *Journeys Through Our Classrooms*. Eds., Dennis Udall and Amy Mednick. Dubuque, IA: Kendall/Hunt, 2000. Print.

Boss, S. "QuadBlogging Connects Student Writers with Global Audiences." *Edutopia*, 25 September 2012. Web. 15 May 2014. <http://www.edutopia.org/blog/quad-blogging-technology-classroom-suzie-boss>.

Clarke, J. *Personalized Learning: Student Pathways to High School Graduation*. Thousand Oaks, CA: Corwin, 2013. Print.

Cornally, S. "Deeper Learning: Performance Assessment and Authentic Audience." *Edutopia*, 20 December 2012. Web. 20 May 2014. <http://www.edutopia.org/blog/making-assessment-relevant-students-teachers-shawn-cornally>.

Fullan, M., and Langworthy, M. *A Rich Seam: How New Pedagogies Find Deep Learning*. London: Pearson, 2014. Print.

Hattie, J., and Timperley, H. "The Power of Feedback." *Review of Educational Research* 77.1 (2007): 81–112. Print.

Hernandez, A. "Where's the Authentic Audience?" *Edtechworkshop*, 29 Sept. 2012. Web. 20 May 2014. <http://edtechworkshop.blogspot.com/2012/09/wheres-authentic-audience.html>.

Miller, M. "Authentic Audiences." *Goldfish Bowl*, 16 June 2013. Web. 15 July 2014. <http://thegoldfishbowl.edublogs.org/2013/06/16/authentic-audiences/>.

Moulton, J. "Learners Thrive with a Public Audience." *Edutopia*, 20 June 2009. Web. 15 Jan. 2014. <http://www.edutopia.org/student-presentations-public-audience>.

Ryan, R. M., & Deci, E. L. "An Overview of Self-Determination Theory." *Handbook of Self-Determination Research*. Eds., Edward L. Deci and Richard M. Ryan. Rochester, NY: University of Rochester Press, 2002. Print.

Wiggins, G. "Seven Keys to Effective Feedback." *Education Leadership* 70.1 (2012): 10–16. Print.

Wiliam, D. "Feedback on Learning." *Journey to Excellence*. Education Scotland, n.d. Web. 11 June 2014. <http://www.journeytoexcellence.org.uk/videos/expertsspeakers/feedbackonlearningdylanwiliam.asp>.

Chapter 4

Tasks That Demonstrate Personalized Learning Evolution in Practice

One week in late 2010 a student presented this paper: Blackawton Bees (*Biology Letters*, November 2010). Of course none of us work on bees, but we were particularly interested in this article because it was written by a class of third graders ... yep, as in eight- to ten-year-old children. As you can imagine, that journal discussion had little to do about the science and much to do about what an interesting approach to science education this is. Third graders had thought of the questions, designed and carried out the experiments, and interpreted the results. How many other students had the same potential? Probably thousands. That got us thinking ... how awesome would it be to promote this kind of research based science and wouldn't it be great if students could publish their research in a peer-reviewed journal created for just that intent?

—Editorial board of *Journal of Emerging Investigators*
(http://www.emerginginvestigators.org/about/)

The walls that separate the "school world" from the "real world" become more porous as learning becomes a shared enterprise. This chapter illustrates how the elements described in chapters 2 and 3 fit together in task designs that have been developed by educators and programs throughout the world. To inspire personalized learning task designs, we offer the saying *go personal, go local, go global* and provide explanations and examples. Finally, we share two examples of how a traditional performance task can evolve based on student interest and broader audience as well as provide a pathway to support student planning.

The Personalized Learning Evolution is repeated in table 4.1 to support your familiarity with the elements, the levels of evolution, and the explanations.

How do you use the elements of the Personalized Learning Evolution to design tasks? The task frame is a graphic organizer that describes the parameters of the assignment to focus the design and the development of the student. Developers of task frames use them to clarify elements of context, task, audience, feedback, targeted disciplinary outcomes, and cross-disciplinary outcomes as well as specify the extent to which students drive the work (that is, minimal student input, some student input, student driven). The first two examples here (tables 4.2 and 4.3) were first referenced in chapters 1 and 2: Water for the Future and Bugsy Breaks. There are more illustrative task frames throughout the chapter and in appendix B. In addition, there is a blank version in appendix B. Again, our goal is to ease the transition from a teacher-designed and teacher-directed task to one that incorporates and values student ideas and actions.

INSPIRATION FOR TASK DESIGNS

How do you invite students to the design table to create with you? We have broken down these examples into three categories: *go personal, go local,* and *go global.* Every example we have featured in these next sections would be, at a minimum, in the Some Student Input column of the shaded sections of table 4.1. These assignments are designed to gain better insight into who students are and how they present themselves to the world. In addition, we include for each category at least two illustrative examples, described in task frames.

Go Personal

To create a sense of belonging (the fourth mindset, as discussed in chapter 2) requires an exploration of who you are and how you present yourself to others. This exploration and communication requires significant student choice as to what to share and how to express it. Following are five examples that students can use to both uncover and share who they are:

- **Six-word memoir (for teens).** Everyone has a story. Can you say it in six words? Students can post their memoir as well as the rationale behind the memoir on the site (http://www.sixwordmemoirs.com/teens/index.php). There are no established

(text continues on page 79)

Table 4.1 Personalized Learning Evolution

	Elements	Minimal Student Input	Some Student Input	Student Driven
Chapter 2	**Disciplinary Outcomes** *What are the subject-specific goals of learning?*	Established standards dictate the content and skills to be learned.	Student has some choice to focus on particular topics, concepts, or skills within established standards.	Student determines the content and skills he or she wishes to learn within established standards.
	Cross-Disciplinary Outcomes *What learning goals cut across subject areas?*	Cross-disciplinary outcomes have been established.	Student has opportunities to develop based on explicit teaching and assessment.	Student identifies cross-disciplinary outcomes from a common set.
	Mindsets *What mindsets are necessary for success?*	Teacher creates a classroom culture that uses the four mindsets (relevance, growth mindset, self-efficacy, sense of belonging).	Teacher guides students to use the four mindsets to strengthen performance and development.	Student uses mindsets to work harder, engage in more productive behaviors, and persevere to overcome obstacles to success.
Chapter 3	**Task** *What is the challenge?*	Teacher, curriculum, or computer generates the problem, idea, design, or investigation.	Teacher guides definition and articulation of the problem, idea, design, or investigation.	Student independently defines and articulates the problem, idea, design, or investigation.
	Audience *Who is the audience? How does that shape communication?*	Teacher is primary audience for student product or performance.	Student has input into or choice of audience.	Student engages with authentic audience to demonstrate learning and to add value through contribution.

(continued)

Table 4.1 (*continued*)

	Elements	Minimal Student Input	Some Student Input	Student Driven
Chapter 3 (continued)	**Feedback** *How is feedback provided, and how is it used?*	Teacher provides formal and informal feedback on the task to help student revise and refine the task.	Teacher and others (e.g., peers, experts in the field) provide feedback to help student revise and refine the task.	Student seeks and uses feedback from teacher and others to guide performance.
	Evaluation *How is performance evaluated on a given task?*	Teacher generates a score and provides explanation of performance.	Student rates performance based on given outcomes to inform teacher evaluation.	Student and teacher interpret evidence of achievement in relation to key outcomes and goals.
Chapter 5	**Process** *Who controls the sequence and pace of learning?*	Learning sequence and pace are specified by the curriculum, teacher, and/or resource.	Learning sequence and pace are specified but somewhat flexible based on student interest and need.	Learning sequence and pace are developed based on student interest and need and flexible based on assessment of progress.
	Environment *Where does the learning take place?*	There is a top-down environment in which teacher instructs and assesses disciplinary and cross-disciplinary outcomes.	The environment is more collaborative; teacher considers student voice and choice in the instruction and assessment of disciplinary and cross-disciplinary outcomes.	Teacher and student work together as learning partners to design and assess learning for disciplinary and cross-disciplinary outcomes.

Table 4.1 *(continued)*

	Elements	Minimal Student Input	Some Student Input	Student Driven
Chapter 6	**Demonstration of Learning** *What constitutes evidence of learning?*	Teacher and district assessments specify the way(s) in which disciplinary and cross-disciplinary outcomes will be demonstrated.	Student chooses among a set of options to determine how disciplinary and cross-disciplinary outcomes will be demonstrated.	Student proposes or shapes way(s) that both disciplinary and cross-disciplinary outcomes will be demonstrated and will provide evidence of learning (e.g., personalized portfolio).
	Time *When can/does learning occur?*	Schooling is defined by "seat time"— prescribed number of school days (e.g., 180 days, Carnegie units)	Schooling is a more variable blend of time-based and outcome-based measures.	Schooling can take place 24/7, 365 days a year and be determined by outcome-based measures.
	Advancement *How does a student progress through the system?*	Student is advanced based on age, irrespective of achievement.	Promotion or retention at the end of the year is based on achievement in the course or grade level.	Advancement is based on demonstrated competency whenever that is achieved.

criteria for submissions. A few examples from the site caught our eye in connection to the topic of this book:

- "Staring upwards, pretending to be elsewhere."
- "My brain is a box of crayons."
- "Second place is never good enough."
- "Cannot wait for freedom to ring."

(text continues on page 81)

Table 4.2 Task Frame: Water for the Future—A High School Algebra Task

Context: Water is becoming an increasingly valuable and scarce resource. Your job is to evaluate water uses in a given community (your town or someplace else) and prepare a briefing/proposal for a town hall meeting with recommendations on future water policy and practices for the next fifty years.	
Task • Minimal Student Input • **Some Student Input** • Student Driven	***What is the challenge?*** This briefing should analyze the current amount of drinkable and nondrinkable water, make predictions about the amount of drinkable water in the future, and provide the status of current water practices, such as: • Historical water usage by categories (e.g., drinking, showering, lawn care, manufacturing, recreational) • Historical cost per gallon to deliver water to a household or business • How much water is wasted each day in homes, local businesses, organizations • Historical share of community taxes that subsidize water • Age of the water infrastructure and projected need for repair • Existing water treatment plants and related operational cost and capacity • Historical population changes in the community The briefing should predict what will happen over the next fifty years if there is no change to water policy and practices. Identify trends in the points listed above. Then make projections for every five years of the next fifty years. The briefing must propose at least two government policies that would conserve water. Consider both costs and benefits of each policy—e.g., possible recycling of wastewater into potable water.
Audience • Minimal Student Input • **Some Student Input** • Student Driven	***Who is the audience? How does that shape communication?*** Local experts and officials from town/city will evaluate presentations (either prior to the town hall meeting or instead of it).
Feedback • Minimal Student Input • **Some Student Input** • Student Driven	***How is feedback provided, and how is it used?*** The following criteria should guide your work: • Analyze and evaluate current water practices • Make realistic predictions based on findings • Prepare briefing/proposal • Make accurate five-year projections based on trends • Make reasonable recommendations based on data

Table 4.2 *(continued)*

Disciplinary Outcomes
• Use functions to model relationships among quantities; analyze and interpret data/evidence to form predictions, discern patterns, or recommend actions • **Common Core Mathematics:** CCSS.Math.Content.HSA.CED.A.2–4; CCSS.Math.Content.HSF.IF.A.1; CCSS.Math.Content.HSF.IF.B.4; CCSS.Math.Content.HSF.IF.B.6–7; CCSS.Math.Practice.MP1, 3–8 • **Common Core ELA:** CCSS.ELA-Literacy.CCRA.W4
Cross-Disciplinary Outcomes
• **Problem Solving:** Frame a question to identify what you don't know; pursue knowledge and conduct research to find a viable solution; draw conclusions and define next steps • **Communication:** Use mode(s) of communication to share information appropriate for a specific purpose, task, and audience • **Metacognition:** Know what you don't know and use mechanisms to deal with problems; think about your thought process; analyze performance along the way; seek and use feedback

An alternative is Dan Pink's one-sentence project. Larry Ferlazzo created a set of links for educators to do this in the classroom (http://larryferlazzo.edublogs.org /2012/09/23/series-of-good-dan-pink-videos-to-use-with-students/). Pink's project is no longer active, but you can offer these examples to inspire students to write statements physically or virtually for a broader audience.

• **Judging a book by its cover: the power of first impressions.** How do we initially judge people? Can a bad first impression be overcome? Examine your "digital footprint" online to determine what first impression is being revealed and how different audiences see specific aspects of who you are. Based on your analysis, take one aspect of how you are presenting yourself to the world via social networking and develop a deliberate plan for rehabilitating or developing your image for a target audience.

• **This I Believe** (www.thisibelieve.org). These are short essays around a personal belief, written by people from all walks of life. Essays are categorized by theme, such as empathy and compassion, discrimination, carpe diem, addiction, setbacks, humor and laughter, legacy, self-knowledge. In order to be considered, you need to adhere to the parameters from the website:

  o Please limit your essay to approximately five hundred words.

  o Tell a story that illustrates how your personal belief was shaped.

(text continues on page 83)

Table 4.3 Task Frame: Bugsy Breaks—Developing a Philanthropic Business Model

Context: Students identified a local, regional, or global need where a philanthropic business model would provide a solution in the form of a service or product. Students explored a variety of issues ranging from water access to poverty to healthy food options. The experience resulted in healthy experimentation with innovation and problem solving among the upper elementary students.	
Task • Minimal Student Input • Some Student Input • **Student Driven**	***What is the challenge?*** Having examined philanthropic business models, this student decided to use the increasingly popular practice of crowdfunding. She started a web-based organization, which accepted contributions for the specific purpose of bringing class pets to classrooms with students like her. Specifically targeting those most likely to help fund such an effort, this student learned how sites like Google, Yahoo, and others can strategically market and cater to specific consumers and investors. The site remains live today and serves as a clear demonstration that when teachers frame a project using a compelling purpose, driving questions, and robust criteria, the conditions are set for students to shape and personalize their learning.
Audience • Minimal Student Input • **Some Student Input** • Student Driven	***Who is the audience? How does that shape communication?*** The audience for this particular project was made up of potential contributors to this cause, which involved the school community as well as anyone finding the website. The student was aware of the potential contributors to her cause and did her best to write in a way that diverse audiences would find accessible, helpful, and clear.
Feedback • Minimal Student Input • Some Student Input • **Student Driven**	***How is feedback provided, and how is it used?*** The following description indicates how students used feedback: Students received feedback from peers using digital tools like Google docs. Students read one another's writing and provided feedback through a "comments" feature. Students also used project checklists as well as writing rubrics to self-score their work. Teachers were also involved in feedback during and after the project products were completed.
Disciplinary Outcomes	

- I can write opinion pieces on topics or texts, supporting a point of view with reasons and information.
- I can write informative/explanatory texts to examine a topic and convey ideas and information clearly.

Table 4.3 *(continued)*

- I can develop and strengthen writing as needed by planning, revising, editing, rewriting, or trying a new approach.
- I can conduct short research projects that use several sources to build knowledge through investigation of different aspects of a topic.
- I can use technology, including the Internet, to produce and publish writing as well as interact and collaborate with others; I can demonstrate sufficient command of keyboarding skills to type a minimum of two pages in a single sitting.

Cross-Disciplinary Outcomes

- **Creative Thinking:** Take a different perspective on the same problem, topic, idea, or object
- **Critical Thinking:** Apply a questioning eye; make predictions, articulate patterns and draw conclusions
- **Communication:** Use mode(s) of communication to share information and ideas for a specific purpose, task, and audience; frame and present a point of view in a way that is compelling and engaging

Developed by Jennifer Carey, teacher/advisor at Aveson Charter School

o Please refrain from writing an opinion piece about a public issue. We want the story of your belief, not an editorial about a current event.

o Tell us what you *do* believe, not what you don't believe.

o Proofread your essay before you submit it, as we do not accept corrections or changes after we receive your essay.

- **Knowing about how your brain controls your attitude and actions.** How does your brain work? How do you use that knowledge of how your brain works to accomplish goals? There are a significant number of programs that focus on student self-empowerment through learning about the brain. There are two notable but very different examples of such programs, which have been implemented in schools and communities internationally. First, Mindset Works (www.mindsetworks.com) is an online brain-based program to teach students about the brain and about how to have a growth mindset. Currently, there are more than fifty thousand students around the world who have worked through the modules to learn how to grow intelligence through effort, resilience, and improvement. A principal in Texas shared this success story: "After completing the modules, one 8th grade boy made the A/B honor roll for the first time since 3rd grade. When I asked him what the difference was, he said that now he understood that learning was not always going to come easy to him and that didn't mean he was stupid, it just meant he needed to work harder on that subject." Girls on the Run, an extracurricular elementary and middle school program, provides girls with tools to develop physical, emotional, and spiritual health. The organization's vision: "a world where every girl knows and activates her limitless potential and is free to boldly pursue her dreams." There are twenty-four lessons that are taught in conjunction with training for a 5K race. Ten-year-old Girls on the Run participant Zoe Zmuda recalls one of the lessons:

> We learned about how what you say to yourself in your head shows up in your attitudes and actions. A positive cord means that you are happy and you are enjoying what is happening in life. A negative cord means that you are angry, sad, or disappointed. If you have a negative cord plugged into your brain, you can recognize that it is there and then unplug that cord based on a change in your attitude. So when I feel like I can't do something, whether it's running or something else I am not the best at, I know I can do this if I believe, try my hardest, and keep doing what they tell me that I need to get better on.

- **Future aspirations.** What do you want to do when you grow up? Students describe their dream and then investigate how to take action through research on training programs, opportunities for internships or service projects, experts, or ideas that inspire. This aspirational work can be done in multiple ways: an advisory program, Career Studies course, English Language Arts class, an independent study structure, or a service learning requirement. In addition, there are several software mapping tools for students to map out their futures, most notably eMAPS from the Consortium for Public Education in Pittsburgh (http://www .theconsortiumforpubliceducation.org/20121011_news.html).

The first task frame (table 4.4) was inspired by a conversation that Allison had on an airplane with a ninth-grade girl, Peyton Brick. As she described what she wanted to do, Peyton became more and more excited that it could be possible as part of her high school experience.

The second task frame (table 4.5) was developed by a team of French and Spanish teachers in Colorado. They wanted to design a task for which students had to conjugate verbs in the past tense to describe a memory.

Table 4.4   Task Frame: My Aspirations

Context: I really want to know more about the health sciences (specifically what pathologists do). I have learned basic information, such as how to graph body parts, do basic paperwork, and address sickness and injuries. One of the things that would help me become more knowledgeable in the medical field would be performing hands-on experiences such as surgeries, autopsies, and seminars of emergency situations. Since many of the medical careers involve fast decision making and evaluating the situation blindfolded, we should be taught how to perform quickly and vigorously. This would enhance our thinking and enable us to react quickly to anonymous situations rather than receiving a rubric and following that verbatim with the scenarios being reiterated.	
Task • Minimal Student Input • Some Student Input • **Student Driven**	**What is the challenge?** I want to intern for a local forensic pathologist over a multiweek period. During this period of time, my vision is observing or assisting a forensic pathologist while they guide me throughout a series of autopsies. During this time, I would gain knowledge and become more fluent with finding the source of deaths and the obstacles to prevent the deaths from reoccurring. **Teacher idea:** Can I use this idea and have every student pursue an internship or research a career in health sciences? What if students aren't interested in the internship or health sciences? Is there another alternative?
Audience • Minimal Student Input • Some Student Input • **Student Driven**	**Who is the audience? How does that shape communication?** Pathologist. There is a high expectation of professionalism both in communication and task completion.
Feedback • Minimal Student Input • Some Student Input • **Student Driven**	**How is feedback provided, and how is it used?** The following describes key criteria that could be used when working with a pathologist: • Ask relevant or pertinent questions • Think through ideas about the possible cause of death • Assist with equipment

Disciplinary Outcomes

From Connecticut State Framework for Medical Careers:
• Develop an understanding of health occupations
• Make informed career decisions
• Demonstrate ability to accurately assess self and others
• Apply academic knowledge and skills to home, community, and workplace environments
• Demonstrate effective communication skills

(continued)

Tasks That Demonstrate Personalized Learning Evolution in Practice   85

Table 4.4 *(continued)*

Cross-Disciplinary Outcomes
• **Critical Thinking:** Make predictions, articulate patterns, and draw conclusions • **Problem Solving:** Pursue knowledge and conduct research to find a viable solution • **Communication:** Use mode(s) of communication to share information and ideas for a specific purpose, task, and audience • **Metacognition:** Analyze performance along the way; seek and use feedback

Go Local

Students consider challenges or problems in the local community and take action on investigating the root of the challenge or problem and developing an idea, design, or prototype to address it. Students can present their ideas to a broader audience both to seek feedback and to garner support for the larger aim. Ideas for local challenges can come from multiple places, including personal experiences, interviews with members of the community, or current events.

The d.school at Stanford University offers two key questions in the selection of the local challenge (answers to both questions should be yes):

• Does the challenge contain a variety of explicit and implicit human needs?

• Does the challenge allow for a range of solutions?

For more information on d.school K–12 design challenges, visit the school's wiki: https://dschool.stanford.edu/groups/k12/wiki/613e8/Creating_Design_Challenges .html.

When considering the integration of local challenges within classroom curricula, teachers can identify how a given design project connects to standards to leverage the appropriate amount of time, staffing, and community outreach. If there is a loose connection with standards but high student interest, a teacher can propose to the student that this is a powerful idea for a service learning project or cocurricular group. If there is a direct association with a few standards and high student interest, teachers can work on part(s) of the design process (delineated in chapter 3) and provide class

(text continues on page 88)

Table 4.5 Task Frame: World Language Task on Memories

<table>
<tr>
<td colspan="2">Context: How do you describe a childhood memory using the target language? How do you use past memories to make a connection to someone else?</td>
</tr>
<tr>
<td>Task
• Minimal Student Input
• Some Student Input
• Student Driven</td>
<td>What is the challenge?
Each student will bring in an artifact representing routine experiences from their childhood (pictures, videos, toys, objects, etc.). They will use this artifact to orally describe fond childhood memories and explain its importance (goal). The student will review, self-evaluate, and rerecord until satisfied (product).
Once the recording is finished, students are encouraged to select two students whom they don't really know that well, listen to the recordings, and make a connection (e.g., pose a question, share a similar story).</td>
</tr>
<tr>
<td>Audience
• Minimal Student Input
• Some Student Input
• Student Driven</td>
<td>Who is the audience? How does that shape communication?
Other students who don't know you that well. You have to describe the artifact but also share a little about what makes you you (e.g., your personality, aspirations)</td>
</tr>
<tr>
<td>Feedback
• Minimal Student Input
• Some Student Input
• Student Driven</td>
<td>How is feedback provided, and how is it used?
The following description indicates how students used feedback:
• Use established speaking rubric to evaluate quality of recording
• Rerecord statement until satisfied that it demonstrates disciplinary and cross-disciplinary outcomes</td>
</tr>
<tr>
<td colspan="2" align="center">Disciplinary Outcomes</td>
</tr>
<tr>
<td colspan="2">• Engage in conversations
• Provide and obtain information
• Express feelings and emotions, and exchange opinions</td>
</tr>
<tr>
<td colspan="2" align="center">Cross-Disciplinary Outcomes</td>
</tr>
<tr>
<td colspan="2">• Communication: Use mode(s) of communication to share information and ideas for a specific purpose, task, and audience; frame and present a point of view in a way that is compelling and engaging; listen to a point of view to verify, deepen, or disagree
• Metacognition: Analyze performance along the way</td>
</tr>
</table>

Developed at ThunderRidge High School, Colorado

time to develop a solution, conduct an independent study, evaluate existing projects, and come up with an action project to carry out one solution or idea. Another option is to partner with a community group to join existing action projects or have student(s) share ideas with a community group to cocreate and carry out a plan. To get you started, here are four ideas that are common in many communities:

- **Art installations.** Students create artwork and install it in local businesses and public spaces. Each piece is accompanied by a short statement that describes relevant information the artist wants to share with the viewer. In addition, there should be a larger explanation of the installation or exhibit to frame the viewing experience.

- **Local enterprises.** Students operate businesses as part of a school-to-career program or on their own time. Common enterprises include catering, auto repair, beauty salon, graphic design, APP design, computer repair, and lessons (for example, guitar, social media, art, animation, 3-D printing). Students learn how to hone their craft, network with local employers, market their business, design customer feedback loops, and improve customer service.

- **Other people's stories.** Students interview and record the stories of senior citizens employing a particular focus (for example, growing up, most important techno-logical innovation, turning point in their lives, greatest love, a day they will never forget). Students create a narrative using a given medium and then present a copy as a gift.

- **Service project.** Students join an existing service project or develop an idea based on an articulated need. This project can be connected to future aspirations and/or course content (for example, cleanup days, food banks, donations to local hospitals, volunteering at shelters) and have conceptual threads and skill sets related to English language arts, social studies, health sciences, foods and nutrition, and environmental science (to name a few).

Tables 4.6, 4.7, and 4.8 are three task frames: two describe how students made sense of a problem and offered a viable solution. Students in an Australian school used their woodworking techniques to give back to their local community (table 4.6); students in Philadelphia applied algebra to determine the safest routes to school (table 4.7). The third task frame for this category (table 4.8) is a youth media project for which students partner with local reporters and studio professionals to capture and create news.

Table 4.6 Task Frame: Wood Technology and Design Project

Context: In Wood Technology and Design class, where typically a student would make pencil holders and other such items (that often see their way to the back of the pantry once they get home!), the students spoke with a refugee family about the type of furniture they need when they arrive in Australia as well as the broader issues that surround being a new arrival to Australia. Designing furniture for this family sparked an idea to partner with other local organizations.	
Task • Minimal Student Input • **Some Student Input** • Student Driven	***What is the challenge?*** As teachers, we built community service tasks directly into the curriculum in the Year 9 Materials and Design course. The students spent half the year making projects to donate to various community groups. The class split itself into groups of three or four students; they researched a variety of community organizations and then contacted them directly to negotiate a project that they would make and then deliver to them. Examples: building toy boxes for Foster Care Association and building raised garden beds for a community house.
Audience • Minimal Student Input • Some Student Input • **Student Driven**	***Who is the audience? How does that shape communication?*** When the projects are completed, the boys contact the organizations, who are over the moon to receive such special gifts. The "clients" collaborate with the boys, make site visits, sometimes work alongside in the design and construction phases. The celebratory aspect of the project is also very significant in consolidating the experience for the students. As one student said, "Materials and Design has been a huge success this year. We first started off by having a guest speaker in. His story of hardship was unimaginable but it also got us in the right frame of mind." ... "The whole class learned a lot this year about making coffee tables and about the hardship of others. We were honored in making the coffee tables for you."
Feedback • Minimal Student Input • Some Student Input • **Student Driven**	***How is feedback provided, and how is it used?*** The following description indicates how students develop and use feedback: Students brainstorm with the teacher to identify criteria for success. The projects then are quality-controlled by the teacher. Teacher and students regularly revisit criteria to evaluate progress and determine next steps.
Disciplinary Outcomes	

• Investigate and make judgments on how the characteristics and properties of materials, systems, components, tools, and equipment can be combined to create designed solutions

(continued)

Table 4.6 *(continued)*

• Apply design thinking, creativity, innovation, and enterprise skills to develop, modify, and communicate design ideas of increasing sophistication • Develop project plans using digital technologies to plan and manage projects individually and collaboratively, taking into consideration time, cost, risk, and production processes

Cross-Disciplinary Outcomes
• **Problem Solving:** Investigation and research stage throughout the project • **Creative Thinking:** Design and development of the product • **Communication:** Throughout the project, with each other and with their chosen community group using Internet and telephone • **Collaboration:** Solving problems jointly through group work • **Metacognition:** Awareness of their own knowledge and their ability to understand, control, and manipulate their own cognitive processes

Developed by Wesley College, Australia

Go Global

When considering how to integrate global literacy into local curricula, there are two basic entry points: (1) investigate the world through a complex problem and (2) recognize different perspectives around a common idea. Brandon Wiley, executive director of the International Studies School Network at Asia Society, asserts: "Learning about problems in far away countries may have been part of the curriculum before, but 21st century technology allows students to actually connect with those problems, serve as actors, and do something about them" (152). Here are just four of many global examples to inspire your students: an engineering competition, a science competition, an illustration of global population, and a common exploration across cultures.

- **Grand Challenges from the National Academy of Engineering** (http://www.engi neeringchallenges.org/cms/8996.aspx). The following are daunting challenges for students who have the background knowledge and developmental skills to think through a possible solution:

  o Determine how to make solar energy more cost effective for home owners and business.

  o Design a plan to supply more clean water to populations with a scarcity of water or make better use of existing water resources.

(text continues on page 92)

Table 4.7 Task Frame: Safe School Routes

Context: This project aims to design a system that can evaluate travel routes for relative safety, so that the most efficient and safest travel routes can be planned and communicated to the community at large. For additional information, visit http://www.samsung.com/us/solvefortomorrow/projects/finding-the-safest -route.html.	
Task • Minimal Student Input • **Some Student Input** • Student Driven	**What is the challenge?** The need for this project was identified by Susan Lee, an Algebra II teacher, and shared with her colleague, Physics teacher Klint Kanopka. Together, the two gathered a group of fifteen students from mixed grade levels interested in the project. The teachers presented the issue, stating, "Here's the problem; fix it," and from there the solution generation process was entirely student driven.
Audience • Minimal Student Input • Some Student Input • **Student Driven**	**Who is the audience? How does that shape communication?** Students submitted their project to the Samsung "Solve for Tomorrow" competition (http://www.samsung.com/us /solvefortomorrow/home.html) and were selected as one of three national winners. The fifteen national finalists traveled to the SXSWedu Conference in Austin, Texas, to present their ideas.
Feedback • Minimal Student Input • Some Student Input • **Student Driven**	**How is feedback provided and how is it used?** The following description indicates how students used feedback in the design of the task: Students began with an open discussion about how "safe" is defined, and distributed a student survey to collect data on community needs (e.g., 50 percent of Academy at Palumbo students walk to school, and the average walk is 5.5 blocks). From there, they assigned values to specific crimes (e.g., shooting = 5 and theft = 2). Students completed walk-throughs of the neighborhood to test their algorithm, walking each of the possible routes to observe differences. Teachers and students together brainstormed possible ways to organize the data, especially when considering such variables as the scope of a crime scene.
Disciplinary Outcomes	

- Describe and/or solve problems using algebraic expressions, equations, inequalities, and functions
- Initiate a plan, execute it, and evaluate the reasonableness of the solution
- Communicate information and ideas based on purpose, task, and intended audience using appropriate language

(continued)

Table 4.7 *(continued)*

Cross-Disciplinary Outcomes
• **Problem Solving:** Frame a question to identify what you don't know; pursue knowledge and conduct research to find a viable solution; draw conclusions and define next steps
• **Communication:** Use mode(s) of communication to share information and ideas for a specific purpose, task, and audience; frame and present a point of view in a way that is compelling and engaging
• **Collaboration:** Build consensus around a shared goal and approach; take individual responsibility for a shared goal and common task; attend to the cohesiveness and quality of the common task

Submitted by Allison Rodman, Mariana Bracetti Academy, Philadelphia Idea generated by Susan Lee, Klint Kanopka, and students at the Academy at Palumbo, Philadelphia

- o Work to restore the natural nitrogen cycle through reducing runoff and erosion of fertilizers, use of organic materials for fertilizer, and strategic planting of plants.

- **Siemens We Can Change the World Challenge.** In this annual national environmental sustainability competition for K–12 students, students learn about science and conservation while creating solutions that impact their planet. Each year, submissions are evaluated on the following criteria: statement of hypothesis, plan and design, analyze and provide results, share it with others, and global impact. The illustrations here are excerpts from the 2013 award-winning proposals, which can be found on http://www.wecanchange.com/.

  - o K–2 example (from Lincoln Avenue Academy, Florida): "Our school is located in an urban center of our city where there are not many green spaces. Even our campus was in bad shape! Green spaces were not taken care of. Runoff polluted our water. And animals had no place to live. We learned about importance of green spaces. Then, we decided to turn our school campus into a certified wildlife habitat and teach others how to create and take care of green spaces in their schools and neighborhoods."

  - o High school example (from Skyline High School, Michigan): "There is a desperate international need for a portable, efficient, and inexpensive method of water purification. Readily available recyclable materials, such as glass, plastic, and foam, could be combined with natural sources of energy to create an efficient,

(text continues on page 94)

Table 4.8 Task Frame: Youth Media

Context: High school youth from across the region served as student journalists during two high-profile civic events after participating in an intensive one-day "Reporters' Boot Camp" that the Consortium organized in partnership with Carlow University, SLB Radio, and a collaborative of nonprofits and media outlets.	
Task • Minimal Student Input • **Some Student Input** • Student Driven	**What is the challenge?** Designed both to cultivate media skills and engage students in civic life, the boot camps brought the trainees together with media professionals from local news outlets to learn reporting techniques and media ethics. Working in teams, the students pulled together stories during the session to practice the media skills among professional journalists serving as their interviewees. As the project progressed, students gravitated toward stories that exerted a pull on them and toward peers and adult mentors who enhanced their work and complemented their style. One student described his experience: "It gave us very interesting insight into the process media undertake to organize coverage of a major event. We watch the news every day, but to learn what it takes to put something like this together, how you need to work together and what you need to be looking for to produce a news story is really fascinating."
Audience • Minimal Student Input • **Some Student Input** • Student Driven	**Who is the audience? How does that shape communication?** Students share their reporting through social media, open-source blogging, and the group's website. Some publish in their school newspapers. SLB Radio, a leading partner in the Pittsburgh Youth Media coalition, has featured the reporters on the air. Adults will sometimes post suggestions for stories to be covered in the region, and often, students will find opportunities and share them with each other. In media ranging from print to audio, video, and still photography, the students last year captured stories from the Remaking Cities Congress, which Carnegie Mellon University and the American Institute of Architects organized to reprise a similar event held thirty years earlier following the collapse of the region's steel industry. In 2012, a different cohort of students covered the One Young World Summit, including the appearances of speakers ranging from former president Bill Clinton to Nobel laureate Mohammed Yunas.

(continued)

Table 4.8 (continued)

Feedback	How is feedback provided, and how is it used?
• Minimal Student Input • Some Student Input • **Student Driven**	The following description indicates how students used feedback in the design of the task: Feedback in this environment operates in a continuous, fluid model of ongoing improvement and refinement. Students learn quickly which adult mentors can help with what: who's the video editing wiz, who can inject humor into a piece, who's the grammar authority? Because no one is aiming for perfection before publication, the kids get excited instead of upset when they are told how to make their work better.

Disciplinary Outcomes
Common Core E/LA: CCSS.ELA.Literacy.CCRA.SL.1; CCSS.ELA.Literacy.CCRA.R.7; CCSS.ELA.Literacy.CCRA.R.8; CCSS.ELA.Literacy.CCRA.SL.4; CCSS.ELA.Literacy.CCRA.SL.4; CCSS.ELA.Literacy.CCRA.SL.5

Cross-Disciplinary Outcomes
• **Critical Thinking:** Evaluating work, theirs and others'; analyzing large, complex issues • **Problem Solving:** Working through technical issues, impossible deadlines, no-show interview subjects • **Creative Thinking:** Generating ideas: What is the story that hasn't been told? the angle that hasn't been taken? the image that no one is noticing at the moment? • **Communication:** How to get the most from an interview • **Collaboration:** Who should take which roles? Doing as a group what one person cannot do • **Metacognition:** Recognizing one's own biases

From the Consortium for Public Education, Greater Pittsburgh, Pennsylvania

inexpensive, and environmentally friendly water distillation system—providing clean drinking water for individuals or small communities. Our solution, the HydroPod, is meant to be inexpensive, reliable, portable, and environmentally friendly. Made of 100% recycled plastic, the HydroPod evaporates water while collecting the condensed remnants, eliminating all deadly bacteria and viruses."

• **100 People: A World Portrait.** The mission of the 100 People Foundation (http://www.100people.org/) is to personalize global statistics by conceptualizing the world's population of seven billion as a representative sample of one hundred people. The goal is to "facilitate communication between cultures and world neighbors [to see] the concept of a world community and shared responsibility for the planet." The website offers lesson plans and project ideas.

- **ePALS projects.** Individual classes (ages one to seventeen-plus) propose an idea to the world, seeking classroom partners. These ideas are framed by subject area, connected to standards, and based on collaboration (for example, email exchange, Skype or video chat, use of collaborative workspace). Here is the website to join an existing project or create one: http://www.epals.com/project-experience.php. The following is a sampling of the dozens of existing tasks:
  - Five- to seven-year-old class in India looking for collaborators on a healthy eating project
  - Eight- to ten-year-old class in Macedonia looking for collaborators on a gaming project
  - Eleven- to thirteen-year-old class in South Korea looking for collaborators on a "Culture in a Box" project
  - Fourteen- to sixteen-year-old class in Jordan looking for collaborators on a cultural fables project

Tables 4.9 and 4.10 are illustrative examples of "go global" task frames. The first is the development of a hero story; the second is creation of a game as part of the Games for Change Festival.

HOW THE ROLE OF THE TEACHER SHIFTS

Many teachers are attentive to student interests, but those interests do not significantly alter how they design and implement assessment and instruction. When moving from left to right in the Personalized Learning Evolution, we grow our partnerships with students as they have a greater stake in the development of the tasks. We deliberately expand student voice and choice in task creation, timely feedback and opportunity to take action, sharing and enlarging the target audience, and taking stock of the accomplishments to consider future goals.

How do you take a typical task and reimagine it? Let's play out two typical units that appear in many elementary schools: a science unit on insects (table 4.11) and a language arts unit on fables and folktales (table 4.12).

Notice that as the descriptions shift from traditional to student centered, the teacher's role shifts as well. These examples illustrate small shifts in design, control,

(text continues on page 98)

Table 4.9 Task Frame: MY HERO

Context: MY HERO is a digital library currently used in 194 countries to empower people of all ages to realize their potential to effect positive change in the world. Students can submit a hero story through narrative (written or audio), art, and/or film. For more information, visit http://myhero.com/go/directory/.	
Task • Minimal Student Input • Some Student Input • **Student Driven**	**What is the challenge?** Students identify a hero and create a written tribute, audio recording, film, or original artwork in accordance with submission guidelines. To inspire, there are current events articles about "heroes in the news" (http://myhero.com/newswire/) as well as categories of heroes (e.g., peacemakers, artists, scientists, explorers; http://myhero.com/directory/). Within a given course or subject area, students can research and/or interview a historical or contemporary hero to portray the significance of that hero to the world.
Audience • Minimal Student Input • **Some Student Input** • Student Driven	**Who is the audience? How does that shape communication?** Global audience—school-age children and adults. Language should be in English or Spanish for written and film pieces.
Feedback • Minimal Student Input • **Some Student Input** • Student Driven	**How is feedback provided, and how is it used?** The following description indicates how students used feedback in the design of the task: Once students send their submissions to the site, they are reviewed (checked for plagiarism) and edited (mechanics, length, language). Most appear on the site. To that end, it is helpful for students to work to polish their piece so as to follow the submission guidelines posted on the site; e.g., submissions must celebrate a hero, explore concepts of heroism, or examine hero-related topics.

Disciplinary Outcomes

• Evaluate information from a variety of sources to construct a written, visual, or multimedia statement

• **Common Core E/LA:** CCSS.W.2, CCSS.W.4, CCSS.W.5, CCSS.W.6, CCSS.W.7, CCSS.W.8, CCSS.W.9, CCSS.W.10, CCSS.SL.4, CCSS.SL.5, CCSS.SL.6

Cross-Disciplinary Outcomes

• **Critical Thinking:** Examine messages and stories presented
• **Communication:** Use multiple mode(s) to share information and ideas for a specific purpose, task, and audience; frame and present a point of view in a way that is compelling and engaging
• **Metacognition:** Analyze performance along the way

Table 4.10 Task Frame: Games for Change

<table>
<tr><td colspan="2">Context: The Games for Change network is a global group dedicated to modeling and solving real global problems using the game format in a safe learning environment. Students model after the Games for Change Festival and evaluate the games honored. Then students describe a problem that they could design a game to help solve. Examples to get students thinking:

• Emotion Motion, from NYC grade 6, at Quest to Learn (http://q2l.org/); training for children about how to recognize and handle their emotions
• Start the Talk (http://gamesforchange.org/festival/gameplay/start-the-talk-underage-drinking/); training for parents in how to speak to their children about underage drinking
• Papers, Please, about immigration questions (http://gamesforchange.org/festival/gameplay/papers-please-2/)</td></tr>
<tr>
<td>Task
• Minimal Student Input
• Some Student Input
• Student Driven</td>
<td>What is the challenge?
Teacher has been using Games for Change website in the classroom. Students have been playing Games for Change, so they are familiar with the format. The teacher will bring the students to the Games for Change Festival website (http://gamesforchange.org/festival/) to view the games nominated for awards. The students will examine the award categories and determine if they agree with the judge's selections or not. They will then create their own award category and criteria, then vote to see what game would win their classroom award (http://gamesforchange.org/festival/gameplay/). Finally, students will research and describe a current global problem and design games that would help solve the problem if enough people played them. This unit may or may not actually involve developing the games—the designs are enough.</td>
</tr>
<tr>
<td>Audience
• Minimal Student Input
• Student Input
• Student Driven</td>
<td>Who is the audience? How does that shape communication?
Gamers from around the world. Presentation should share either the design concept or the full development.</td>
</tr>
<tr>
<td>Feedback
• Minimal Student Input
• Student Input
• Student Driven</td>
<td>How is feedback provided, and how is it used?
The following description indicates how students used feedback in the design of the task:
The Games for Change network has hubs and festivals for all players and designers to share their ideas and solutions. The network also has a feedback system for games that are submitted so that students will get feedback as a group from the target audience.</td>
</tr>
</table>

(continued)

Table 4.10 *(continued)*

	The class should generate some samples to submit to the Games for Change website for approval and feedback. There is also a discussion board that they can post on and monitor to field-test some options if they cannot agree as a class. The class should also incorporate survey data from the school community to help make choices.
Disciplinary Outcomes	

Common Core E/LA: CCSS.W.2, CCSS.W.4, CCSS.W.5, CCSS.W.6, CCSS.W.7, CCSS.W.8, CCSS.W.9, CCSS.W.10, CCSS.SL.4, CCSS.SL.5, CCSS.SL.6

Cross-Disciplinary Outcomes

- **Critical Thinking:** Examine messages and stories presented
- **Creative Thinking:** Take a different perspective on the same problem, topic, idea, or object
- **Communication:** Use mode(s) of communication to share information and ideas for a specific purpose, task, and audience; frame and present a point of view in a way that is compelling and engaging
- **Collaboration:** Build consensus around a shared goal and approach; take individual responsibility for a shared goal and a common task; attend to the cohesiveness and quality of the common task
- **Metacognition:** Know what you don't know and use mechanisms to figure it out; think about your thought process; analyze performance along the way; seek and use feedback

Developed by Marie Alcock

management, and scope to provide a stronger student voice and stewardship of their own learning.

From the point of view of a classroom teacher, there are three pertinent questions to make this learning approach challenging, possible, and worth the effort. First, *Do I know my content standards*—what they say, what they mean, how they interrelate? Fluency with content standards means that a teacher can see the forest (overarching expectations) and the trees (grade-level expectations). The teacher can then take the standards language, which is often obtuse, dense, or overly detailed, and translate it so that students can be clear about the disciplinary outcomes. Some content standards are more important than others, and the teacher can focus on what is pivotal (developmentally, in the PreK–12 scope and sequence) rather than "covering" every standard.

(text continues on page 102)

Table 4.11 A Science Unit on Insects, Grade 1

Minimal Student Input	Some Student Input	Student Driven
Task Description: Students research ants and produce an illustration as well as identify basic facts and represent those on their illustration. Then students write one or two sentences to articulate an interesting fact they learned about how ants interact with their environment (e.g., how they get food or work together as a community).	**Task Description:** Students produce a bug field guide for budding young scientists. Every student selects a bug, finds key information about that bug, and works to represent findings both visually and in words. Once a draft is completed, each student seeks feedback from two individuals: a classmate and someone outside the classroom (e.g., a family member or friend). Using the feedback, each student creates a final draft that is included in the bug field guide for publication.	**Task Description:** Students identify a task within the bugs unit and an audience for their work. Examples: • Create photo(s) and recorded explanation(s) of insect(s) for personal scientific observation journal • Create Illustrations and find interesting facts about each stage of an insect's life cycle for young science readers • Identify key information about an insect and turn that into a story (using Eric Carle's *A Very Hungry Caterpillar* as a model text) to be read aloud to young children • Create "What am I?" clues to identify a particular insect using pictures and facts for a PreK–2 audience Student(s) work with the teacher to articulate a set of multidisciplinary learning goals that the task measures. They also collaborate to create a set of criteria to guide and evaluate task development. As students work on their drafts, they elicit feedback from others, specifically their target audience of young scientists. At the end of the task, students reflect on their learning, share the reflection with their teachers, and identify areas of success and areas for continued growth.

(continued)

Tasks That Demonstrate Personalized Learning Evolution in Practice

Table 4.11 (continued)

Minimal Student Input	Some Student Input	Student Driven
Teacher Role: • Provides the directions for the assignment on ants • Preselects resources on ants for students, to ensure that they can access key information • Organizes whole-class learning chunks based on each phase of the assignment: identifying and recording key information, creating an illustration, labeling external structures, sharing interesting ideas found out about the bug • Creates a checklist for students to help them keep track of what they are doing • Creates a rubric to evaluate students that mirrors the checklist; may or may not share the rubric with students	***Teacher Role:*** • Develops a set of goals that the task measures. For example, this task can measure the content and inquiry in science; comprehension, analysis, and communication in ELA; and the process skills of self-navigation and collaboration • Develops a student-friendly checklist to inform work on what a quality submission looks like for the bug field guide • Organizes whole-class learning chunks for locating resources and identifying and recording key information • Provides "just-in-time teaching" on creating an illustration, labeling external structures, and sharing interesting ideas found out about the bug • Develops a student-friendly set of questions for the students to use to seek feedback from a classmate and someone outside the class • Takes individual student submissions to create the bug field guide • With student, reviews progress toward larger learning goals and sets targets for future learning experiences	***Teacher Role:*** • Consults with students to identify how they will focus their work toward these goals and standards • Collaborates with the student to develop a student-friendly checklist to inform work on the task • Plays the role of facilitator, raising questions for students to consider about task, purpose, and audience • Documents observations and provides "just-in-time teaching" to address student roadblocks (e.g., not finding any information on a particular bug, difficulty with group dynamics) • Helps students identify and access external audiences who will provide feedback on the task design and the emerging and final product • Collaborates with the student to identify areas of success and areas for future learning and growth

Table 4.12 English Language Arts Unit on Fables and Folktales (Upper Elementary)

Minimal Student Input	Some Student Input	Student Driven
Description: Students read/listen to fables and folktales and identify the central message or theme. Students use these examples as models to create a fable/folktale with a specific theme (e.g., patience, self-confidence, generosity).	**Description:** Students read fables and folktales to identify a central message. There is a blend of individual, small-group, and whole-class discussion around how they "figured out" the message and what made one fable or folktale more powerful than another. Then students select one central message that they read, and re-create that message in a contemporary context. Once the writing is completed, each student buddies up with a kindergarten classmate and shares the story.	**Description:** Students read a range of fables to identify what makes a good fable. The class then creates a set of characteristics to inspire their own production. Each student then produces a fable to submit for a virtual fable anthology (can be hosted by classroom teacher or the school) based on a current issue. Students seek feedback from at least two individuals: a classmate and one person outside the classroom (e.g., a family member or friend). Using the feedback, each student makes modifications to his or her final copy and posts it online. Readers of the site (including participating students) are encouraged to leave feedback on one another's stories.
Teacher Role: • Preselects fables and folktales for students organized around a specific theme • Identifies whole-class theme and provides assignment direction for writing of fables and folktales	**Teacher Role:** • Provides the frame for the assignment and describes how students can make it their own by taking an identified message and re-creating it based on what is familiar in a young child's world. (For example, "The Tortoise and the Hare" could become "The Run-Down Car and the Race Car" to illustrate the same message that slow and steady wins the race.)	**Teacher Role:** • With students, develops a set of goals that the task measures, including content, comprehension, analysis, and communication in ELA; and process skills of self-navigation and collaboration • Develops a student-friendly checklist to inform work on what a quality submission looks like for the class anthology of fables

(continued)

Table 4.12 (*continued*)

Minimal Student Input	Some Student Input	Student Driven
Teacher Role: • Organizes whole-class learning chunks based on each phase of the assignment: identifying the central message and creating the fable or folktale (planning, drafting, revising, and editing) • Creates a checklist for students to help students keep track of what they are doing • Creates a rubric to evaluate students that mirrors the checklist	***Teacher Role:*** • Organizes whole-class learning chunks based on each phase of the assignment: identifying and sharing fable/folktale, determining a theme, and creating a fable to publish and share with kindergarten students • Creates a checklist for students to help them keep track of what they are doing • Creates a rubric to evaluate students that mirrors the checklist • Provides an opportunity for students to share their fables with a kindergartener	***Teacher Role:*** • Organizes whole-class and small-group learning chunks for both comprehension and production of fables • Provides "just-in-time teaching" on such topics as selecting a theme and using feedback to inform revisions • Develops a student-friendly set of questions for the students to use to seek feedback from a classmate and someone outside the class • Assembles individual student submissions to publish the classroom anthology • Confers with students to determine students' progress within the larger learning goals and standards and to set goals for the future • Provides students with time to review, reflect, and revise based on feedback on the site

Developed by Lorena Kelly and Allison Zmuda

Second, *Do I trust my students to be true learning partners*—in a dynamic rather than hierarchical exchange, one in which we collaborate often to frame tasks, evaluate progress, and consider next steps? The teacher creates the conditions (the four mindsets in chapter 2) and uses two vital strategies as part of regular practice. One essential strategy is to establish key criteria for quality work. How the work will be evaluated must be transparent to students, and they must have access to several examples that demonstrate work meeting those criteria. This is true whether the criteria have been developed externally or by the students. The use of key criteria becomes the basis for feedback and identification of next steps. The second essential strategy is to use formative assessment to gather detailed information to improve instruction and student learning while it's happening. The teacher can determine the appropriate next steps on the basis of what the learner needs: just-in-time teaching, more practice, additional development time, seeking out expert advice, and so on. The teacher has the flexibility to focus on the desired disciplinary and cross-disciplinary outcomes (as measured through independent performance) instead of following a rigid pacing guide.

Third, *Do I have tolerance for mess, uncertainty, and failure* — change that takes me out of my comfort zone? Structure and planning are still important, but the focus is no longer implement-assess-repeat until the curriculum is over. Instead, the structure and the plans are in service to the development of students' disciplinary and cross-disciplinary outcomes. Therefore, if our best-laid plans do not work, as educators we have an obligation to figure out alternate routes for student success. We are not suggesting that the student has no role in his own achievement; we advocate that self-regulation is pivotal to success for both teacher *and* student. The messiness of this type of learning experience requires considerable rapport between teacher and student as learning partners so that when there is a roadblock or a dead end, partners see it as an obstacle, not a death blow.

HOW THE ROLE OF THE STUDENT SHIFTS

As students become stewards of their own learning experience, it helps both teacher and student to have a planner that describes the problem or challenge, design process, pathway to action, and reflection on mindsets. This planner integrates the design elements of a personalized learning task, as described in chapter 3, for students to consider and respond to. Typically this planner should be used when the *task* and *audience* are classified as student choice or personalized learning.

- My design problem or challenge:
  What is it? Why does it matter?
- My design process:
  Generate: *How do I approach it?*
  Focus: *How do I make sense of it?*

Ideate: *How do I create?*

Act: *Is it working?*

Build: *How do I move it forward based on data and/or feedback?*

(REPEAT AS NEEDED)

- My pathway to action:
What's my plan?

- My mindset:
Relevance: *Why do I care? Why does the work matter? Is this the only way?*

Growth mindset: *What are the criteria I am holding myself to? How am I doing right now? How do I feel right now?*

Self-efficacy: *Where am I in my process? What are my next steps?*

Sense of belonging: *How does this impact my connections with others?*

The role of a teacher is one of advisor: he or she provides feedback both on the plan and task development. The role of the student is one of creator: he or she better understands the problem or challenge and goes through a dynamic design process until the goal is realized.

We have shared an illustrative example (see table 4.13) of the planner in action, cocreated by Allison and her son, Cuda, about a personal challenge. (There is a blank version of the template in appendix B [table AB.4].)

NEEDED SYSTEMS AND SUPPORTS BEYOND THE CLASSROOM

There are four considerations that typically are beyond the individual classroom; they require not just systematic permission but considerable support. First, we propose more *transdisciplinary tasks* that are meaningfully aligned to multiple content standards and disciplinary outcomes. Specialization in a particular discipline is not as desirable as applying knowledge to address the multifaceted nature of complex problems, collaborating with diverse partners, and creating something powerful, elegant, or joyful. Yet we acknowledge that traditional organizational forms (for example, subject-area courses in secondary school, X number of minutes per day/week for elementary school) are still the reality at most public, private, and charter schools. Second, we propose that more tasks be done *off the classroom clock*—projects and challenges that require full immersion. It is incredibly difficult to design and carry out

(text continues on page 106)

Table 4.13 Personalized Learning Vision-to-Action Project Planner

MY DESIGN PROBLEM OR CHALLENGE
Type 1 Diabetes
What is it? Why does it matter?
I am a 13-year-old boy who has Type 1 diabetes. That doesn't define who I am, but it helps people understand what I have gone through over the past two years. I thought my life was over because it changed the way I think about food. For a while, food was the enemy. I had to take shots of insulin for the carbs at each meal. Early on, I learned that the fewer carbs I ate, the fewer shots I had to take. My family tried to help me, but I was miserable. One day toward the end of last school year, my mom asked me what I wanted to do when I got older. I said that I had wanted to be a chef, but because I had diabetes I didn't think I wanted to do that anymore. My mom asked, how come? I said that there are no great recipes that I can look at anymore that have carb counts on them. Either they are gross and have a carb count or they are good and have no carb count. My mom said that I had identified a need that not only I had, but lots of other kids may have as well, and I should create recipes not only to fill that need but also to still pursue my dreams of being a chef.

MY DESIGN PROCESS
Generate (1st cycle): *How do I approach it?* **Focus:** *How do I make sense of it?* **Ideate:** *How do I create?* **Act:** *Is it working?* **Build (repeat cycle as needed):** *How do I move it forward based on data and/or feedback?*
Generate: I wanted to make a cookbook of kid-friendly recipes that only list carb counts. But I also wanted to see if the recipes were good. So I wanted to test them. I found lots and lots of ideas in books that I wanted to try, but it was pretty overwhelming to start.   **Focus:** I want to focus on one recipe at a time, but it will take me forever to assemble enough for a cookbook. I will do this as a blog instead.   **Ideate:** I will take an existing recipe that I like the sound of, tweak it to fit my tastes (appropriate substitutions based on flavor, carbs, personal preferences), research carb counts for each ingredient, create the dish, take a picture of it, and write up the ingredients, description, and directions.   **Act:** I have a goal of doing twenty recipes during summer vacation: both creating and posting online.   **Build:** I get super excited when people comment on the blog, but I don't really get enough feedback. I created a space where people can send email about their favorite food, but I don't have any responses yet. I know that I am doing this for me and for other people, but I get depressed sometimes when I feel like no one is listening. I need to figure out how to get more people to see my site …

MY PATHWAY TO ACTION
What's my plan?

WHAT *Task and Resources Needed*	WHO *Key Partners*	WHEN *Timeline*	ACHIEVEMENT *Evidence of Progress*
Develop and learn how to use WordPress site	Me My mom	Two weeks	Site is up and I can use it to post recipes
Find recipes that I like (use cookbooks from my house, the library, and what I research online)	Me My dad (former chef) who will help me evaluate the level of difficulty of the recipe	Ongoing	Number of recipes that I have flagged for my blog

(continued)

Table 4.13 *(continued)*

WHAT *Task and Resources Needed*	WHO *Key Partners*	WHEN *Timeline*	ACHIEVEMENT *Evidence of Progress*
For each recipe, identify accurate carb counts for the recipe based on single portion size. Resources such as The Calorie King Calorie, Fat & Carbohydrate Counter 2012	Me	Ongoing	All ingredients used in the recipe have an accurate carb count.
Write the steps down as I am making the food item.	Me	Ongoing	My steps are in order, and I use appropriate measurement terms and descriptions.
Take photo of each food item.	Me	Ongoing	Quality photo that shows the finished food
MY MINDSET			
Relevance *Why do I care? Why does the work matter? Is this the only way?*	Doing the blog helps me feel better, like I am taking a little bit of control over living with diabetes. One challenge I am having now is staying motivated now I am back to school. I don't have the time and the energy after my homework is done.		
Growth Mindset *What are the criteria I am holding myself to?* *How am I doing right now?* *How do I feel right now?*	I want it to be kid-friendly. A kid not only should like it, but also can make it (with help as needed). I want the description to make the reader want to make it. That should happen with the sentence I am writing before the recipe and the picture I take. I am pretty worried that I am not so good at taking pictures. Is it because I am using the phone on my camera? Or maybe it is the lighting? How I put things on the plate? I need some help with this.		
Self-Efficacy *Where am I in my process?* *What are my next steps?*	I get overwhelmed by taking on too much at once. One recipe at a time. I can handle the concreteness of that, especially when I have a good structure going. Find a recipe. Research carb count. Tweak it to meet my needs and write those tweaks down as I am doing them. Take a picture. Type in ingredients and directions. Post.		
Sense of Belonging *How does this impact my connections with others?*	Having diabetes makes me feel pretty alone sometimes. I am trying to turn my disease into something that can help other people. I feel good when someone makes a comment on the site, like "I want to try this!" even if they don't care about carb counts.		

Developed by Allison Zmuda with Charlotte-Mecklenburg Schools; example by Cuda Zmuda

on-site experiences, involve experts who consult with students to provide feedback on their work, create substantive research/production assignments, and engage in creative acts within the time constraints of a given class period. Schools can examine how they allocate time on a daily or weekly basis to make the design of these tasks more feasible. Third, we propose moving from a typical academic prompt, hypothetical problem, or "make-believe" audience to *imagining what a task can be:* a task that is complex, substantive, and authentic. The inspiration for these tasks can come from

- An existing idea—something that you have seen, heard, or read and are excited to play with

- A student-generated idea—something that comes from dialogues, journaling, or blogging to unearth what students are fascinated by, problems they are struggling with both in and outside school, or projects they want to pursue

- A problem or project that is already in play—something that inspires student(s) in class to become involved and to collaborate with experts (journalists, scientists, art historians, and so on), classes across the globe, and local organizations

To design and execute these tasks requires "research and development" space where teachers and students have the time, resources, and latitude to create. Fourth, we propose the deliberate incorporation of *student choice* in the design and development of tasks. "Student centered" denotes that students are respected and are responsible for making decisions both inside and outside of the school walls. This is a pedagogical shift for many teachers: to entrust students with both a higher level of responsibility for work that they may theoretically crave and a task design process with which students have minimal experience.

CONCLUSION AND REFLECTIVE QUESTIONS

The ultimate intention of moving along the Personalized Learning Evolution is to have students believe that the work they are doing matters. It comes with a shift in the pedagogical capacity of teachers to collaborate with students and peer teachers; to provide frequent, robust, and action-oriented feedback; to model curiosity about the world and their work; to share ideas with students as learning partners; to be a trusted mentor; to discover new challenges, texts, and problems; and to shepherd the publication of new knowledge, texts, designs, and ideas. Before moving on to the next chapter, consider the following questions:

1. When reading the illustrative examples, what were your initial reactions?
2. The examples may be compelling, but the reality of designing and developing tasks may be overwhelming and perhaps a little extreme. What "Yes, buts" popped into your head?

3. To what extent do you support more of a role for students in the design and development of their own ideas? When should that experience take place—at what age? what time of day/week/year?

4. Reread the examples of the two tasks and the teacher roles that move along the Personalized Learning Evolution (tables 4.12 and 4.13). What might the student's role be in each?

WORK CITED

Wiley, B. "Leading for Global Competence: A Schoolwide Approach." *Leading the New Literacies*. Ed., Heidi Hayes Jacobs. Bloomington, IN: Solution Tree, 2013. 123–159. Print.

Chapter 5

What Personalized Learning Looks Like at the Instructional Level

Our school is a place where kids can learn in their own ways. You may have difficulties, but you are always able to find a way to take in information yourself. You are not controlled by teachers all the time. You can make some of your own choices. When I walk into our school I feel very at home. I see a happy place where I can learn, but also be myself. Kids here have different frustrations. Teachers and other kids in your community are all there to encourage you.

—Grade 5 Student #1

We can work at our own pace, no matter how slow or how fast. It does not matter how smart the kids are, but only if they learn, and are happy. And all the teachers have special bonds with each and every one of their pupils. Smiles are always visible at our school.

—Grade 5 Student #2

In chapter 1, we discussed the reasons we commit to personalized learning as a vital approach to achieving deeper engagement in student learning that produces high-level disciplinary and cross-disciplinary outcomes. Chapters 2, 3, and 4 delineated the first seven elements of the Personalized Learning Evolution and shared illustrative examples of such tasks both in and outside school. In this chapter, we turn our attention to process and environment: the growth of our students based on how we design instruction. These two elements open up reflection on how to meaningfully incorporate technologies in the classroom; they also reinforce the needed shift in roles for teacher and student. In a recent blog post on *MindShift*, Shawn McCusker elaborates: "The role of the teacher moves from being a distributor of information to one of nurturing students as they collect, evaluate, and process information into unique learning products. The students' role consequently moves from that of a receiver of the teacher's knowledge to that of a researcher, curator, and creator. Products of student creation and individual expressions of learning become important parts of the learning process that are shared, evaluated by classmates, and built upon by the teacher."

This chapter will not be a list of packaged instructional strategies, but rather a sampling of tools, recommendations, and narratives to expound on the two elements.

ELEMENT 8: PROCESS

The element of process (see table 5.1) encompasses both the planning and implementation of the learning sequence and the pace. Traditional education generally is a teacher-centered enterprise: the teacher's job is to develop, implement, and assess a sequence of lessons based on the coverage of agreed-on topics at the course or grade level. The student's job is to keep up with the teacher's pace, organization, and preferences. In a personalized learning classroom, teachers create the conditions or "tilt the environment" toward success for each individual. As we move to the right in the evolution, we begin to see a different focus, which requires attention to four key components: the way that disciplinary and cross-disciplinary outcomes are developed; the multiple or flexible pathways that students can pursue to demonstrate learning; the teacher's role in relation to the learner at different stages of the process; and a cumulative evaluation of learning.

Table 5.1 Personalized Learning Evolution: Process

Element	Minimal Student Input	Some Student Input	Student Driven
Process *Who controls the sequence and pace of learning?*	Learning sequence and pace are specified by the curriculum, teacher, and/or resource.	Learning sequence and pace are specified but somewhat flexible based on student interest and need.	Learning sequence and pace are developed based on student interest and need and flexible based on assessment of progress.

Let's start with how disciplinary and cross-disciplinary outcomes are identified within the instructional sequence. First, the teacher (either alone or with the student) identifies (in student-friendly language) specific disciplinary outcomes that frame a unit of study (for the class or for an individual student) and are paired with broader disciplinary and cross-disciplinary outcomes. Consider an example from a seventh-grade mathematics class:

Specific Disciplinary Outcomes for a Unit on Algebraic Manipulation

- I can solve for a variable using properties of operations. (7.EE.1, 7.EE.2)
- I can solve real-life multistep problems using simple equations. (7.EE.3, 7.EE.4)
- I can combine like terms and use the distributive property. (7.EE.1, 7.EE.2, 7.EE.3)

The broader disciplinary outcomes might be as follows:

- Compose and decompose numbers to establish relationships, perform operations, and solve problems
- Describe and/or solve problems using algebraic expressions, equations, inequalities, and functions

The broader cross-disciplinary outcomes might be

- **Problem solving:** Based on an understanding of *any* problem, initiate a plan, execute it, and evaluate the reasonableness of the solution
- **Critical thinking:** Articulate how mathematical concepts relate to one another in the context of a problem or in the theoretical sense
- **Metacognition:** Know what you don't know and use mechanisms (for example, tools, strategies, context) to deal with a given math problem

The teacher then can design a playlist of resources, learning experiences, and/or tutorials for students to navigate in preparation for solving an authentically messy mathematics problem. In this scenario, the student has a lead role in selecting resources and learning experiences to guide her work.

Now that disciplinary and cross-disciplinary outcomes are identified and learning resources are collected, the teacher works with students to identify multiple ways to demonstrate learning. A simple way to open up the space for students to identify alternatives is to have a "standing offer" to develop an independent project that is teacher approved (for example, rigorous, meets targeted outcomes, doable). A second

Table 5.2 Tasks Options for Wind Turbines

Tasks	Disciplinary and Cross-Disciplinary Outcomes
Task 1: Design and build a home wind turbine that can generate the most power	• (Task 1 only) Design a model using appropriate scientific tools, resources, and methods • Collect, analyze, and evaluate the quality of evidence in relation to a question
Task 2: Evaluate the design of a wind turbine prototype found on Kickstarter	• Develop a valid scientific conclusion, assess its validity and limitations, and determine a future course of action to inspire further questions
Task 3: Do a cost-benefit analysis of a standard wind turbine, including financial and environmental costs and benefits	• Communicate scientific information clearly, thoroughly, and accurately

way is to provide a few ideas from which students can select. For example, two science teachers from ThunderRidge High School in Colorado designed three task options for students to evaluate technologies to harness alternate energy resources (see table 5.2).

A third and the most student-driven approach is to clarify the targeted disciplinary and cross-disciplinary outcomes that the task should measure but leave the rest of the assignment for students to design. For example, a Civics and Government teacher wants students to make connections between the abstract ideals of the founding documents of the United States and real-life events. The disciplinary and cross-disciplinary outcomes might be as follows:

- Actively engage in a problem or idea that is meaningful to self and society

- Create question(s) or statement(s) that advance research and analysis

- Access and analyze text for context, reliability, and accuracy to determine relevance

- Use textual evidence to form generalizations, make predictions, and draw conclusions

- Communicate information and ideas based on purpose, task, and intended audience, using appropriate language

In this example, the design of *what* to pursue and *how* to pursue it rests on the shoulders of the student. Many students may need some initial guidance and illustrative models of communication formats that can be a mix of student and professional examples (for example, a blog post, white paper, or stump speech). The teacher may need to provide significant scaffolding for some students, especially if they are unaccustomed to such autonomy.

To teach in a personalized learning classroom calls for a shift in how we provide support to the learner depending on the stage of the project or individual challenge. To make this shift, consider three instructional stances in relation to students: in front, deliver knowledge for students; behind, observe work by students; and beside, collaborate with students. In a personalized learning environment, an effective teacher adjusts his stance depending on where the student is in her learning journey. We call this "differentiation by position," and it is an important consideration in the delivery of instruction. Aside from some of the elements that we have decided should be delivered "in front" of students, facilitation is really a matter of conducting the group and individuals on their learning journey. This requires frequent check-ins, supporting students in progressing through their plans, and offering a suggestion here and there as to how a student can succeed or resolve a dilemma; we are engaged in a constant process of mentoring. As mentors, we need to stay in regular contact, use structures for project management, and be very agile in how we support students. We need to be aware, at all times, of where a student or group is within a larger task and to know their strengths and weaknesses well enough to support them appropriately, even anticipating some potential areas of need.

It is helpful for teachers to keep project journals on each student or group throughout this process so that they can stay on top of what can sometimes seem like chaos. This ongoing documentation and reflection also helps with the overall assessment of student performance. Jesse Gloyd, teacher/advisor at Aveson Charter School in California, describes what you might see when walking into his classroom:

> Much of my time is spent meeting with students as a means of developing frames that might best facilitate good, solid, production and output. Occasionally I will workshop in small groups (or have my instructional assistant workshop as well); however, the deeper we get into the school year, the more I begin to understand my students, the majority of time spent comes in the form of small-group/one-on-one topic prep and idea selection ... The end goal is to get students to a place where they are creating their own tasks, developing them, looking for help, and, in the end, assessing themselves at such a high level that they are really self-monitoring and moving through the process with as little help from me as possible. The frames that we've set up for mastery seem to be working toward helping students exist more and more without needing us as educators—which

really is, at the end of the day, the most important thing. We want to set up systems that get students to a place where they can, with confidence, exist without us guiding them each step of the way.

Table 5.3 is a sampling of instructional strategies and resources at Aveson.

Personalized learning does not negate the need to "teach." There is nothing wrong with direct instruction as long as it is used judiciously. There will always be a need

Table 5.3 Instructional Design Strategies and Resources, Aveson Charter School

Literacy	Math	Projects
• Small-group instruction (I) • Mini-lessons with advisors (I) • Spelling city (I) • Book clubs (C, I) • Peer work/workshopping writing (C) • One-on-one instruction (I) • SAI (specialized academic instruction) support (C, I) • Fluency cards (O) • Graphic organizers (C) • Google Docs for digital conferencing (C, I) • One-on-one conferencing/mentoring (C, I) • Anchor documents—exemplary writing samples used as models of expected writing, products, published works (O) • Study Island—online software (I) • Starfall—online software (I) • Handwriting Without Tears program (I) • Project-based writing (O, C) • SRA—reading comprehension (I) • Audiobooks (O) • earobics—online software (O) • SIPPS (I) • CARS—online software (I) • Wordly Wise—vocabulary reinforcement (C) • The Literacy Lab—online software (I)	• Small-group instruction (I) • Mini-lessons with advisors (I) • Skills-based small groups (I) • SAI (specialized academic instruction) support (C, I) • One-on-one instruction (I) • Khan Academy (I, C) • Math jobs (use Montessori-based materials) (O) • Singapore lessons (I, C) • Sensorial manipulatives (O) • Fluency cards (O) • Fact fluency (O) • Focus choice (O) • Individual conferencing (C) • TenMarks—online software (I) • Google Docs for digital conferencing (C, I) • Graphic organizers (C) • Guided practice—teacher directed (O, C) • Starfall—online software (I, O) • Conferring about writing one-on-one (C) • Tiers (I) • Positive reinforcement (C) • Group work—student directed (O) • Scaffolded worksheets (O) • Four-step process to solving math problems (I, C) • Concrete-pictorial-abstract instructional sequence (I, O)	• Mini-lessons with advisor (I) • Interactive notebooks (O, C) • Videos and review games (I, O) • Google Docs for digital conferencing (C, I) • Pair share (O) • One-on-one instruction (I) • BrainPop (online software) (I, O) • Graphic organizers (I) • Eye Openers—leveled informational texts for research projects in younger grades (O, C) • Group work activities (O) • Small-group instruction (I) • Outlines—teach and use outlines to manage time, stages of projects (I, O) • Four-step process to solving math problems (I, C) • Differentiation—without diminishing the quality of the finished work (I, C) • Individual conferencing (I) • Focused choice—individualized voice-driven pieces (O)

Note: (I) = sequence of instruction—either delivered by teacher or software program; (O) = observation of student work; (C) = collaboration between teacher and student(s)

to teach students "stuff," but you want to choose the stuff that is most appropriate and effective for students to learn through direct instruction. Structure modules that students can work through with appropriate checks along the way. These modules can be delivered either through digital means (and there are many solutions that exist for this method) or through the packaging of physical learning modules around important outcomes. The most import element to reinforce here is that these common elements should be ones that *every* student is going to need to access and use when moving into more personalized elements of the process.

Finally, the evaluation of student performance in a personalized learning environment can be challenging for those new to the process. However, if we have defined appropriate demonstrations of success in the design phase and kept close contact with students throughout the process, evaluation can be very manageable. Assessment of student learning becomes less *summative* in nature and more *cumulative*. If we have been in constant contact with students, we will recognize that they have been demonstrating their learning all along. Shauna Stafford, a teacher/advisor at Aveson Charter School, explains:

> We have created outcomes that cover every skill we would like students to master over the course of the semester. While I assign some tasks for the entire class to complete, such as a writing piece where students describe their growth from the previous semester, discuss their work habits, and create goals for the current semester, most tasks are created by students. They use the outcomes as a guide, we conference together, my instructional assistant checks in with them frequently, and they conference with their peers, but ultimately they decide what they want to read and write. During silent writing time, my instructional assistant and I hold one-on-one conferences with individual students about their writing. Every student must always be in the process of a writing piece—this becomes second nature to students, even those who struggle with motivation or lack requisite skills. We ask them the same questions over and over again and take notes on their answers: What are you working on? Can I read your draft? How's it going? What specific feedback would you like? How can I help you? Where are you in the writing process? And our advice usually begins with the same sentence starters or question starters: I notice … , I wonder … , Do you think … ? What is the purpose of … ? Do you need … ? Do you want to try … ?

Our assessment won't be based simply on the product, performance, or presentation; it will be based on all of the ingredients that have created the "meal," not just the meal itself. Students have collected ingredients throughout the process, not necessarily following a recipe as much as creating one. Their collecting, discarding, refining, and discovering of ingredients are perhaps more important than following the set recipe correctly. If we believe this to be true, an assessment of student performance should include metrics that allow us to evaluate the ingredients they have amassed and to interpret how they used these to create a meal that demonstrates the important disciplinary and cross-disciplinary outcomes we have broadly defined as "success."

Personalized Learning Recommendations

1. *Introduce the area of focus or outcomes to stimulate inquiry and task definition.* Success in a personalized learning environment relies to a great extent on the clear framing of the process for learners. Students should know the parameters for the larger, more personalized tasks and how they are going to attain and demonstrate success. This may seem self-evident, but it is often neglected. In traditional environments, we often roll out a unit day by day or provide only a linear description of lessons, chapters, quizzes, and tests. This approach will not support students in a personalized environment. Teachers need to foreshadow the "big picture" so that students can navigate in an environment where the act of learning is more important than the product.

2. *Consider a redesign of the learning space.* The layout of the room indicates what type of work is expected. For example, there could be a corner of the room designated for intense concentration, with table space to spread out and noise-canceling headphones. Or there could be a collaborative space complete with a painted wall (chalkboard paint, dry-erase-board paint) for students to capture ideas, develop plans, or work on a problem. Again, invite your students to join in on this experience; working together on design and execution creates shared ownership and promotes upkeep. For more information, visit *Edutopia*'s 2013 blog series on how to remake your classroom: http://www.edutopia.org/remake-your-class-collaborative-learning-video.

3. *Consider a redesign of a course structure.* A teacher can develop a course structure opening up the task possibilities but still honoring the disciplinary and cross-disciplinary outcomes. For example, take a look at this graphic that illustrates a reimagined high school World History course (figure 5.1).

   As illustrated in figure 5.1, the structure creates a matrix out of two elements of the course: the horizontal headings represent traditional topics (various historical periods selected as focus areas of the course); the vertical headings indicate key drivers that represent constant forces and systems that drive change throughout periods of history. This adds a level of conceptual and "big idea" thinking to the course beyond learning *about* periods in history, rich intersections between crucial periods of human development and powerful drivers of change. The drivers become both desired learning goals and the vehicles for higher-level learning and understandings of the forces of change over time. The *X*'s in the figure represent an individual student's area of focus for each topic or unit of study; the student will use a different driver as a lens to explore each historical era. Her classmates will explore the intersection between another driver of change and the same era. At the end of each unit, they will share the understandings

Figure 5.1 Example of How to Redesign a Course

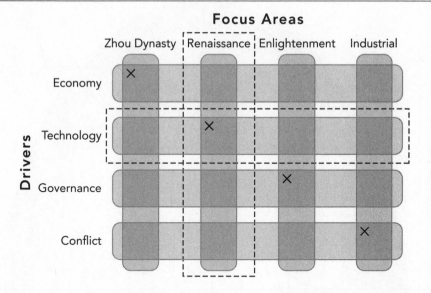

attained and attempt to synthesize these. They will have time for this, as they attain most of the content for each historical era through flipped and modular methods and will have more face-to-face time to interact with others. The culminating project of the course, as represented by the open rectangles, is for students to pursue important questions by looking at the effect of a single driver of change across all historical periods (and our present one) *or* to look at the forces of change within a period of history by looking through the lens of all drivers.

The same structure could be used with the study of science. Drivers such as balance, systems, or cycles could be used as ways to view a number of topics in science in the elementary grades. Major themes in literature can become drivers for looking across various pieces of fiction. Fundamental principles of art can help deepen and focus our inquiry into various movements. Certainly, many teachers already utilize this mixture of recurring concepts and disciplinary topics, but it is often not leveraged to bring personalized learning into the regular classroom. Again, this structure is not meant to illustrate "radical" or transformational personalization, but it does demonstrate elements that can be worked into all settings.

4. ***Consider a redesign to create a cross-disciplinary structure.*** Another recommendation is to reimagine how a cross-disciplinary or grade-level team could integrate multiple subject-area disciplinary and cross-disciplinary outcomes in the design. This example comes from Greg's work with a "school-within-a-school" model at various schools. These academies are intended to be innovative "hothouses" where larger strategic goals are developed, prototyped, evaluated within a smaller, more agile environment and spread to the rest of the school. There are several layers to this program structure. (See figure 5.2.)

Figure 5.2 Example of How to Create a Cross-Disciplinary Structure for Multiple Courses

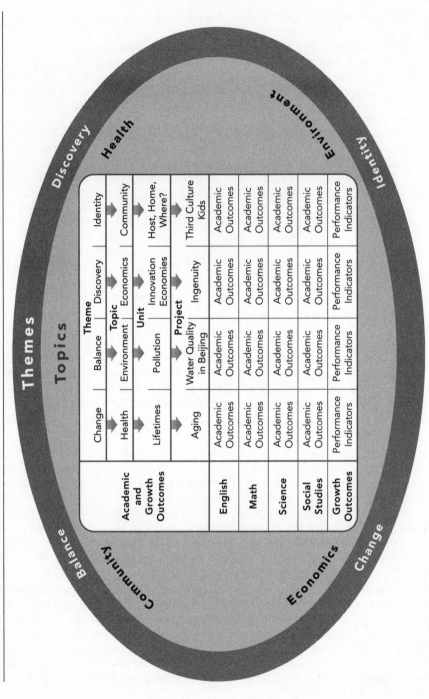

Developed by Greg Curtis

Similar to the previous course example, there are themes to represent bigger concepts that recur and spiral throughout the environment, often revisited through different entry points. In this case, the **themes** are *change, balance, discovery,* and *identity*. There is a set of **topics** to provide the context within which we can apply each theme: *health, environment, economics,* and *community*. There are **units:** logical "blocks" of learning organized around the convergence of themes and topics that will draw relevant disciplinary and cross-disciplinary outcomes into the mix. This structure will frame learning experiences through a rich blend of disciplinary and cross-disciplinary outcomes as well as personalized experiences. Figure AC.1 in appendix C shows how the intersection between a theme and a topic can result in interesting units, or areas of study, inquiry, and personalized ***projects.*** It is in these projects that students explore possibilities and pursue an idea based on investigation and analysis. For example, students could "combine" the theme of change with the topic of health and decide that aging was a great area for a project. One student could decide to focus his project on helping the elderly connect with family by teaching them some basic social networking and technical skills. Another could try to design a solution to a common problem among the elderly. Yet another student might choose to design a play-based program for people in the early stages of Alzheimer's disease to help slow the deterioration of memory and cognitive function. Skillfully supported, each student could define and demonstrate a set of desired disciplinary and cross-disciplinary outcomes while having a great deal of control and choice.

ELEMENT 9: ENVIRONMENT

For personalized learning to flourish, teachers (and all members of the school community) have a broad view of where learning can take place (see table 5.4). The following

Table 5.4 Personalized Learning Evolution: Environment

Element	Minimal Student Input	Some Student Input	Student Driven
Environment *Where does the learning take place?*	There is a top-down environment in which teacher instructs and assesses disciplinary and cross-disciplinary outcomes.	The environment is more collaborative; teacher considers student voice and choice in the instruction and assessment of disciplinary and cross-disciplinary outcomes.	Teacher and students work together in a learning partnership to design and assess learning for disciplinary and cross-disciplinary outcomes.

three areas require not just classroom teacher support but also buy-in from administrators, families, community members, and local boards:

- Students *shift* according to the learning need: staff promote movement among physical and school spaces as well as flexibility in grouping.
- Students *connect* with a wide range of authentic audiences and experiences: online sources, placements within the community, service and experiential learning.
- Students *navigate* virtual learning activities and resources: goals and resources are organized into smaller, targeted sets to make specific modules accessible and encourage independence based on their learning trajectory.

Let's explore each point in a little more depth.

Students shift according to the learning need: staff promote movement among physical and school spaces as well as flexibility in grouping. At Aveson Charter School, for example, staff consider the design of the environment in terms of specific student needs or opportunities; disciplinary and cross-disciplinary outcomes; and task(s). Staff then design "spaces" based on the metaphors of campfires, watering holes, and caves.

- Campfires — learning from an expert or storyteller in a more formal learning setting
- Watering holes — cooperative, collaborative, more informal learning
- Caves — individual-focused learning, study, reflection, quiet reading, and creative flow

On any given day, students move from one space to another depending on what they need. Within those spaces, the instructional practices are a blend of physical and virtual experiences designed to provide students what they need when they need it.

Students connect with a wide range of authentic audiences and experiences: online sources, placements within the community, service and experiential learning. This expectation tears down the walls between the "school world" and the "real world" to create a unified learning experience grounded in problems, challenges, and ideas. Field trips, guest speakers, and community service are no longer "add-ons"; information, ideas, action, and feedback gained from these experiences bolster the significance of the task and the opportunity for students to see the impact.

Students navigate virtual learning activities and resources: goals and resources are organized into smaller, targeted sets to make specific modules accessible and encourage independence based on their learning trajectory. Technology should be seen as a catalyst for and an enabler of learning, rather than as a separate category on the Personalized Learning Evolution. Author and education consultant Michael Fisher shared with Allison:

> Personalized learning is not necessarily technology dependent. While it's good for students to have both physical and digital toolboxes of resources to use while learning and solving problems, there is no magic technology elixir. The task must drive the operational decisions around method, resources, and outcome. I don't think that the question "How can we integrate technology?" is a good question to ask anymore. A better question, especially in terms of personalized learning, might be "What choices does the student have to learn and perform?" Or maybe "What's in the student's toolbox?" This demands that technology is a ubiquitous expectation, like the usage of books or pencils, and is not something we have to plan for—because it's already there.

Integration of technology tools and platforms into the classroom can satisfy students' desire to use devices to make sense of problems and challenges, and educators' need to improve student achievement. Therefore, we offer three broad categories of technologies to frame the potential benefit of technology within various contexts:

- **Access technologies** shift control of learning from the teacher and the textbook publisher to the learner. By appropriately shifting some of the acquisition of knowledge and skills to a tech-supported environment, we can focus our time on extending student learning in meaningful ways. "Flipped" environments off-load traditional uses of our time with students to make space for active and engaged learning experiences. Face-to-face time with and between students is too valuable to remain shackled to traditional transmission tasks. Access technologies also put more control and responsibility into the hands of learners to direct their own inquiries. Although there is an abundance of resources regarding the digital tools available, table 5.5 lists a few examples that are particularly well suited to a personalized learning environment.

- **Facilitative technologies** provide space for us to work and learn individually and together, and facilitate many of the cross-disciplinary outcomes that are central to the aims and success of personalized learning. These technologies empower students to organize, plan, and refine ideas to become independent, self-directed learners. Using mind-mapping software to introduce concepts to students, maintaining your

Table 5.5 Sample Access Technologies

Sample Tools	Uses
World Digital Library	A small yet growing repository of primary source documents spanning centuries and continents. These great artifacts can spur critical and creative thinking around key points in the development of humankind.
Khan Academy	A well-known compendium of "self-help" videos on various topics (especially in the areas of math and science). The individual modules make good resources for students who would benefit from some reteaching and attention to identified areas of learning needed to succeed at larger tasks.
Brain Pop	Another site that has been around for a long time, by digital standards. The series of short presentations around various topics is engaging and can help students plug gaps or extend their learning in identified areas.

own blog to engage students, and using project management tools to help chart out the course of a project are all ways that you can model the use of technology to support and extend students' work (see table 5.6).

- **Adaptive technologies** "learn" about us as we use them and then react accordingly. We see this clearly in the way that websites will position advertisements based on what they can learn about us (our location, browsing history, past activity on that website, and so on). In the context of personalized learning, adaptive technologies tailor learning opportunities to the student based on his ongoing performance. A software program might present appropriately challenging texts for him based on the level of comprehension demonstrated in previous tasks, or a problem-solving scenario chosen to nudge him forward based on his previous performance; or it might use complex heuristics to assess a student's writing ability and present him with tasks to focus attention on areas of weakness and strength. Typically used in blended or flipped learning environments, adaptive technologies should release teachers from the stand-and-deliver model and students from the dutiful learner role. Adaptive technologies should connect students with their learning and assist them in a thoughtful process of ongoing improvement and reflection.

The first step is to carefully select appropriate adaptive support for student learning. Adaptive technologies (see table 5.7) should help students acquire necessary

Table 5.6 Sample Facilitative Technologies

Sample Tools	Uses
Trello	Trello is a simple project management tool that allows individuals and groups to manage various tasks within larger projects. It supports collaboration, problem solving, and planning skills, and can also be used for metacognitive purposes that involve some creativity.
MindMeister	There are many mind-mapping tools out there, and this is but one example. This tool is geared toward teachers, but can also be used by students. There are also a number of sites and software tools out there for students. Visualization helps hone communication skills, especially with complex issues or concepts, and aids in developing critical thinking and problem-solving skills.
WordPress	WordPress is but one of many tools that can be used for student blogging. However, this particular one has many tools and "widgets" that students can use for some very effective forms of communication. Blogs can support communication, collaboration, creative and critical thinking, and metacognitive development.

Table 5.7 Sample Adaptive Technologies

Sample Tools	Uses
Knewton	Knewton is an adaptive engine to power e-learning experiences developed by others. It can be used with any content, but allows teachers to customize each student's interaction with the material and uses analytics to support students along the way.
Smart Sparrow	This is an adaptive e-learning platform from Australia. It is used in higher grades and into the postsecondary environment, but can be used by teachers at other levels to develop courseware. It includes some analytical tools to help capture and mine learning data.
ScootPad	ScootPad is an adaptive learning tool for K–5 students utilizing the Common Core. It is promising to see tools tailored to developmental needs in elementary education.
WriteItNow	This area of adaptive technology has proponents and detractors. WriteItNow is an example of a tool that supports the development of student writing. It would be wrong to think that this is the silver bullet for creating fabulous writers, but there are elements that can support students through the draft stages and allow them to get instant and useful feedback on basic elements of their writing in progress.

knowledge and skills in an individualized and growth-oriented way. Students should not just be "turned loose" to plow through modules in a simple "get to the end" fashion; they should be supported in gaining insights about their learning throughout the process. Most adaptive technologies are still geared toward supporting the development of foundational skills, but in the not-so-distant future, they will present students with complex scenarios and engaging real-world tasks based on their trajectory as learners.

Along with introducing students to new tools for learning and working, we must help them in their conscious choice of the right tool for the job at hand. This can involve engaging students in experimenting with different tools to capture the pros, cons, and uses of each.

A DAY-IN-THE-LIFE NARRATIVE

It is helpful to get a glimpse into what a personalized learning environment might look like. To that end, we have developed a narrative to illustrate the process and environmental shifts we have examined in this chapter. The example may be idealized or unrealistic right now given your conditions and resources, but it challenges you to see what could be, to craft a collective personalized learning vision, and to pose questions about "how" rather than "why." As you read through this elementary school example, physically track (with highlighting or margin notes) the "Yes, buts" that come up for you, so that you can discuss them with other educators. At the end of the narrative, we will pull back the curtain a little to describe, very briefly, some of the elements that the example represents. This "decoding" of the narrative (shown in table 5.8) will focus on

- How disciplinary learning was demonstrated
- How identified cross-disciplinary outcomes were developed and demonstrated by the student(s)
- Feedback given to further investigation, revision, or reflection
- Features of the environment and technologies used
- Mindsets engaged in and expanded by the example

Katie enters school at the usual time. As she waits for her classmates to gather, she checks her daily calendar on her tablet. She makes a mental note as to whether she's

Table 5.8   Decoding a Day in the Life: Elementary Example

Elements	Commentary
Disciplinary Outcomes	Clearly, Katie and Rasheed are engaged in tasks that demonstrate the learning at the heart of the narrative. These include English language arts (writing and character development through the documentary), social studies (documentary), math (challenge lab and practice activities), and science (insect field guide).
Cross-Disciplinary Outcomes	Creativity, critical thinking, communication, and collaboration are all used to access the learning experiences described and hinted at in the narrative. The development of metacognition, creativity, critical thinking, and communication is supported through the processes, tools, and teacher support provided.
Feedback	Teacher: offers keywords for web search based on Katie and Rasheed's vision for the field guide; sets up a checkpoint (having them show him an image that communicates the interaction between insects and their environment) Student: Rasheed located resources and asks Katie to review
Environment	Communication tools, such as a class website and individual learning logs, figure prominently in many personalized environments. You'll also notice mention of "project spaces" and other tools to support project planning and collaboration. Technology is used to communicate learning and ideas in multiple modes. An online writing tool and online learning modules are also mentioned as ways to move tasks from the classroom environment into the personalized one.
Mindsets	**Relevance:** Katie and Rasheed focus on making their field guide useful for a younger audience through illustrations and by showing how important insects are in the environment. **Growth Mindset:** Both students focus on the improvement of the task. **Self-Efficacy:** Katie checks to see what she needs to accomplish based on resources and teacher instruction; Katie and Rasheed work together to plan and to talk with their teacher about progress. **Sense of Belonging:** Classmates work together in small teams to work through questions and challenges.

done what she needed to do in preparation for today's work. The day begins with the teacher outlining the day's activities.

"So," he says, "We have a couple of group sessions today. The first one is a math activity to help you prepare for tomorrow's challenge lab. You all have the information for that on your class site, so use that to figure out what areas you might need to work on to prepare properly. You'll also find instructions about what modules to use in the math center to work on these specific needs. Then I'll outline some common things you might want to consider in your prep for this task.

"Later, we'll meet to share some of what you've learned about character development as you have been working on your documentary script for your social science movie. Remember, you should focus on what you've learned about portraying a fictional or historical character through images, interview questions, and character monologues. The prompting questions for your sharing are in your project outline. I'll also share some tips about how to make your character's dialogue realistic and use it to reveal who he or she is.

"For the rest of these blocks of time, I'll meet with each small team for a few minutes as you work on your science field guide. I'm interested in the progress you are making and the challenges you might be facing as you look at the content and delivery of your information for your particular audience. OK, let's get to work … "

With that, some of Katie's classmates go straight to the math center to find the practice modules they need to work on to prepare for tomorrow's math challenge. Others open the class site on their tablets and go through the self-assessment to check on the areas they need to work on.

Katie's partner on the field guide project, Rasheed, approaches: "If you get your math prep done a little early, can we meet for five minutes so we can talk about what we'll share about the field guide?"

"Sure," says Katie. "Last night I went through some of the math stuff online, so I have time. Find me when you're ready."

After the math prep session, small groups share their challenges and insights in depicting character through their documentary. Classmates make quick notes on their tablets and discuss their reflections, such as, "We had the same thing! Have you thought about using pictures to show where your character comes from instead of having them explain it?"

Later in the day, small groups meet to work on their field guides. Some students are putting together documents for their guide, some are making illustrations, and some are recording an audio guide. Katie and Rasheed meet to go through their project plan and check their progress. Rasheed starts the conversation: "I found some good resources last night, and I put them in our project space. I think they might help to explain how the insects we're focusing on are important to the environment."

"Great, thanks! I'll have a look at those after I finish this graphic that shows all the insects we're going to use, and I guess I'll start to put the pieces we have into a single document."

After a short period, their teacher arrives with their project plan on his tablet. "So, Rasheed and Katie, how's it going? Do you feel you're pretty much on plan?" Rasheed answers, "Yeah, I think so. Some of the pieces shift around a bit, but we've got it under control."

"Good," replies their teacher. "Now, tell me how you plan to make this field guide useful for your audience. You're making this for younger students, right?"

"Yes," says Katie. "We thought we'd use more pictures and illustrations to show the insects and not use so much text. But it's kind of hard to take all of our research and figure out how to help them understand it through pictures."

The teacher acknowledges their difficulty. "Yes, that certainly is a challenge. What types of information do you find easier to put into illustrations?"

"Well," says Rasheed, "the descriptions and parts of the insects are easy to put into images. So are the types of things they eat and where they live."

Katie joins in, "Yeah, that part is easy. But we want kids to think about how important these insects are in their environment. You know, that they have a purpose."

"So the relationship between these insects and other parts of the environment?" asks the teacher.

"Yeah, something like that," agrees Rasheed.

"There are some visual models you might want to think about," offers the teacher. "Why don't you search on 'food webs' or 'ecosystem' images and see if any of those things help you think through it. And remember, your audience is five years old. Keep it simple and direct."

"OK, we'll try that," says Katie.

"Good. And why don't you check in with me when you think you've found the type of image you might use to communicate that idea?" concludes the teacher.

"OK. I'll do some looking after I look at Rasheed's resources. Rasheed, maybe if you get some of the pieces in the document, we can find a place for an image about this," says Katie.

The day concludes with instructions for Katie and her classmates on using the online writing assessment tool to check the text of their field guides. They will need to submit their final draft for peer review in three days and need to check it for clarity and correct use of punctuation and word choice. Before they leave, students use their tablets to update their daily calendar with what was accomplished today and verify what they need to do tonight and tomorrow to complete tasks.

Appendix C includes day-in-the-life narratives for middle and high school as well as a blank table for decoding. Feel free to use these to "spot the personalization" and explore other ideas and environments.

CONCLUSION AND REFLECTIVE QUESTIONS

Before we leave chapter 5, we want to remind you of two salient instructional points in a personalized learning environment. The importance of "good teaching" and the role of the teacher don't go away; the teacher works as a facilitator to empower students to take a more significant role in the design and development of the learning experience. Second, there are alternate ways to restructure programs, courses, or units to increase student ownership of the learning experience and achieve desired disciplinary and cross-disciplinary outcomes. Do not feel overwhelmed, but instead feel supported by the number of options to help make the shift meaningful for you and your students. Consider these possibilities:

- Personalized learning formats through which individuals or small groups pursue a project or problem that they deeply care about, and use the "experts" (in and out of school) to provide them with information and feedback

- Authentic community-based formats, such as internships, projects, and workplace employment, that value the application of learning

- Online or blended learning, guided by schools and teachers, that values students' time and engagement by using a setting that they are comfortable with to explore, connect, and make sense of texts, problems, and challenges

Here are a few reflective questions that may help you consolidate your thinking:

1. What does this chapter tell you about the "feel" of a personalized learning environment?

2. How do the process and environment mesh with your own identity as a teacher?

3. Do you tend to spend most of your time in front, behind, or beside your students?

4. Which elements of technology do you currently use, and how do you use them?

5. What elements from the examples in this chapter do you recognize from your current practice?

6. What elements from the examples in this chapter do you think might provide you with an entry point to further develop a personalized learning environment?

WORK CITED

McCusker, S. "Teachers Most Powerful Role? Adding Context." *MindShift*, 7 April 2014. Web. <http://blogs.kqed.org/mindshift/2014/04/teachers-most-powerful-role-adding -context/>.

Chapter 6

What Personalized Learning Looks Like at the Systems Level

Student voice, like teacher voice, should be integral—not an afterthought, or even a means of validation. There is a tangible attitude in education that children are to do what the adults say, since the adults know best. They can complain and protest, but their voices should be dismissed because, well, it's petulant and uneducated. This philosophy is synonymous to a physician ignoring his patient's report of pain or symptoms because he clearly knows more about the human body. Just as a physician must, our educational legislators should know more than children about the specifics of engineering an education system. But this is no reason to dismiss students' input and ideas.

—Ethan Young, high school senior in Tennessee

We now address the ripple effect that many readers have anticipated from the first few pages of the book: how we organize school needs to become personalized as well. A **personalized learning system** transforms schooling by providing voice and choice on what, where, and how students learn in relation to disciplinary and cross-disciplinary outcomes aligned with standards. In *Why School?* Will Richardson asserts, "In this new story, real learning happens anytime, anywhere with anyone we like—not just with a teacher and some same-age peers, in a classroom, from September to June. More important, it happens around the things learners choose to learn, not what someone else tells us to learn."

Therefore, in this personalized learning system,

- **Every teacher** creates a classroom culture of respect grounded in high expectations and provides feedback and guidance in learning content, developing skills, and thinking strategically.
- **Every learning community** both in and outside school offers students opportunities to learn from experience through application in authentic situations.

In this chapter, we focus on elements generally not within the locus of teacher control but are absolutely vital to making personalized learning a reality: *assessment of learning, time,* and *advancement.* All three of these elements are connected to local policy as well as to state, ministry, and/or national requirements.

As we explore each element, consider the "Yes, buts," both those that come up for you as a reader and those that you can imagine other members of the school community might say.

ELEMENT 10: DEMONSTRATION OF LEARNING

A personalized learning system captures student learning through the use of multifaceted assessments (see Table 6.1). This robust and rigorous system creates the opportunity for students to develop pride in their work, agonize over details, and work through challenges. Ron Berger eloquently described this difference in student pride and performance when students have a voice and choice built into assessment of learning: "Rather than seeing school as something done to them, students are given the

Table 6.1 Personalized Learning Evolution: Demonstration of Learning

Element	Minimal Student Input	Some Student Input	Student Driven
Demonstration of Learning *What constitutes evidence of learning?*	Teacher and district assessments specify the way(s) in which disciplinary and cross-disciplinary outcomes will be demonstrated.	Student chooses among a set of options to determine how disciplinary and cross-disciplinary outcomes will be demonstrated.	Student proposes or shapes way(s) that both disciplinary and cross-disciplinary outcomes will be demonstrated and will provide evidence of learning (e.g., personalized portfolio).

responsibility to carry out original academic projects, save work in portfolios, display their work, and reflect publicly on their work and their learning" (53).

Demonstrations of learning value the solution, interpretation, creation, or conclusion and the explanation or justification that led to that result. In a 1989 *Phi Delta Kappan* article, Grant Wiggins poses a powerful question that is as timely then as it is now: *What is a true test?*

We have lost sight of the fact that a true test of intellectual ability requires the performance of exemplary tasks that replicate the challenges and standards of performance that typically face writers, businesspeople, scientists, community leaders, designers, and historians. A genuine test of intellectual achievement doesn't merely check standardized work in a mechanical way. It reveals achievement on the essentials, even if they are not easily quantified.

As Wiggins reflects in a recent blog post, "Authenticity in Assessment," he advocates that this is a curriculum design challenge into which local educators can make significant inroads if they focus on the following components: structure and logistics, design features, grading and scoring, and fairness (see table 6.2).

Reimagining what a true test looks like opens the door for students to take a lead role in the learning experience. Students can use clear criteria (aligned with standards and disciplinary and cross-disciplinary outcomes) to investigate, create, and analyze problems of interest that are at the heart of various disciplines.

To illustrate this point, in the summer of 2014, curricular designers and administrators from Learn4Life Charter Schools in California worked with Allison to articulate artifacts that are evidence of student learning outside a given content area, but worthy of accomplishment and documentation (see table 6.3). Working from the Personalized Learning Evolution chart, they categorized student artifacts as either *minimal student input* (authentic task with clear parameters) or *some student input/student driven* (authentic task that requires significant development from student to establish parameters and what success looks like).

We advocate for the inclusion of three major assessment types to measure and motivate student performance as well as hold schools accountable for the growth of every child: (1) summative assessments; (2) digital portfolios, gateways, or exhibitions; and (3) large-scale assessments.

In a personalized learning system, **summative assessments** primarily are rich performance-based tasks for which students have to apply their learning to novel situations to demonstrate the strategy, skill, and perseverance needed to be successful. Summative assessments provide information to the student, her family, and staff about

Table 6.2 Authentic Assessment Tasks

Component	Authentic Tasks
Structure and Logistics	• Are more appropriately public; involve an audience, panel, etc. • Do not rely on unrealistic and arbitrary time constraints • Offer known, not secret, questions or tasks • Are not one-shot—more like portfolios or a season of games • Involve some collaboration with others • Recur—and are worth retaking • Make feedback to students so central that school structures and policies are modified to support them
Design Features	• Are "essential"—not contrived or arbitrary just to shake out a grade • Are enabling, pointing the student toward more sophisticated and important use of skills and knowledge • Are contextualized and complex, not atomized into isolated objectives • Involve the students' own research • Assess student habits and repertories, not mere recall or plug-in • Are representative challenges of a field or subject • Are engaging and educational • Involve somewhat ambiguous (ill-structured) tasks or problems
Grading and Scoring	• Involve criteria that assess essentials, not merely what is easily scored • Are not graded on a curve, but in reference to legitimate performance standards or benchmarks • Involve transparent, demystified expectations • Make self-assessment part of the assessment • Use a multifaceted analytic trait scoring system instead of one holistic or aggregate grade • Reflect coherent and stable school standards
Fairness	• Identify perhaps hidden strengths (not just reveal deficit) • Strike a balance between honoring achievement while mindful of fortunate prior experience or training (that can make the assessment invalid) • Minimize needless, unfair, and demoralizing comparisons of students to one another • Allow appropriate room for student styles and interests (some element of choice) • Can be attempted by all students via available scaffolding or prompting as needed (with such prompting reflected in the ultimate scoring) • Have perceived value to the students being assessed

Table 6.3 Artifacts of Student Learning

Minimal Student Input	Some Student Input/Student Driven
• Record of achievement (GPA and credit completion) • Letters of recommendation and supervisory reports based on internships, workplace experiences, and service learning projects • Updated resume (for example, awards, scholarships, work experience, participation in team sports or cocurricular clubs) • Personal narrative (entering Learn4Life and exiting) • Significant research tasks that generate findings, patterns, predictions/generalizations for a given course, competition, or local/global project that is already under way • Evidence of identifying a problem and creating a viable solution for a given course, competition, or local/global project that is already under way • Evidence of dynamic communication for a given purpose (for example, email threads, social media, discussion boards, blog posts, online course conversations) for a given course or local/global project that is already under way • Formal presentations for a given purpose and audience (for example, Key Club, YouTube, Skype, church, Toastmasters, student council, student-led conference, graduation) • Development of technical skills as demonstrated by certification exams (for example, Microsoft, CISCO, food handling)	• Service learning project (demonstration of cross-disciplinary outcomes and ideas for next steps or next projects) • Demonstration of acquired creative and/or technical skills based on independent tasks (for example, coding, graphic design, game design, original writings, video creation, art pieces) • Tangible timelines (calendars, project management, and so on) associated with projects (academic and extracurricular) that focus on quality outcome while still managing the realities of life • Goal tracker for a significant project that shows goal setting, action taken, resetting, recalibrating • Trajectory (short-term/long-term goals and accomplishments based on course selection, internships, postsecondary plan, and so on) • Significant research tasks that generate findings, patterns, predictions/generalizations • Evidence of identifying a problem and creating a viable solution • Evidence of dynamic communication for a given purpose (for example, email threads, social media, discussion boards, blog posts, online course conversations) • Accomplishments/recognition in cocurricular endeavors (for example, enterprise program, community service, entrepreneurship, organized groups)

Developed by staff at Learn4Life Charter Schools

the student's mastery of given competencies. Generally these assessments occur toward the end of a unit, semester, or year. Grading is not something "done" to the student but rather with the student, where she has clarity on how the work will be judged and uses that clarity to continue to inform the development of the task. The teacher provides feedback to the student to inform revision of a given task, validate competency levels, and clarify readiness for taking a state or national assessment. For example, Albany Senior High School in New Zealand is featured on the Ministry of Education's website for the design of its Impact Project. The four principles of the Impact Project are as follows:

- **Student Ownership and Agency:** *How excited are you about this project?*
  The project focuses and builds on you and your group's strengths and passions. The project matters to you, you care about what you are doing.

- **Substantial Learning beyond the Classroom:** *How will your new skills change the world?*
  Your project supports substantial learning that deepens the understanding, skills, and dispositions of the group and yourself. The learning offers challenge to all group members over a sustained period of time.

- **A Quality Product:** *How will you make your product awesome?*
  Meets the aim of your project and involves something you are interested in and/or passionate about. A quality product will be useful and provide a solution to a need your group has identified. It will be useful after the term of the project.

- **Participating and Contributing with the Community:** *Who wants it and who cares?*
  The project enables you to participate and contribute to your community in a meaningful way. The "community" is anything larger than yourself. For example, identifying a stakeholder who the project group will work with for developing their project in some way.

For more details on the project structure, rubric, and rationale, visit http://elearning .tki.org.nz/Teaching/Pedagogy/Personalised-learning#stories and http://wikieducator .org/Albany_Senior_High_School/Impact_Projects. In addition, table AC.2 in appendix C lists the reflective questions centered around each of the four principles.

Digital portfolios, gateways, and exhibitions are formal collections and presentations of what students have learned throughout one or multiple years of schooling. In a personalized learning system, the student owns the work: a demonstration of mastery of competencies through a student-created, student-led conversation about content and skill development over time. Students can showcase a variety of authentic tasks to demonstrate mastery; audiences for these presentations typically consist of parents, staff, and practicing experts.

For example, in his book *Personalized Learning: Student-Designed Pathways to High School Graduation,* John Clarke describes the power of students creating and organizing learning for a public audience. He highlights how preparing a range of artifacts (for example, films, photos, essays, diagrams) causes students to reflect on the meaning of what they have done over time and the accomplishment and growth they have experienced. Then, in an hourlong presentation to peers, advisors, mentors, and parents, students use artifacts and highlights from their e-portfolio to discuss personal and academic growth. To prepare for this formal presentation, each student leads a fifteen-minute conference to summarize current performance on a range of competencies and delineate next steps.

Another powerful example of authentic assessment is the creation of digital portfolios at High Tech High School. School leaders provide a rationale for *why* a digital portfolio is necessary: to capture learning that is much richer than a "collection of letter grades." Staff at High Tech High expect that "each student will create and maintain a portfolio of work to communicate who they are, what they have learned and what they have accomplished. They will be able to demonstrate their true skills and abilities." The digital portfolio includes a cover page, a personal statement, work samples, a resume, and contact information. For more information and to see several examples of e-portfolios, visit http://www.whatkidscando.org/archives/portfoliosmallschools/HTH /portfolios.html.

Large-scale assessments provide information to students, their families, school and district staff, and the state/ministry/national government about student performance and schoolwide challenges. Typically these assessments are administered for every student in that grade or course level at a predetermined time of the year. Ideally, in a personalized learning system, a student takes a large-scale assessment when he is ready, not on a time schedule. These criterion-referenced large-scale tests are likely to become more innovative over time, using advances in assessment technology to address different contexts of the learning. For example, the external assessment for the International Baccalaureate Diploma Program (http://www.ibo.org/diploma /assessment/methods/) comprises essays; structured problems; short-response, data-response, text-response, case study, and multiple-choice questions; a theory of knowledge essay (a reflection on how we know what we know); an extended essay (self-directed piece of research culminating in a four-thousand-word paper); and world literature assignments. Another example comes from the New Hampshire State Department of Education, which has partnered with the Center for Collaborative Education to develop a performance assessment system to measure student mastery of college- and career-ready competencies that balances local control with statewide accountability and comparability. On the New Hampshire Department of Education website (http://www.education.nh.gov/assessment-systems/), the following description outlines the parameters of the statewide performance-based system: "This system, the Performance Assessment for Competency Education (PACE) option, will include: common performance tasks that have high technical quality, locally designed performance tasks with guidelines for ensuring high technical quality, regional scoring sessions, and local district peer review audits to ensure sound accountability systems and high inter-rater reliability, a web-based bank of local and common performance tasks, and a regional support network for districts and schools."

Although a sizeable number of schools have been dabbling in the development of robust performance tasks, digital portfolios, exhibitions, student-led conferences, service learning projects, and expanded forms of independent study, they all face the challenge of documenting those pieces in a traditional reporting system. Personalized learning can be a messy process, which is one of the reasons that traditional education has held it at bay for so long. It's difficult to offer a multitude of learning opportunities for individual students based on their needs and interests. It's even more difficult to capture student performance on these personalized journeys and to organize results in a way that both students and educators can make sense of, let alone draw insights from.

In a personalized learning environment, a great deal of learning, especially in the area of cross-disciplinary outcomes, is demonstrated within the learning environment and alongside learning tasks. As mentioned, evidence of learning and performance in personalized learning environments can be messy. Evidence of performance may come from different sources, such as artifacts of student learning, metacognitive journals, reflections, and input from various audiences. Evidence may also come from different places — personalized modules, adaptive technology, online sources outside the school setting, and the like. To top it all off, criteria for success are not always standardized, especially in the area of cross-disciplinary outcomes, which tend to be derived from an organization's vision and mission. Not only does the articulation of cross-disciplinary outcomes vary from place to place, but students may demonstrate achievement of the same outcomes in different ways. Lining up everyone for the end-of-unit test is not likely to be the norm in personalized learning environments, especially where cross-disciplinary outcomes are involved.

In a personalized learning environment, a rich and varied set of student performances demonstrate valid indicators of learning that must be captured and organized to be both recognized and useful. Current grade books and report cards are not equipped to deal with this rich messiness. We need a platform to

- *Capture* a diverse set of learning experiences in order to make sense of a student's personal learning journey and what this evidence says, as a whole, about student achievement and performance
- *Aggregate* individual student learning and performance in unique ways
- *Organize* these unique demonstrations and interpret their performance around common areas, such as our disciplinary and cross-disciplinary outcomes
- *Equip* students with powerful tools to both understand and direct their own learning

Here, again, is where contemporary technology can help. There are an increasing number of learning management systems (LMSs) that will track student performance on learning modules. These systems can capture all of the actions and results of students using the system, from the amount of time spent on a particular learning module to the number of times a student attempted a problem to the aggregate score accumulated by a student across many learning modules within a particular area of study. For example, Khan Academy (www.khanacademy.org) enables students to access their learning modules and their performance on related assessments. These results are then presented back to the student in useful infographics that allow him to gain an overview of his learning over time and make observations about his progress. Project Foundry (www.projectfoundry.org) is a system designed to support personalized learning. This platform has been around since the mid-1990s and supports learning in project-based learning environments. The system enables students to develop personalized projects and align them to existing disciplinary standards. Assessment of student performance is entered into the system, which will generate standards-based report cards from these projects and allow students to "drill down" into their performance on various standards. Summit Public Schools (www.summitps.org) has chosen to develop its own Personalized Learning Plan platform to support its vision of learning in the twenty-first century. The platform offers students learning modules from a menu supported by a third-party delivery platform. Students can access their assessment results, set goals, and manage their learning within an environment that has removed many of the obstacles to personalized learning. A mixture of projects, face-to-face time, and digital delivery and tracking tools help Summit's students pursue learning anywhere, anytime, and through a variety of modes.

The challenge for the modern LMS is to provide for existing needs while at the same time innovating to meet emerging needs, all in a comprehensive package. This requires an openness and agility with which more traditional and monolithic software companies have difficulty. Developers are often more adept at creating tools to support linear processes than tools to support the relationships and messiness involved in personalized learning. But they are getting closer. For example, Schoology (https://www.schoology.com/home.php) integrates many tools to support the processes involved with "being a teacher" or "being a student." It is much more open in its architecture, allowing innovative connections with other systems and apps. However, like most comprehensive LMS systems, it organizes the learning environment using a set of structured rules and relationships. These are often one-way in nature. They help us achieve existing tasks, but do not have the flexibility to accomplish new ones. The challenge is to break from these established patterns.

Although these systems are examples of valuable components of a personalized learning environment, their focus is primarily on the attainment of disciplinary outcomes through standardized methods and assessments, although Summit Schools has woven this into a reengineered learning environment. However, the school system misses one of the main goals of our vision for personalized learning: cross-disciplinary outcomes. Although there are some assessments out there for critical thinking and creativity, these tend to be isolated and separated from an environment within which students can authentically demonstrate them. Also, we have yet to see an LMS or other system that adequately captures performance on cross-disciplinary outcomes *alongside* performance on disciplinary outcomes. For a couple of years now, Greg has been working with a few "lighthouse" schools around the world and an educational technology company, EduTect (http://edutectinc.com), to design such a dynamic platform. The platform is called LearningBoard, and we believe it has great potential to support personalized learning from both the student and school perspective. The LearningBoard may seem like a leap from most forms of assessment and reporting, but this platform helps students, staff, and families see the richness and diversity of student performance in a personalized learning environment.

The LearningBoard combines elements to both capture student learning and provide tools (such as project planners, goal-setting and tracking tools, and student-led conference planners) to support learning in a personalized environment. Let's briefly explore the two types of performance elements:

- *Disciplinary outcomes.* This area provides both a place to contribute evidence of the attainment of disciplinary outcomes and access to evidence captured around these outcomes. It includes analytical and querying tools to allow students to inquire into their performance so that they can gain insights and metacognitive understandings that will assist ongoing improvement. This tool also allows the "tracking" of student performance against defined and common disciplinary outcomes to gauge student readiness for advancement. In this way, the platform is similar to the examples mentioned earlier.

- *Cross-disciplinary outcomes.* The LearningBoard also focuses on the cross-disciplinary outcomes articulated for our personalized learning environment. Students submit evidence that they believe shows their performance or growth against these outcomes. They reflect on their development through different experiences, and self-assess. Teachers or other assessors submit evidence using performance areas and indicators developed for each cross-disciplinary outcome. These indicators become criteria for success *alongside* of disciplinary criteria within rich performance tasks. Student demonstration of these cross-disciplinary outcomes is also captured *in situ* through observational matrices and rubrics.

In this way, the LearningBoard moves beyond a content delivery system or a data warehouse for students' marks on assessments. It becomes a dynamic tool that encapsulates the organization's vision of successful learning in a personalized environment, where performance on both disciplinary and cross-disciplinary outcomes engages students in their own development and growth.

Within this platform, there are three types of evidence of student learning (see table 6.4).

When evidence of student learning is captured and interpreted with explicit alignment to clear disciplinary and cross-disciplinary outcomes, we can develop an extremely rich picture of student learning that continues to grow, in contrast to a set of separate assignments that are averaged together to produce a score. Because each LearningBoard belongs to a unique individual, the picture that emerges is equally unique, and the entire platform is a demonstration of personalized learning. Schools can use this to help navigate the messiness of personalized learning and maintain accountability. Key stakeholders (staff, students, family members) now have the data to support ongoing improvement efforts and a culture of attention to the individual within the whole.

Table 6.4 Types of Evidence in the LearningBoard Platform

Type of Evidence	Contributed by ...	Source	Interpreted through (Criteria)
Artifact	Student	Any tangible product of learning	Demonstration of disciplinary outcomes and cross-disciplinary outcome performance indicators
Reflection	Student	Any learning experience	Reflection on how cross-disciplinary outcomes, performance indicators, and mindsets are demonstrated in the work, and on areas of possible improvement
Assessment	Teacher	Any culminating or summative assessment	Demonstration of disciplinary outcomes and cross-disciplinary outcome performance indicators

Personalized Learning Recommendations

We propose a series of shifts that a local system may need to make in conjunction with state, ministry, and/or national authorities:

1. ***Shift from primarily structured (for example, multiple choice, short answer) and constructed response (for example, academic prompt, summary of information) items to measure acquisition to primarily performance-based tasks to measure acquisition, conceptual understanding, and application.*** There are times when it is appropriate to hold students accountable for memorization so that they can fluently recall information in service to more complex problems, texts, and challenges. However, the overreliance on these forms of assessment perpetuates the misunderstanding that the teacher's job is to cover the curriculum and the student's job is to keep up. We want students to play an active role in which they struggle, make sense of the material or evidence, and revise their work until they are satisfied with the quality of the performance. The assessment of learning tasks mentioned earlier in this section expects students not only to apply learning in novel situations but also to demonstrate progress in both disciplinary and cross-disciplinary outcomes. This is not a far-fetched dream; progressive departments of education are advocating such policies. For example, on its website, the Maine Department of Education (http://www.maine.gov/doe/plan/education_evolving/cpa3.html) promotes that "students design meaningful assessments to demonstrate learning and to be active participants in setting and meeting expectations."

2. ***Shift from the use of texts and tasks solely determined by the teacher to more student voice and choice.*** Perhaps this shift may be more of a pedagogical one that goes to the heart of the question "What's my job as a teacher?" We contend that the job of the teacher is to grow students to become competent and capable of figuring out messy problems on their own, independent from explicit direction or scaffolds. As

educators, we must show our students the worthiness of struggle and the power of revision, and offer them the opportunity to see growth over time. The enlistment of students in cocreation of summative assessments makes this acclimation much more likely because they take ownership of the questions they pursue, the texts they wrestle with, and the challenges they face.

3. *Shift from the completion of assignments that are done for the teacher as audience to exhibition or presentation to demonstrate learning to broad audiences, with continual guidance, monitoring, and assessment by the teacher.* The role of an authentic audience was discussed in chapter 3, but it is worthwhile to mention this here as well in relation to expectations of the learning community, both in and outside school. The examples shared throughout the book ask educators, other students, community members, and professionals in a given field to provide feedback, guidance, and expertise to enable students to learn by doing. If the walls between the school world and the outside world become more porous, then we need volunteers in and outside school to spend time listening, sharing, and refining work with one another.

4. *Shift from having the teacher report progress and achievement to the student and family to having the teacher and student conference regularly to evaluate progress, achievement, and appropriate next steps, with continual communication and engagement with parents.* We hope that the days of reports to families at the end of a nine- or twelve-week period will soon be over. Although it is important to keep students and their families apprised of progress, this predictable reporting system has outlived its usefulness. We propose that communication among teacher, parent, and student will be much more robust and proactive through the use of e-portfolios, student-led conferences, LMSs, and formal presentations of learning. This shift requires not only the adoption of these platforms and practices but also the clear articulation of disciplinary and cross-disciplinary outcomes aligned with standards.

ELEMENT 11: TIME

A personalized learning system uses time as a flexible resource depending on the nature of the challenge and the skill level of the students (table 6.5). Blended learning approaches to support student mastery of the competencies are more meaningful and

Table 6.5 Personalized Learning Evolution: Time

Element	Minimal Student Input	Some Student Input	Student Driven
Time *When can/does learning occur?*	Schooling is defined by "seat time"— prescribed number of school days (e.g., 180 days, Carnegie units).	Schooling is a more variable blend of time-based and outcome-based measures.	Schooling can take place 24/7, 365 days a year and be determined by outcome-based measures.

practical to students, staff, families, and community members. If we are moving toward learning that can occur anywhere, anytime, then what we do in the brick-and-mortar, online, or community learning space to further the competencies is more important than the set number of minutes assigned to a particular class.

With greater time flexibility, every student will receive customized supports and accelerated opportunity both in and outside school to ensure that they stay on track to graduate ready for college and career. The goal is to provide learning opportunities and meet the educational needs and interests of all children. This opens the door for

- Intensive development in areas of student interest and/or need during and outside the school day

- Focus on a student's demonstration of competencies rather than arbitrary endings (end of a lesson, unit, or marking period)

- Opportunities for off-site projects or virtual course offerings that go beyond the school day and tap into outside expertise

Using time as a resource rather than as a fixed structure will require leadership at the local, state, ministry, and national levels to change policies and practices that continue to define learning as "seat time" moments rather than as demonstrated learning accomplishments.

Personalized Learning Recommendations

In addition to the series of shifts we proposed in the previous section, we also recommend that a local system, in concert with the state, ministry, and/or national authorities, make the following shift in how it works with time:

Shift from a predictable school day and school year to learning 24/7, 365 days a year, monitored and validated by teachers. Students have grown up in a world with an expectation that learning is everywhere; there is a constant stream of information, much bigger than any teacher or textbook, waiting to be consumed, added to, and shared. Students no longer wait for permission to play, publish, or problem-solve. They have high expectations of a learning environment that is on-demand, constantly connected, and personalized. Therefore, a personalized learning system honors the student by creating variable time structures, providing every student the time she needs to make progress toward the defined competencies. The opportunity to learn is not limited by the school building, the school day, or the school year.

ELEMENT 12: ADVANCEMENT

Robust and varied advancement strategies should be implemented to inform students, families, school and district staff, and state officials about individual and group progress in relation to the competencies (see table 6.6). Such strategies should feature an evidenced-based collection of student tasks and tests designed around clearly defined competencies. Advancement can be used as a meaningful feedback loop through which students, staff, and family members check progress toward competency targets. This would likely make formal reporting cycles unnecessary, which would prevent an artificial rush to get marks in by a certain date. Communication with the family still remains essential and is perhaps more robust, through student-led conferences, formal demonstrations (for example, portfolios or exhibitions), and opportunities for family members to log on to a system (for example, LearningBoards) and engage with the teacher.

At the state or ministry level, policymakers and education officials are beginning to open up what school can become. For example, on its website, the Maine Department of Education (http://www.maine.gov/doe/plan/education_evolving/cpa3.html) advocates for a learner-centered model based on demonstration of mastery rather than movement based on age: "The system of schools we have today is one in which time is the constant and learning is the variable. Teachers and students are given a fixed period of time in which to cover a fixed curriculum. The result is a model that falls short of meeting the needs of all students. In a learner-centered, proficiency-based system, students advance upon demonstration of mastery, rather than remain locked in an age-based cohort that progresses through a fixed curriculum at a fixed pace, regardless of learning achievement."

Again, we continue to reinforce that *standards are not the barrier to personalized learning*; the barrier lies in the design of local curriculum and related instruction with an emphasis on standardized assessment and teacher control.

Table 6.6 Personalized Learning Evolution: Advancement

Element	Minimal Student Input	Some Student Input	Student Driven
Advancement *How does a student progress through the system?*	Student is advanced based on age, irrespective of achievement.	Promotion or retention at the end of the year is based on achievement in the course or grade level.	Advancement is based on demonstrated competency whenever that is achieved.

Personalized Learning Recommendations

The following delineates the advancement shifts that a local system may need to make in concert with the state, ministry, and/or national authorities:

1. *Shift from limited flexibility in where schooling happens to appropriate flexibility in locations for learning (for example, online, workplace, community) based on a student's needs and ability.* On the US Department of Education website (http://www.ed.gov/oii-news/competency-based-learning-or-personalized-learning), national policymakers submit that students can "progress as they demonstrate mastery of academic content, regardless of time, place, or pace of learning." A leading example in promoting personalization is the New Hampshire State Department of Education, which approved in 2005 that students who participate in site-based experiences (for example, job shadowing, internships, informational interviews, business tours) can earn credit toward graduation. There is an increasing number of state virtual schools (Florida, Georgia, Illinois, and Texas, to name a few) that typically offer more than one hundred middle and high school courses tuition free for those students who reside in the state. In addition, there are a growing number of private, charter, and local schools that provide opportunities for students to earn credit through virtual coursework.

2. *Shift from a system that awards credits using a seat-time system to a competency- or outcomes-based system that measures disciplinary and cross-disciplinary standards on local and state assessments.* On the US Department of Education website (http://www.ed.gov/oii-news/competency-based-learning-or-personalized-learning) is the following statement: "Depending on the strategy pursued, competency-based systems also create multiple pathways to graduation, make better use of technology, support new staffing patterns that utilize teacher skills and interests differently, take advantage of learning opportunities outside of school hours and walls, and help identify opportunities to target interventions to meet the specific learning needs of students."

   In the United States, for example, currently thirty-six states have policies that provide school districts and schools with some flexibility for awarding credit to students based on demonstrated mastery of content and skills (as opposed to seat time). New Hampshire has eliminated the Carnegie unit completely and replaced it with a competency-based system that promotes student choice and flexibility in where and when learning occurs. To see the latest developments in competency-based education, check out the Education Commission of the States site: http://www.ecs.org/html/educationIssues/ECSStateNotes.asp?nIssueID=290.

3. *Shift from systems that record scores to systems that track student advancement.* Many schools have adopted a web-based platform to record scores so that students and families can be up-to-date on current performance; however, numbers alone fail to capture an individual student's progress. Collecting more data around mastery of skills and pieces of content is significantly different from documenting students' demonstration of what they can produce leveraging the content and skills. Scores will still have a place in a transformed tracking system, but we propose that they are part of a bigger picture to reveal the whole student. An LMS such as LearningBoard has great promise to bring this approach to scale.

CONCLUSION AND REFLECTIVE QUESTIONS

This chapter has described elements of a very different type of schooling: one that is bound by rich and varied artifacts to demonstrate growth over time rather than a collection of scores, bound by mastery rather than seat time, and bound by learning that happens 24/7 rather than at certain times of the day and year. The system shifts described in relation to assessment of learning, time, and advancement call into question the assumptions we have about how students demonstrate mastery or competency on disciplinary and cross-disciplinary outcomes. As teachers' and students' roles evolve, so, too, should those of leaders and policymakers.

Consider these questions:

1. In your estimation, how far are we from the tipping point where personalized learning is more widespread? What might that tipping point look like? What are you doing in preparation for this?

2. In what ways are there design innovations occurring in your classroom, school, or program? (These can be officially sanctioned pilots, quiet campaigns, or covert actions.)

3. What is still standing in the way of the evolution of schooling in your community?

4. What was your reaction when you read the various policy examples in the chapter?

WORKS CITED

Berger, R. *An Ethic of Excellence: Building a Culture of Craftsmanship with Students.* Portsmouth, NH: Heinemann, 2003. Print.

Clarke, J. *Personalized Learning: Student-Designed Pathways to High School Graduation.* Thousand Oaks, CA: Corwin, 2013. Print.

Richardson, W. *Why School? How Education Must Change When Learning and Information Are Everywhere.* New York: TED Conference, 2012. Web.

Wiggins, G. "A True Test: Toward More Authentic and Equitable Assessment." *Phi Delta Kappan* 70.9 (1989): 703–713. Print.

Wiggins, G. "Authenticity in Assessment, (Re)defined and Explained." *Granted, and …* Grant Wiggins, 26, Jan. 2014. Web. <http://grantwiggins.wordpress.com/2014/01/26/authenticity-in-assessment-re-defined-and-explained/>.

Wiggins, G. "Engagement and Personalization: Feedback Part 2." *Granted, and …* Grant Wiggins, 19 April 2014. Web. 20 May 2014. <http://grantwiggins.wordpress.com/2014/04/19/engagement-and-personalization-feedback-part-2/>.

Chapter 7

Leading the Change for Personalized Learning

Followers want comfort, stability, and solutions from their leaders. But that's babysitting. Real leaders ask hard questions and knock people out of their comfort zones. Then they manage the resulting distress.

— Ronald Heifetz and Donald Laurie, "The Work of Leadership," *Harvard Business Review,* Dec. 2001

The evolution to personalized learning is an adaptive change; it's hard, it's disruptive, and it creates uncertainty. These deep and transformative changes require leaders, teachers, and students to examine and oftentimes abandon deeply held beliefs in order to reframe the role of the teacher and the student, the nature of what is to be learned, and the way in which it will be learned. This chapter explores how leaders can successfully navigate adaptive change by clearly articulating and creating urgency for the change, releasing the control of the work to teachers, and managing change as it is occurring. By focusing on these strategies, leaders can increase the probability that personalized learning will become a reality. As opposed to technical change, which can be achieved with relatively simple alterations to existing practice, adaptive change takes place in situations where there are no readily available answers that tell us what to do and how to do it (Heifetz and Linsky). We are creating the road map as we go.

This often creates conflict and uncertainty, but also can be the source of new and transformative solutions.

CLEARLY ARTICULATING AND CREATING URGENCY FOR PERSONALIZED LEARNING (THE "WHY")

At its core, personalized learning places its faith in students' ability to unearth what is important, meaningful, and relevant in their world. Personalized learning gives students increasing voice and choice in the creation of learning tasks; timely feedback and opportunity to take action; and time and space to share and create impact on their intended audience. In order to create this type of learning environment, teachers will need to learn new ways to manage academic and growth outcomes, attend to individual interests and needs, connect students to authentic audiences and opportunities, and track individual progress. We recognize that as we evolve toward more and more sophisticated ways of sharing the learning process with students, there are no manuals, guides, or "how-to" texts that tell us how to accomplish this change. In essence, personalized learning pushes our thinking about virtually every aspect of schooling as we know it.

One way a leader can begin to tackle an adaptive change is to step back from the details of the change she seeks, in an effort to develop her own broad understanding. Heifetz and Linsky call this "getting on the balcony in order to see the dance floor." Balcony thinking offers a comprehensive perspective from which a leader can begin to navigate the complex change process that lies ahead. Being able to clearly and concisely describe the overall vision is the first step toward being able to articulate the "why" of the change for others in a way that captures the imagination and intellect and creates a sense of urgency. The vision grounds the leader in what needs to be accomplished long term and helps her delineate the individual elements of the change that lead to the end goal.

Given that personalized learning represents a significant departure from established practice, a clear and compelling vision that communicates the urgency and the "why" of personalized learning can provide teachers with a reason to invest the time and effort that is needed to learn the content and undergo the pedagogical shifts that personalized learning demands. Consider Simon Sinek's "Golden Circle" as a way of conceptualizing the process of evolving a school toward personalized learning (see figure 7.1).

Figure 7.1 The Golden Circle

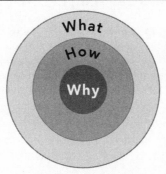

Source: Adapted from S. Sinek, "How Great Leaders Inspire Action," *TED*, September 2009, Web, 15 May 2014.

As Sinek explained in his TED talk: "Everybody knows 'what' they do 100 percent of the time. Some know how they do it. But very very few people or organizations know *why* they do it." The most transformative organizations (with the most loyal subscribers, participants, and users) start with the "why."

Why is personalized learning a better way of "doing school"?

A clear articulation of the vision enables teachers to understand where they are headed and why they are headed in that direction. As Sinek notes, "After all, the goal is not just to get people to buy what you are selling, but to believe what you believe." The process of articulating a vision begins by comparing what learning currently looks like with what learning will look like when personalized learning is fully developed. Wiggins and McTighe underscore that without a clear vision, "schools are likely to remain mired in unexamined habits and rituals, and limited by incoherent practices and structures that continue to miss the mark in preparing students for the demands of today's 'real world.' The challenge is not to invent some ideal school that is unmoored from reality, but to build exemplary schooling 'backward' from its long term goal of making students thoughtful and accomplished at worthy tasks" (1, 2).

Rather than a collection of vague and lofty statements, a powerful vision of personalized learning creates a sense of direction that helps shape what learning will be accomplished (academic and growth outcomes), how it will be accomplished (redefined roles for teacher and students, and cocreated learning tasks), and how it will be evaluated.

Personalized Learning Recommendations

1. *Use the power of stories to communicate the "why."* Stories, such as the opening vignettes in chapter 2 and the ideas from the task frames in chapter 3, can capture the hearts and minds of the school community; they have the power to make a significant and difficult change feel worth the investment. Sharing stories that illustrate the vision of personalized learning is an effective way to clarify and create a sense of urgency.

2. *Take the time to engage stakeholders in understanding what it is you are trying to do and why it is so important to do it.* If both the "what" and the "why" aren't in place, your efforts can be derailed. In a private conversation with Diane on moving forward with personalized learning, one superintendent reflected, "I just didn't do a very good job of bringing the community along with what I was trying to do and why I was trying to do it. Now there are questions about funding, whether or not it is going to impact postsecondary admissions, and student performance on standardized testing." Questions from all stakeholders (teachers, students, parents, and community members) arise because they do not understand what teaching and student learning will look like if this shift takes place. A skillful leader works to develop a shared language around the elements of personalized learning and pushes for clarity about the practices, structures, and use of time and resources necessary to support teachers' growth and development as they navigate this complex change. The leader also pushes for clarity about how school will be different for students as a result of this change (for example, varied success measures of academic and growth outcomes, exhibitions of student work, flexibility in time). As leaders work with stakeholders to articulate what personalized learning is and why it is so important, the vision becomes the North Star for the difficult journey ahead.

GIVING BACK THE WORK TO TEACHERS (THE "HOW")

As leaders set about helping teachers and students feel at home with personalized learning, it only makes sense that they attend to the mindsets described in chapter 2.

- **Relevance:** As leaders, how can we help teachers feel that the work they do as adult learners is relevant to their students and their professional practice?

- **Growth mindset:** How can we support teacher practice so that they have the opportunity to continuously incorporate feedback in order to improve their practice?

- **Self-efficacy:** How can we highlight incremental successes so that teachers build stamina as learners?

- **Sense of belonging:** How can we create learning communities for teachers so that they can learn from one another and acquire the same growth outcomes we value in student learning?

Leaders also need to pose questions rather than provide answers, helping teachers push through the discomfort of not knowing the answer and seek solutions through problem solving on their own and with others.

If adaptive change is going to take hold, leaders must create the conditions that will allow teachers to learn, test out, and acquire new skills. Kate Bean, director of Aveson Charter Schools in California, explained an early but significant miscalculation in opening a school devoted to personalized learning:

> Our biggest miscalculation was our belief that we could institutionalize the practice ... with three weeks of professional development prior to school starting and no real plan for ongoing coaching. It was ironic for a team of educational consultants to have underestimated the amount of collaboration and coaching needed to create an unprecedented personalized learning model. There lies the crux of our challenge ... We knew that we wanted students to experience personalized learning, but we didn't know really what it looked like or how to do it, and unfortunately there were no exemplars to copy. We had fallen into the same trap as many reform models in predicting that structure and programs of the school would drive the learning outcomes. We attempted to implement every best practice and some untested practices in the first year with new students, new parents, and new staff. We did not anticipate that taking students from traditional schools and immersing them in our model would prove to be stressful for many students, parents, and staff. However, the strength of Aveson lived in our willingness to see the failures and be nimble enough to make changes expeditiously.

The shift from a traditional model to a personalized learning model does take collective attention, conversation, and action as individuals embrace, learn, and grow into their new roles and responsibilities.

In order to promote deep learning and sustained change, teachers must have the opportunity to master element(s) of personalized learning before moving on to additional challenges. The research of Bruce Joyce and Beverly Showers has shown that in order for change in teaching practice to be successfully implemented and sustained, teachers need to learn the theory behind a change, see examples of the change, and be coached in implementing that change. Without classroom coaching, there is only a 10 to 15 percent chance that the new practices will survive. As mentioned at the beginning of this chapter, it is inevitable that conflicts will arise as teachers struggle to learn new roles, establish new relationships, and take on new responsibilities. Successful navigation of these conflicts requires leaders to treat conflict as an opportunity for growth rather than as evidence of failure. Facing conflict openly and honestly within structures that allow teachers' voice and influence to surface can spur development of the entire learning community.

Releasing the work back to teachers signals a dramatic shift in culture and the way work gets done in schools. It creates an environment in which teachers can own their work, build sustained relationships with peers, and continuously improve their knowledge and skills. Among the most powerful levers for transforming school culture is the formation of "communities of practice" in which teachers with similar content needs, interests, or students meet regularly to solve problems of practice and learn from one another. These communities of practice mirror the classroom community of practice in which teachers and students collaborate around learning goals and processes. Communities of practice require a commitment of time and an investment by each individual in the collective work, which can produce exciting transformation in teachers' knowledge and skill. Communities of practice are especially effective when there are structures within the organization that allow the learning, insights, and decisions that emerge from the communities of practice to bubble up to the rest of the organization, creating a flow from one community to the whole. It is far more powerful to develop teacher knowledge and skill in communities of practice than to tackle skill development one teacher at a time (Hargreaves and Fullan).

Personalized Learning Recommendations

Here are some moves that can help leaders navigate the rough waters of individual and organizational change.

1. *Acknowledge teacher concerns.* As described in the Concerns-Based Adoption Model (Hord, Rutherford, Huling-Austin, and Hall), individuals progress through predictable stages of concern as they implement new practices:

   o Staff start with personal concerns. (How is this going to affect me?)

   o Then they move to management concerns. (How am I going to get it all done?)

   o Finally, staff experience concerns about the success of their work and its impact on students. (How is what I am doing affecting my students?)

   In the beginning stages when teachers have personal and management concerns, effective leaders not only acknowledge the legitimacy of the concerns but also address the concerns to the extent possible. They provide venues in which teachers can surface their concerns and address them. This can occur as teachers work with peers or in faculty

---

meetings and professional development sessions. The leader must set up mechanisms through which these concerns can be generally recognized and addressed.

2. ***Manage the pace and sequence of change.*** In addition to acknowledging the level of concern that teachers have, leaders who successfully navigate complex change manage the pace and sequence of change. They seek a pace that is fast enough to sustain momentum but slow enough that teachers have a fair chance to learn and successfully implement new practices. Successful leaders are careful to articulate a doorway into this work—a starting point that is connected to other aspects of the change. Focusing on the cocreation of tasks can be a productive doorway into personalized learning.

3. ***Consider the adoption of a learning management system (LMS) to assist teachers and students track progress over time.*** An LMS, such as LearningBoards, creates a repository where teachers can upload feedback and enter marks as well as review past progress to offer students guidance and next steps. An LMS also assists with the development of student-led conferences, exhibitions, and portfolio reviews. For more information, refer back to the discussion of element 10, demonstration of learning, in chapter 6.

4. ***Plan for continuous refinement.*** Aveson Charter School collaborated with Allison to revamp their Personalized Mastery Learning Continuum. Kate Bean, director of Aveson Charter Schools, explained:

> The next big step is to shift more of the learning process to student-led practices based on their strengths and passions. The original charter document of Aveson schools envisioned a K–12 continuum of gradual release of teacher-directed learning and projects to student-directed learning and projects. There are numerous examples of this being done across our schools; the anecdotes of "student passion" projects and "take action" projects can be found on a daily basis. Yet at Aveson we are not satisfied and will continue to refine and grow our philosophy of Personalized Mastery Learning. With the assistance of Allison Zmuda, … we have once again entered into a period of reflection, refinement, and reinvention. The … Personalized Mastery Learning Continuum is the new bar we have set for ourselves.

MANAGING CHANGE AS IT IS OCCURRING (THE "WHAT")

Managing the predictable concerns and needs that will emerge as teachers begin to evolve their work toward personalized learning is a critical step in the change process. As Heifetz and Linsky (134) so eloquently state: "because a leader must strike a delicate balance between having people feel the need to change and having them feel overwhelmed by the change, leadership is a razor's edge." Personalized learning lives on that razor's edge. The instinct of most leaders is to avoid the messiness, discomfort, and new learning that accompany adaptive change; they want to provide answers and smooth out conflict. Yet working through adaptive change requires just the opposite: leaders and teachers must give up known and familiar ways of doing their jobs for unknown territory. Distress and frustration will result with the emergence of the new roles, responsibilities, relationships, and skills that are needed to successfully navigate the change.

The work of the leader is to help teachers grapple with this complexity and learn the new skills that will make them successful practitioners of personalized learning. The "Instructional Core" is a helpful way to organize and communicate each of the personalized learning elements. First described in 2003 by the Public Education Leadership Project at the Harvard Graduate School of Education (City, Elmore, Fiarman, and Teitel), the Instructional Core consists of four components: **teacher** knowledge and skill, **student** engagement in learning, **content** they are learning, and the **tasks** that students are given (see figure 7.2).

The Instructional Core helps explain what personalized learning is and helps you understand how changing one component (for example, a student's opportunity to pursue something that he finds fascinating) impacts the others (for example, content may need to shift or be eliminated). Let's examine each component in more detail.

Role of the teacher. The teacher's role in personalized learning shifts from one of deliverer of information to one of facilitator/coach of learning through questioning, conferences, and feedback to students. This is a far different role from the one that

Figure 7.2 Instructional Core

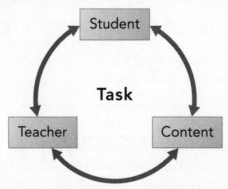

Adapted from E. A. City, R. F. Elmore, S. E. Fiarman, and L. Teitel, *Instructional Rounds in Education: A Network Approach to Teaching and Learning.* (Cambridge, MA: Harvard Education Press, 2009). Print.

preservice teachers are taught and that the vast majority of teachers have experienced. We cannot assume that the shift from "teacher in charge" to shared power in the classroom will happen without explicit development of new strategies and behaviors, and coaching on those behaviors. In fact, without careful attention to helping teachers manage their new role as it plays out in the design, implementation, and assessment of tasks, we can predict that personalized learning will be a passing fad.

Role of the student. In personalized learning, the student's role shifts from one of compliance to one of codeveloper of her learning experience through cocreating tasks, seeking out partners for collaboration and feedback, and proposing how their disciplinary and cross-disciplinary outcomes will be demonstrated. Thus the role that students play in personalized learning is dramatically different from the one they experience in a traditional classroom. Like teachers, students have been socialized to assume a certain role in the teaching and learning process. Students are accustomed to asking, "Is this going to be on the test?" "What do you want me to remember?" "How long does this assignment have to be?" These questions indicate that they see their role as complying with their teacher's demands.

The content to be learned. Chapter 2 describes how academic and growth outcomes should be integrated into task design. Academic outcomes are derived from overarching content standards (for example, Anchor Standards in Reading), and cross-disciplinary outcomes are broader transdisciplinary skills and dispositions that are essential to success outside school. Shared understanding of the academic and growth outcomes and what they look like in student work will go a long way in the development and management of content. One clear challenge for teachers is to understand how the content standards for which they are accountable can be managed and met in an environment in which students have significant choice in what and when they learn. This is where chapter 3's task frames and other related ideas demonstrate how content standards can align with tasks in which students have significant input.

Task. In personalized learning, teacher-developed tasks and lesson plans give way to codesigned tasks and plans for learning. This final component of the Instructional Core represents a significant departure from current practice as well. Teachers will need to coach students in task design and execution; and, because a range of tasks will be in play, they'll need to engage in "just-in-time" teaching instead of front-loading information. Students will need to become more accustomed to struggle as they navigate through problems, challenges, and dead ends without feeling defeated. This is where the articulation and development of mindsets (relevance, growth mindset, self-efficacy, and sense of belonging) will promote a healthy and vibrant learning culture.

As stated earlier in this chapter, the role of the leader is to help teachers grapple with the complexity of change that the evolution to personalized learning demands. This can best be accomplished by the creation of a clear, focused plan that articulates the desired outcomes, indicators of success, and specific actions that will lead to success. Such a plan memorializes what the learning community has come to understand about the larger purposes of personalized learning as well as the specific actions that will lead to achievement of that larger vision. To that end, table 7.1 is a "vision-to-action plan" that can help facilitate the organization and management process.

Personalized Learning Recommendations

1. *Articulate a theory of action that describes the evolution to personalized learning.* A theory of action, a series of "if-then" statements, makes explicit how you think change will occur and allows you to target actions appropriately. For example, the following might be one aspect of a personalized learning theory of action:

   > **IF** students have a voice in determining the learning tasks, **THEN** they will be more engaged and invested in the learning tasks.

   This provides a clear articulation of how personalized learning will improve student learning. Guidance on creating a theory of action can be found in *Instructional Rounds in Education* (City et al.).

2. *Provide models and offer structures and supports to engage teachers in personalized learning.* A leader can greatly enhance teachers' ability to understand the shift in classroom roles by giving teachers the authority and responsibility to design their own work as adult learners. Seek input on the yearly agenda for the data team. Ask them to design an upcoming professional development session on the topic of growth outcomes. Have teachers in a grade-level team or vertical team select one of the mindsets to investigate further. When teachers have input into the design of their own learning (through the use of many of the elements in Personalized Learning Evolution), it demonstrates a level of trust in them as professionals but also models what you expect them to do with students.

3. *Create an action plan that connects the "why" and the "how."* Why we are doing what we are doing and the development of actions have to directly correlate with each other. This connection between the "why" and the "how" should be constantly communicated with teachers, both to refine actions and to support teachers through an adaptive change. There is a blank version of the "Vision-to-Action Plan" (table AD.1) as well as an illustrative example (table AD.2) in appendix D. Notice that it has clear parallels to what we ask students to do in the "Vision-to-Action Project Planner" in chapter 4 (table 4.13) and in appendix B (table AB.5).

Table 7.1 Personalized Learning Vision-to-Action Plan

OUTCOMES *What is your vision for personalized learning?*		
Design • How will we design a personalized learning pathway toward academic and growth outcomes? • How will we know if our design is viable?	**Implement** • How will we ensure quality control? • How does the plan evolve over time?	**Institutionalize** • How will we ensure sustainability?

INDICATORS *What is evidence of success at each stage?*

PATHWAYS TO ACTION
WHAT: What actions will we take? What is the optimal sequence?
WHO: Who should be involved, in what role/capacity? How will we build ownership?
WHEN: How much time is needed? When will this occur? What timing is optimal?

INDICATORS *Connection to Evidence of Success (listed above)*	WHAT *Task and Resources Needed*	WHO *Key Partners*	WHEN *Timeline*

(continued)

Table 7.1 *(continued)*

CULTURE AND MINDSET *In what ways will current values, beliefs, and behaviors support attainment of our vision?* *In what ways will current values, beliefs, and behaviors challenge attainment of our vision? What changes may be needed?*		
CHALLENGES AND OPPORTUNITIES *What are potential challenges? Immediate? Long term?*		
Personnel	Job descriptions (What's my job?)	
	Staff development	
	Staff appraisal	
Financial	Priority budgeting	
	Support (e.g., substitute, stipends, instructional coaches)	
	Incentives (e.g., conference attendance, iPads)	
Structures	Schedule for students	
	Schedule for staff	
	Grading and reporting	
External Factors	State/national accountability tests	
	College tests (SAT, AP, ACT)	
	Graduation requirements	
	GPA/college admissions	

Cocreated by Allison Zmuda and Jay McTighe

CONCLUSION AND REFLECTIVE QUESTIONS

By its nature, adaptive change cannot be achieved by the leader alone; innovative and workable solutions arise only by partnering with the people responsible for the work. Therefore, in developing a personalized learning system, every leader creates an organizational culture of respect grounded in high expectations, and provides feedback and guidance in instructional strategies and task design. Every learning community, both in and outside school, offers students opportunities to learn from experience through application in authentic situations. Staff meetings are dedicated to the empowerment of students as agents in curriculum, instruction, and assessment to demonstrate college-, career-, and citizenship-ready skills.

When reflecting on the magnitude of this adaptive change, consider the following questions:

1. Why personalized learning? What would the role of the student look like? the role of the teacher? the role of the leader? the role of the parent? the role of the community member? Describe these in clear, compelling language.

2. How can we engage the school community in a dialogue about personalized learning that will build a shared understanding of why this work is important, how we will go about it, and the changes that will occur in teaching and learning as a result?

3. What incentives do students, teachers, and leaders have as motivation in circumstances where defining the problem, developing a solution, and working through implementation issues all require new learning?

4. How can we restructure our use of time and resources so that we are modeling collaboration and the learning environments that we want teachers to provide their students?

WORKS CITED

City, E. A., Elmore, R. F., Fiarman, S. E., and Teitel, L. *Instructional Rounds in Education: A Network Approach to Teaching and Learning.* Cambridge, MA: Harvard Education Press, 2009. Print.

Hargreaves, A., and Fullan, M. *Professional Capital: Transforming Teaching in Every School.* New York: Teachers College Press, 2012. Print.

Heifetz, R., and Linsky, M. *Leadership on the Line: Staying Alive through the Dangers of Leading.* Boston: Harvard Business School Publishing, 2002. Print.

Hord, S. M., Rutherford, W. L., Huling-Austin, L., and Hall, G. E. *Taking Charge of Change.* Alexandria, VA: Association for Supervision and Curriculum Development, 1987. Print.

Joyce, B., and Showers, B. *Student Achievement through Staff Development.* Alexandria, VA: Association for Supervision and Curriculum Development, 2002. Print.

Sinek, S. "How Great Leaders Inspire Action." *TED.* TED, September 2009. Web. 15 May 2014. <http://www.ted.com/talks/simon_sinek_how_great_leaders_inspire_action>.

Wiggins, G., and McTighe, J. *Schooling by Design: Mission, Action, Achievement.* Alexandria, VA: Association for Supervision and Curriculum Development, 2007. Print.

The Conclusion of the Era of "One-Size-Fits-All Schooling"

> Schools are not "broken" and in need of fixing. They are social institutions under stress that need to evolve.
>
> —Peter Senge et al., *Schools That Learn*

The opening paragraphs of this book described schooling as a series of required experiences where students are relegated to the sidelines in the development of what to learn, how to learn, and how to demonstrate learning. We challenged you to reconceptualize learning as a process in which students access, create, and share new knowledge through the elements of personalized learning. In personalized learning, the typical student experience is marked by doing work that is innately interesting to her and worth her time and effort. Students see the connections between the work and broader academic and growth outcomes. They see how their work affects the world outside their classroom, which spurs them to keep learning and growing. Students track their progress as they become more skillful and sophisticated, and they recognize improvement over time. Feedback from their teachers and others, and flexibility in terms of location and how their time is structured, help students feel supported. Students record individual accomplishments on a learning management system to demonstrate achievement and reflect on future goals.

A distressing "Yes, but" may have accompanied your reading experience—"Yes, but how can I do this in a curriculum that is jam-packed and where accountability looms over me?" The current educational climate poses significant challenges, but the cost of inaction is that students will continue to go through the motions of schooling and leave unprepared for the future. Just start—find a window into the work and let it grow from there. Collaborate with one student on a question he finds fascinating. Make space on your physical and virtual walls to describe disciplinary and cross-disciplinary outcomes in student-friendly language. Bring in an expert to review student work and offer feedback. Talk about mindsets with students and use them as a guide for how you communicate and motivate. Invite students to the design table to imagine what is possible and rediscover how joyful teaching and learning can become.

Additional Resources for Chapters 1–3

WHAT IS PERSONALIZED LEARNING?

Here is a sampling of more recent definitions that break through the boundaries of "one-size-fits-all" schooling:

- *Personalized Learning Foundation:* Personalized learning is a blended approach that combines the delivery of education both within and beyond the traditional classroom environment. The personalized learning model fosters a collaborative partnership among the teacher, parent, student, and school that designs a tailored learning program for each student according to the needs and interest of each individual student (Clarke 6).

- *Personalized Learning in British Columbia:* learning that is increasingly student-initiated, self-directed, and interdisciplinary and that is facilitated by the teacher and co-planned with students, parents and teachers. Personalized learning combines the "how" and "what" of learning. A personalized approach recognizes that there are still core requirements and expectations. However, with personalized learning there will be increased emphasis on competencies: social responsibility, global and cultural understanding, environmental stewardship, healthy living, ethics, collaboration, creativity, innovation, critical thinking and problem solving, digital literacy. (From "An Interactive Discussion Guide," by the Ministry of Education in British Columbia, http://www.sd33.bc.ca/news/personalized-learning-interactive -discussion-guide 10)

- *A+ Schools:* Personalized Learning is a 21st century, student-centered model that puts the needs of students first by: tailoring an individualized learning plan for each and every student; honoring and supporting each student to reach his or her greatest potential, providing choice and flexibility in how, what, when, and where students learn; supporting parent involvement in their children's learning plan and process; encouraging collaborative partnerships between the student, parent, teacher, school, and greater community; fostering positive, meaningful relationships between each student and teacher; engaging and motivating students by supporting learning in a manner that is relevant and valuable to each student's life, interests, and goals; and preparing students to be life-long learners and productive, successful 21st century citizens. (http://www.theaplus.org/personalized-learning.php)

- *Glossary of Education Reform:* Personalized learning is intended to facilitate the academic success of each student by first determining the learning needs, interests, and aspirations of individual students, and then providing learning experiences that are customized—to a greater or lesser extent—for each student. (http://edglossary .org/personalized-learning/)

What is your definition? Is it the same as that of your colleagues? your students? your parents?

Create a collective definition of personalized learning.

DEVELOPMENT OF DISCIPLINARY OUTCOMES

Long-term disciplinary outcomes have the following characteristics:

- They emphasize independent application when the student is facing new challenges both in and outside school.

- They establish purpose and relevance for students. For example, they answer common student questions: "Why should I learn this?" or "How/where/when will I use this?"

- They create coherence across grade levels within the subject-area program.

Prosper Independent School District in Texas articulated disciplinary outcomes for each subject area. Here are its disciplinary goals in the arts, special education, and social studies.

Visual and Performing Arts

- Communicate effectively based on purpose, task, and audience using appropriate vocabulary
- Find meaning and interest in varied works and performances of art
- Create a work or performance to evoke mood and emotion through application of technique and methodology
- Evaluate a work or performance to determine its value
- Demonstrate professionalism through exhibiting attentiveness, growing from feedback, continuing to make a good impression, and adhering to industry standards
- Create a portfolio of accomplishments through documenting training and experience to promote themselves as an artist
- *Advanced high school courses:* Develop a career pathway by exploring and pursuing viable options based on interests, experience, and aspirations

Special Education

- Function in the community through their training and experience
- Communicate effectively based on purpose, task, and audience using appropriate vocabulary
- Develop a pathway by exploring and pursuing viable options based on interests, experience, and aspirations
- Demonstrate professionalism through exhibiting attentiveness, growing from feedback, continuing to make a good impression, and being mindful of social/cultural norms
- Advocate based on personal needs (academic, behavioral, emotional, and physical) to determine an appropriate solution

Social Studies

- Evaluate claims and analyze issues to verify the credibility of that point of view

- Analyze documents and data to establish generalizations, make predictions, or draw conclusions

- Determine relevance of historical lessons (for example, ideas, documents, tactical errors, and events) and apply to a given situation, problem, or challenge

- Evaluate the interdependent nature of a given situation or conflict

- Communicate effectively based on purpose, task, and audience using appropriate vocabulary

DEVELOPMENT OF CROSS-DISCIPLINARY OUTCOMES

Cross-disciplinary outcomes are transdisciplinary learning goals with a clear set of descriptions and performance indicators. In chapter 2, we offered the following as an illustrative example (see table AA.1).

Here are four other sets of illustrative cross-disciplinary outcomes that were identified, defined, and described to clarify the performance indicators across students' K–12 education.

- *Henry County Public Schools, Virginia:* critical thinking and problem solving, creative thinking, communication, collaboration

- *Katy Independent School District, Texas:* creative thinking, critical thinking, problem solving, information literacy, collaboration, social contribution, communication

- *Lake Havasu Public Schools, Arizona:* critical thinking, creativity and innovation, problem solving, information literacy, communication, collaboration, social and civic engagement, self-direction and initiative, task management

- *Oneida-Herkimer-Madison Board of Cooperative Educational Services, New York:* global competence, social responsibility, critical thinking, problem solving, creative and innovative thinking, information and media literacy, collaboration, initiative and self-direction, communication

FIVE STEPS TO DEVELOP CROSS-DISCIPLINARY OUTCOMES

The following are five steps to articulating cross-disciplinary outcomes:

Step 1. Identify a list of cross-disciplinary outcomes that reflect your school community. Keep in mind that each outcome requires a related set of skills. Focus on what is essential, as identifying too many areas will bog down both

Table AA.1 Illustrative Examples of Cross-Disciplinary Outcomes

Cross-Disciplinary Outcomes	Related Skills
Creative Thinking	• Assemble raw material and let the collection define the purpose and intent • Take a different perspective on the same problem, topic, idea, or object • Sample, mix, and repurpose information into new forms
Critical Thinking	• Apply a questioning eye • Make predictions, articulate patterns, and form conclusions • Examine messages and stories presented
Problem Solving	• Frame a question to identify what you don't know • Pursue knowledge and conduct research to find a viable solution • Manage information effectively and ethically • Draw conclusions and define next steps
Communication	• Use multiple mode(s) to share information and ideas for a specific purpose, task, and audience • Frame and present a point of view in a way that is compelling and engaging • Listen to a point of view to verify, deepen, or disagree
Collaboration	• Build consensus around a shared goal and approach • Take individual responsibility for a shared goal and common task • Attend to the cohesiveness and quality of the common task
Metacognition	• Know what you don't know and using mechanisms (for example, tools, strategies, context) to deal with problems • Think about your thought process • Analyze performance along the way • Seek and use feedback

the development and implementation processes. Involve as many stakeholders as possible to identify the outcomes, but once the list is created, it should go to a "heavyweight" team for the next step.

Step 2. Create a heavyweight team to articulate the cross-disciplinary outcomes.
A heavyweight team is one that is assembled for a deliberate purpose; once

the team's purpose has been achieved, the team is disbanded (Christensen, Horn, and Johnson). Ideally, representatives from the local community and PreK–12 staff will be included. The work will then move to more permanent "middleweight" teams (that is, departments, grade-level teams, longstanding leadership committees) to revise.

Step 3. Define each of the skills or competencies. Coming up with a list of skills is the easy part; the first real challenge is crafting definitions. Parent and community representatives should take a leadership role in defining the skills because they are employed outside the school walls. Their life and work experience is great fodder for not only developing the definitions but also clarifying how students can become more sophisticated and skillful over time.

Step 4. Take the definitions and related skills out for a test drive. Feedback from the full staff and community both demonstrates the seriousness about this endeavor and broadens it by having individuals wrestle with the concepts and the language. Whether this work results in minor tweaks or significant improvements, the real objective is for stakeholders to own the work. When it comes to soliciting feedback from the community at large, it is important to use a blend of low-tech and high-tech tools. For example,

- Post a direct link that is prominently featured on your school or district web page.

- Send Twitter and/or Facebook messages to remind stakeholders of their value in this process, inform them of deadlines, and provide direct links to more information.

- Describe cross-disciplinary outcomes and related skills at the next monthly meeting (of the board, the PTO or PTA, the student council) and then elicit immediate feedback.

- Use survey software (such as Poll Everywhere) to collect responses to such prompts as "Identify the three most important cross-disciplinary outcomes in the workplace" or "Provide an example of a task in or out of school that illustrates cross-disciplinary outcome(s)."

Step 5. Reexamine assessment and instructional design. Once the cross-disciplinary outcomes have been articulated, it is vital to turn attention to how they impact existing classroom routines, instructional practices, and assignments.

CONNECTING CROSS-DISCIPLINARY OUTCOMES AND TASK FRAMES "BY DESIGN"

Newport News School Division in Virginia worked with Allison to articulate what they named College, Career and Citizen Ready Skills (or cross-disciplinary outcomes) and then describe task frames to be embedded in every curriculum (all subjects, K–12). The collective dialogue that led to the description of each task frame illuminated what primary cross-disciplinary outcomes are to be measured, making it less overwhelming for task designers who think they have to measure everything (see table AA.2).

STRATEGIES AND TOOLS TO SUPPORT GROWTH AND DEVELOPMENT IN METACOGNITION

Metacognition is a vital cross-disciplinary outcome, ambiguous to describe and even more elusive to implement in classroom practice. Metacognition is highly individual; students need skills cultivated through direct prompts, questions, and tasks that reveal the thought process that led to the solution, the next step, or the reflection. Here are five practical examples that can be integrated into your classroom practice.

   1. **Metacognitive awareness inventories.** There are many tools online that can be adapted for the classroom. According to a review of the research literature, student scores on these inventories correlate with general cognitive gains (Tokuhama-Espinosa). Tables AA.3 and AA.4 are examples of inventories for reading and for problem solving, respectively, that can be rated on a five-point Likert scale.

   2. **Sentence stems.** To develop metacognitive skills, these sentence stems can be used by students to reveal the steps that the student took to arrive at the conclusion, answer, or insight. Make these visible in classrooms and model their use in one-on-one conferencing, small groups, and class conversations.

   o   This makes me think of …

   o   I wonder …

   o   I notice …

   o   I picture …

   o   My strategy is …

   o   My question is …

   o   I am figuring out …

   o   I am puzzled …

   o   I was surprised …

   o   I thought that …

Table AA.2 Task Frames

Task Frame: Authentic and Transdisciplinary	Cross-Disciplinary Outcomes That *Should* Be Measured	Cross-Disciplinary Outcomes That *May* Be Measured
Problem/Solution. Identify and define a problem and generate a possible solution(s) (or solution paths), evaluate the viability of each solution, and offer a recommendation.	• Problem solving • Critical thinking • Communication	Creativity and innovation; social responsibility; information literacy; collaboration
Inquiry/Investigation. Systematically develop questions and pursue an explanation/pattern based on, but not limited to, known information.	• Critical thinking • Problem solving • Initiative and self-direction • Information literacy	Creativity and innovation; communication; collaboration; social responsibility
Source/Comparative analysis. Analyze data, information, artifacts, and/or textual evidence to develop an explanation or interpretation, and/or to determine impact.	• Critical thinking • Communication	Collaboration; information literacy
Critique/Self-Analysis. Evaluate a given text, performance, or problem based on established criteria.	• Critical thinking • Communication	Initiative and self-direction; collaboration; problem solving; information literacy
Debate, Panel, Role Play. Present and participate in a debate, panel, or role play to provide information, gain insight, and/or promote a particular point of view.	• Critical thinking • Communication	Social responsibility; information literacy; collaboration
Performance/Product. Generate a performance/product using visual, multimedia, sound, writing, and/or speech to demonstrate understanding and/or communicate creative intent.	• Critical thinking • Communication • Initiative and self-direction	Information literacy; collaboration; creativity and innovation
Modeling/Simulation. Given a model or set of criteria/data/experiences, create representations to illustrate/predict outcomes or to deepen understanding.	• Critical thinking • Creativity and innovation	Problem solving; communication; collaboration; information literacy

Table AA.2 *(continued)*

Task Frame: Authentic and Transdisciplinary	Cross-Disciplinary Outcomes That *Should* Be Measured	Cross-Disciplinary Outcomes That *May* Be Measured
Correspondence/Interviews. Appropriately communicate to an audience and/or respond to an idea, point of view, concern, request, or proposal to achieve a desired result.	• Communication • Critical thinking	Collaboration; social responsibility; information literacy
Persuasive statement. Develop an argument/artifact using supporting information and persuasive techniques to promote a particular point of view and/or to cause action.	• Communication • Critical thinking	Creativity and innovation; social responsibility; collaboration; information literacy
Portfolio/Reflection. Collect work over time to demonstrate mastery in one or more modes of expression, reflect on growth, and/or set goals.	• Communication • Critical thinking • Initiative and self-direction	Creativity and innovation

3. <u>**Thinking journals.**</u> Have students regularly use journals to describe ambiguities, difficulties, and inconsistencies. The journal can be a daily exercise employing a common set of prompts:

o What did you learn today? Describe where you feel more accomplished based on your work.

o What are the struggles that you need to continue to work through? Describe areas that are challenging right now.

o What strategy or next step can you take based on the challenges you faced?

o (If you are using these prompts on a daily basis) Based on your work over the past _____ days, what strategies or next steps were most helpful/effective? What strategies or next steps were unhelpful/ineffective? How might this change what you will do next time?

Table AA.3 Reading Strategies Inventory

1. I have a purpose in mind when I read.
2. I take notes while reading to help me understand what I'm reading.
3. I think about what I know to help me understand what I'm reading.
4. I preview the text to see what it's about before reading it.
5. When text becomes difficult, I read aloud to help me understand what I'm reading.
6. I write summaries to reflect on key ideas in the text.
7. I think about whether the content of the text fits my purpose.
8. I read slowly but carefully to be sure I understand what I'm reading.
9. I discuss my reading with others to check my understanding.
10. I skim the text first by noting characteristics like length and organization.
11. I try to get back on track when I lose concentration.
12. I underline or circle information in the text to help me remember it.
13. I adjust my reading speed according to what I'm reading.
14. I decide what to read closely and what to ignore.
15. I use reference materials such as dictionaries to help me understand what I'm reading.
16. When text becomes difficult, I begin to pay closer attention to what I'm reading.
17. I use tables, figures, and pictures in text to increase my understanding.
18. I stop from time to time to think about what I'm reading.
19. I use context clues to help me better understand what I'm reading.
20. I paraphrase (restate ideas in my own words) to better understand what I'm reading.
21. I try to picture or visualize information to help me remember what I'm reading.
22. I use typographical aids like boldface type and italics to identify key information.
23. I critically analyze and evaluate the information presented in the text.
24. I go back and forth in the text to find relationships among ideas in it.
25. I check my understanding when I come across conflicting information.
26. I try to guess what the text is about when reading.
27. When text becomes difficult, I reread to increase my understanding.
28. I ask myself questions I like to have answered in the text.
29. I check to see if my guesses about the text are right or wrong.
30. I try to guess the meaning of unknown words or phrases.

Source: K. Mokhtari and C. A. Reichard, "Assessing Students' Metacognitive Awareness of Reading Strategies," *Journal of Educational Psychology* 94.2 (2002): 249–59. Print.

Table AA.4 Metacognition in Problem Solving

Knowledge of Cognition: How much learners understand about the extent and utilization of their unique cognitive abilities and the ways they learn best

- I can make myself memorize something.
- I use different ways to memorize things.
- When it comes to learning, I can make myself learn when I need to.
- When it comes to learning, I know how I learn best.
- I use learning strategies without thinking.
- When it comes to learning, I know my strengths and weaknesses.
- When I am done with my schoolwork, I ask myself if I learned what I wanted to learn.
- I think about how well I am learning when I work a difficult problem.
- I ask myself if there are certain goals I want to accomplish.
- I ask myself how well I am doing while I am learning something new.
- I think of several ways to solve a problem and then choose the best one.
- I try more than one way to learn something.
- I ask myself what is the easiest way to do things.

Problem Representation: Understanding the problem fully before proceeding

- I try to understand what the problem is asking me.
- I read the problem more than once.
- I read the problem over and over until I understand it.
- I think to myself, do I understand what the problem is asking me?
- I try to understand the problem so I know what to do.
- I make an extra effort to pay attention to what's important.
- I use different learning strategies depending on the problem.

Subtask Monitoring: Breaking the problem down into subtasks and monitoring the choice of learning strategies and completion of each subtask

- I use different ways of learning depending on the problem.
- I try to break down the problem to just the necessary information.
- I identify all the important parts of the problem.
- I try to eliminate information in the problem that I don't need.
- I pick out the steps I need to do this problem.
- I think about what information I need to solve this problem.
- I think about all the steps as I work the problem.

Evaluation: Double-checking throughout the entire problem-solving process to evaluate if it is being done correctly

- I go back and check my work.
- I double-check to make sure I did it right.
- I check to see if my calculations are correct.
- I look back to see if I did the correct procedures.
- I check my work all the way through the problem.
- I look back at the problem to see if my answer makes sense.
- I stop and rethink a step I have already done.
- I make sure I complete each step.

Source: B. C. Howard, S. McGee, R. Shia, and N. S. Hong, "Metacognitive Self-Regulation and Problem-Solving: Expanding the Theory Base Through Factor Analysis," Annual Meeting of the American Education Research Association, New Orleans, April 2000. Paper. Full text: http://files.eric.ed.gov/fulltext/ED470973.pdf.

If you want to have students journal regularly, but not daily, consider the following set of prompts:

Preferences

o The most interesting thing about _____was …

o I prefer to work by myself on activities that …

o I like working with others when …

Learning Style and Strategies

o If I can, I try to avoid activities that …

o I find it easiest to understand when …

o When I don't understand something, I …

Strengths

o I'm getting much better at …

o One good question I asked (or thought of) today was …

o One of the things I do best is …

Areas in Need of Improvement

o I'm still not sure how to …

o I need to get help with …

o The part I found the most difficult was …

4. <u>Self-navigation plan.</u> Provide students with a common template to chart their own course: create an action plan that includes estimation of time, needed resources, and steps necessary to complete a larger project. We also want them to adapt in response to new information, challenges, and ideas. These additional questions are designed for self-evaluation.

Given My Goal (and My Deadline) …

o What information have I learned that may shape my direction? (either confirms or suggests another pathway)

o What feedback have I received that may shape my direction? (either confirms or suggests another pathway)

o Where do I need to reconsider my timeline? project scope? format and audience?

5. Self-evaluation prompts. After the learning experience or project is finished, it is important to have students reflect back on the broader accomplishments that go beyond the task itself.

o What have you learned?

o What did you find most interesting?

o What did you find easy about learning to … ?

o How would you do things differently next time?

o What did you find most challenging while you were learning to … ?

o What helped you when something got tricky/complicated/frustrating … ?

o How would you change this task/assignment for another group/class that was learning to … ?

STRATEGIES AND TOOLS TO SUPPORT GROWTH AND DEVELOPMENT IN QUESTIONING

What questions are *worth* pursuing? As educators, we are trained to look at our topics and articulate questions for our students that are thought-provoking, that channel inquiry, challenge assumptions, and generate more questions. We think that if we come up with a powerful or beautiful question, then the students will be more likely to be engaged in the related inquiry. But oftentimes we take up too much of the thinking: students use *my* (thought-provoking) question on *my* terms (to channel inquiry on my assignment, challenge assumptions that I already have thought through, and generate questions that are related to the assignment). Students are expected to work within our inquiry frame rather than be part of the design process. We can teach students to pose and pursue their own inquiries based on a given topic, problem, or idea. We also need to create a culture of questioning and challenging others' assumptions as a vital feature of learning environments.

1. *Questioning can be modeled, taught, and encouraged only when it is valued in the organization.* Powerful questions challenge authority figures to examine current assumptions to see if the prevailing approach is "the only way." When someone lower down the hierarchy poses such a question, it is easy to dismiss him as less knowledgeable or invested. Yet any organization committed to growth must create a culture where it is safe to ask a question. Therefore, how we respond and how we train others to respond, matter.

2. *Powerful or beautiful questions start with an awareness of what we don't know*—the willingness to embrace ignorance. In fact, many powerful questions come from a "beginner's mind" (someone who has little or no knowledge of the subject) or from experts who constantly challenge themselves on "why." The following are some examples of these actionable, powerful questions:

o Why do some keep questioning while others stop? (Was it something in the genes, in the schools, in the parenting?)

o How do cars work?

o What should we stop doing?

o Do aliens exist?

o Can animation be cuddly?

o Who is to blame?

o What trends are having the most impact on my field, and how is that likely to play out over the next few years?

o Why are some people mean?

o What if a human leg could be more like a cheetah's?

o Why is the sky blue?

o Can a school be built on questions?

o Is sugar bad for you?

o Why do I get bored?

o Why should I believe you when you tell me something can't be done?

Warren Berger offers a "Why, What If, How" framework to develop powerful questions.

Ask **Why.** Why does it have to be this way? Why does this exist? Why will it benefit you to invest time and energy thinking about this problem? The "why" should lead to action: improvements, solutions, ideas, possibilities.

Ask **What if?** Imagination begins to go to work, and that focus, germination, or stewing will typically lead to possibilities that can be acted on. We sit with a problem for as long as it takes until we arrive at an insight. We can research, wonder, and pursue other people's attempts, but we are not fenced in by existing knowledge.

Ask **How.** Use discipline and focus to work through possibilities and "fail forward." Ask questions to hone in on a better solution or idea.

MINDSETS: WHAT MOTIVATES STUDENTS TO MEET A CHALLENGE?

The text that follows is from a blog post by Kathleen Cushman and Allison Zmuda.

When we question our students about "what it takes to get really good at something" and give them the space to respond, it is amazing how insightful they can be—and how much of it lines up with the neuroscience of learning. Here are nine answers that students gave in Kathleen Cushman's book *Fires in the Mind,* along with suggestions for related teacher actions to incorporate into your classroom practice.

1. Let us see what we're aiming for.

   o Show models of exemplary work

   o Show real-world connections to questions, problems, and challenges that experts are facing in various fields

2. Break down what we need to learn.

   o Identify the knowledge and skills needed

   o Set realistic goals to create an achievable challenge

3. Give us lots of ways to understand.

   o Present concepts and skills in different ways to help students find a foothold

4. Teach us to critique and revise everything we do.

   o Provide multiple opportunities for students to make changes as they learn from mistakes

   o Keep good records of student progress on key concepts and skills

5. Assess us all the time, not just in high-stakes ways.

   o Use diagnostic and formative assessment to monitor learners' progress

   o Focus less on the grade and more on the information you receive about your teaching from looking at student work

6. Chart our small successes.

   o Make sure all students know their individual goals—and acknowledge their progress toward them

7. Ask us to work as an expert team.

   o Teach key skills of collaboration (how to come to consensus on a plan, how to manage time, how to make sure everyone pulls her weight)

   o Evaluate collaboration skills when assessing a group project, presentation, or performance

8. Help us extend our knowledge through using it.

   o Build meaningful applications of concepts and skills into daily instruction and larger projects

9. Use performances to assess our academic understanding.

   o Seek out audiences for student work so as to underline its authenticity and relevance

   o Make time for students to rehearse, critique, and revise before their presentations

WORKS CITED

Berger, W. *A More Beautiful Question: The power of inquiry to spark breakthroughs.* New York: Bloomsbury USA, 2014. Print.

Christensen, C. M., Horn, M. B., and Johnson, C. W. *Disrupting Class: How Disruptive Innovation Will Change the Way the World Learns.* New York: McGraw-Hill, 2008. Print.

Clarke, J. *Personalized Learning: Student Pathways to High School Graduation.* Thousand Oaks, CA: Corwin, 2013. Print.

Cushman, K. *Fires in the Mind: What Kids Can Tell Us About Motivation and Mastery.* San Francisco: Jossey-Bass, 2010. Print.

Cushman, K., and Zmuda, A. "What Motivates Students to Meet a Challenge?" *Learning Personalized.* 2 Sept. 2013. Web. 5 Jan. 2014. <http://learningpersonalized.com/2013/09/02/what-motivates-students-to-meet-a-challenge-student-answers-and-teacher-actions/>.

Tokuhama-Espinosa, T. *Making Classrooms Better: 50 Practical Applications of Mind, Brain, and Education Science.* New York: Norton, 2014. Print.

Appendix **B**

Additional Resources for Chapter 4

TEMPLATES AND ILLUSTRATIVE EXAMPLES TO GENERATE IDEAS

The design of a worthy task may seem daunting, but the good news is that you are not alone. There is inspiration everywhere: rich problems worth figuring out, ideas that are worth tinkering with, and texts that are worth consuming and producing. You also have the talents, inspiration, and focus of students who can seek out information, hone an idea, and investigate what's best given a set of parameters. Table AB.1 is the blank version of the template for you to consider in developing a new idea or practicing using Michael Fisher's commentary on "Butterfly Story" or Scott Houston's projects on the Laws of Motion (both at the end of this appendix).

Tables AB.2 and AB.3 are two illustrative examples from public school educators: a high school civics and government example and an upper-elementary cross-disciplinary example on evaluating media messages.

Table AB.1 Task Frame Template

Task Frame:	
Context:	
Task • Minimal Student Input • Some Student Input • Student Driven	*What is the challenge?*
Audience • Minimal Student Input • Some Student Input • Student Driven	*Who is the audience? How does that shape communication?*
Feedback • Minimal Student Input • Some Student Input • Student Driven	*How do students use feedback?*
Disciplinary Outcomes	
Related Standards:	
Cross-Disciplinary Outcomes	
• **Critical Thinking:** • **Problem Solving:** • **Creative Thinking:** • **Communication:** • **Collaboration:** • **Metacognition:**	

Table AB.2 Task Frame: Electoral College Project

Context: For this first-time project in ninth-grade Government/Economics (college preparatory and academic level classes), I wanted students to have a working knowledge of the Electoral College. I pulled an electoral map from the 2008 election off Google images, and asked kids to partner up and become campaign advisors to both a Republican and a Democratic candidate. Each candidate had a million dollars to spend on TV ad bundles and state visits. The project required students to budget to spend at least $900K and to articulate one of their strategies using VoiceThread. A spreadsheet of expenses, a paragraph explanation of each strategy, and the VoiceThread were the final products submitted.	
Task • Minimal Student Input • Some Student Input • **Student Driven**	**What is the challenge?** Given that these are ninth graders without too much background knowledge, I wanted a map that was already partially complete (some blue and red states were considered "givens"). I also limited what kids were buying (ad bundles and travel, but two other factors could have served the same purpose). The expectation was that they needed to spend as much of their money as they could, but the where and how was up to them. VoiceThread was a piece of technology I had wanted to try with my classes, and so we all needed some direction from one of the school tech experts. Class time was allotted so we could handle questions and problems as they came up, as opposed to this being a group project totally outside of school.
Audience • Minimal Student Input • **Some Student Input** • Student Driven	**Who is the audience? How does that shape communication?** The spreadsheets and VoiceThreads were the final products, but kids were asked to present one of their strategies to the class. Next year I would probably keep the project the same in scope and expectation, but allow a bit more time for the technology (if VT is new to kids, it takes time for log-ins and instructions). In a presidential election year, this would be a must-do, and might allow for more ongoing study, tracking of candidates and poll numbers, as well as electoral predictions. It would be a much larger and more engaging project then, since it would be following the news at its pace, not ours.
Feedback • Minimal Student Input • **Some Student Input** • Student Driven	**How do students use feedback?** Rubric was developed by me, but with a sense of what students could be expected to do with a project that: (1) required the building of a lot of background knowledge, (2) required technology that was new to most of us, and (3) involved kids working on different levels across a variety of classes. Class time allowed for questions and easily monitored progress, as well as the occasional mini-lesson or reminder of how this system actually worked.

(continued)

Table AB.2 (*continued*)

Disciplinary Outcomes
Pennsylvania Civics & Government: 5.3.9.E, F **Pennsylvania Core Standards:** CC.8.5.9– 10.A, E, F, H; CC.8.6.9– 10.A, C– H
Cross-Disciplinary Outcomes
Problem Solving: Frame a question to identify what you don't know; pursue knowledge and conduct research to find a viable solution; draw conclusions and define the next steps **Communication:** Use mode(s) of communication to share information and ideas for a specific purpose, task, and audience; frame and present a point of view in a way that is compelling and engaging **Collaboration:** Build consensus around a shared goal and approach; take individual responsibility for a shared goal and common task; attend to the cohesiveness and quality of the common task

Developed by Paul Wright

GENERATING A TASK FRAME BASED ON AN ILLUSTRATIVE EXAMPLE: COMMENTARY ON "BUTTERFLY STORY" BY MICHAEL FISHER

The following was written by author and education consultant Michael Fisher based on his musings after reading this manuscript. As you read, consider what you would record in elements of the task frame. In addition, consider how this example or another child-centered example could be integrated into the schooling experience.

While putting together materials for a workshop on digital storytelling, I came across a video called "Butterfly Story," accessible here: https://www.youtube.com/watch?v=88ZQE_Kcfr0. In this digital story, three sisters, ages 14, 11, and 9, wrote, directed, filmed, and narrated a video that brought the life cycle of a butterfly alive. The script they wrote detailed the steps in the cycle of butterfly growth, from egg to larva to caterpillar to chrysalis to butterfly, with all stages vividly depicted on film.

This was not a school project. They did this at home because of an interest in nature and a desire to create something interesting that they could share with others. As of this writing, they have more than nine thousand hits on YouTube. They've also received comments from multiple people praising their work and describing how they've found the video useful.

These children designed their own project with very little peripheral help from their parents. In fact, their parents were relegated to small roles in the process and

Table AB.3 Task Frame: Making Sense of Media Messages—Grades 4–6 English Language Arts/Library Media

Context: Media messages surround us and have powerful impacts on our lives. *Media* refers to any means (e.g., digital, print, visual, audio) used to share a message. These messages affect the way we think, feel, and behave. In order to be a productive and responsible member of society, one must be a critical consumer of information. Understanding that everyone has biases and that media messages are constructed for a purpose for specific audiences helps recipients (readers, viewers, listeners) be critical analyzers of information.

Task	What is the challenge?
• Minimal Student Input • **Some Student Input** • Student Driven	Students collect and analyze media messages for a specific time frame (journal). As students analyze the media messages they selected, they determine the authorship, format, content, purpose, and intended audience of the media messages. Students identify a trend in their data (e.g., gender bias, race bias, age bias, body image, lifestyle) that has impacted their life. Students work in groups based on the trend they select. Students will show evidence of the trend and develop a plan to decrease the reinforcement of the stereotype they observed in media messages. Students will construct a media message as the vehicle to share the plan. Throughout the process, students will work with local media sources based on the format of the media message they select, and media messages will be shared through the local media source.
Audience	**Who is the audience? How does that shape communication?**
• Minimal Student Input • **Some Student Input** • Student Driven	Local media sources (radio, television, Internet) based on format of media message. Students consider their personal bias, content, purpose, format, and audience as they prepare their plan.
Feedback	**How do students use feedback?**
• Minimal Student Input • **Some Student Input** • Student Driven	• Further analysis of selected media messages • Reexamination and/or further articulation of trend • Continued development of plan to work through challenges • Refine media message based on audience reaction
Disciplinary Outcomes	

- To be critical consumers of information by analyzing and evaluating information
- Deconstruct and analyze media messages to determine purpose and impact (includes author's purpose and author's use of language, image, and sound)
- Investigate and determine trends in multiple media messages
- Develop and produce creative/informational media messages
- **Common Core E/LA:** CCSS.ELA-Literacy.RI.6.2, CCSS.ELA-Literacy.RI.6.7, CCSS.ELA-Literacy.W.6.4, CCSS.ELA-Literacy.SL.6.2, CCSS.ELA-Literacy.SL.6.5

(continued)

Table AB.3 *(continued)*

Cross-Disciplinary Outcomes
• **Critical Thinking:** Examine messages and stories presented; apply a questioning eye • **Communication:** Use mode(s) of communication to share information and ideas for a specific purpose, task, and audience; frame and present a point of view in a way that is compelling and engaging • **Collaboration:** Take individual responsibility for a shared goal and common task; attend to the cohesiveness and quality of the common task • **Metacognition:** Think about your thought process

Submitted by Lorena Kelly

are mentioned in the credits at the end of the video as having the roles of Executive Producer, Larva Wrangler, and Location Scout. These children had a coach and a guide through this process, but they were allowed to make all of the decisions for the finished product.

In terms of feedback, there are comments on the video, though these do not amount to much more than praise. To be fair, these children weren't looking to be assessed; they just wanted to learn. When you, the reader, watch the video, what is your assessment? Do these children understand the life cycle of the butterfly? Are they adept at creating something through collaboration that is accessible to multiple audiences? Does this creation lay the foundation for future efforts both in learning and in demonstrating learning through the creation of media?

What interests me the most about this is that it is a content-rich product created solely on the basis of interest in butterflies, without regard to a grade they would get. I absolutely think it exemplifies quality work as well as demonstrated collaboration and communication. It is extremely creative, both in cinematography and structure. The attention to detail has a high degree of precision, evidenced by the clever script, the interaction with the music, and the text and titles used. My only wish is that this *was* a school project. What would our classrooms look like if deep interactions with content and the creation of new resources were the focus, rather than a high-stakes test or a pop quiz on Fridays or a canned project that is well past its expiration date? What if students were partners in their choices for learning rather than just recipients of content gifts?

GENERATING A TASK FRAME BASED ON AN ILLUSTRATIVE EXAMPLE: LAWS OF MOTION BY SCOTT HOUSTON, AN AVESON PHYSICS TEACHER/ADVISOR IN CALIFORNIA

The following is an illustrative example from a high school Physics class for a unit on motion and forces. As you read, consider what you would record in elements of the task frame. The physics outcomes (referenced at the end of the description of each option) are as follows:

1. I can explain how motion deals with the changes of an object's position over time.

2. I can describe motion through the concepts of velocity and acceleration.

3. I can describe motion using Newton's three laws.

4. I can discuss how fundamental forces in nature govern the physical behavior of the universe. One of these fundamental forces, gravity, influences objects with mass but acts at a distance, or without any direct contact between the objects.

5. I can use the concept of gravity to discuss the circular motion of objects.

Option 1: You work for a toy company that wants to market toy cars. Your idea is to take ten different cars and determine their speed to see which one is fastest. You will use the winning car as the cover model for the ad campaign. You should have a slogan with a picture of the car that indicates its speed. You will build a sloped track on which to conduct this competition. Each car should go at least five times so you can set an average for each car. If you would like to, you can build two identical tracks and have races as well to determine who is the fastest. You will still need to record time for this, though. You will calculate the speed of each run for each car and then turn in your report. You will also have the car strike something at the end of the ramp and determine the force with which it hits for each car. This project is for one or two people. *The purpose of this project is to get better at calculating speed, average speed, and force. Connects to outcomes 1 and 3. You may want to choose this project if you enjoy conducting experiments and playing with cars.*

Option 2: You are a trial witness with an expertise in speed mechanics. Many times lawyers try to get their clients acquitted by saying that a person's speedometer is broken or that a speed gun isn't properly calibrated. Your job is to learn how one of these devices really works and explain what could go wrong with it. You will research your device and the types of malfunctions it has, and can even take one apart and put it back together if you can get your hands on one and show me what you learned about how it works. Your report should be about four pages long typed, and with pictures to emphasize your points. This project is for one or two people. *The purpose of this project is to get students familiar with how physics is being used to design machines that can gauge velocity. Connects to outcome 1. You may want to choose this project if you enjoy learning how things work or have an interest in mechanical things.*

Option 3: You have your own YouTube channel and are trying to help other people who are in physics. You feel that physics is boring and hard and want to take confusing concepts and make them simple to understand. You also know that people who watch YouTube do not like to be bored, so your video has to be not only educationally sound but also entertaining. You will do a video that compares Newton's Three Laws of Motion. You must make sure that all three laws are included in the video and discuss how they are different from one another. This project is for one to three people. *The purpose of this project is to be able to understand Newton's Laws of Motion in depth. Connects to outcomes 2, 3, and 4. You may want to choose this project if you enjoy designing scientific examples, teaching others, and being on camera.*

Option 4: You are a model designer for a company that deals in historic memorabilia. They have asked you to build mini working catapults that can be used to throw small objects across an area. They also want to be able to market this to physics teachers to be able to teach their students about projectile motion. You will research how to build a mini-catapult, design it to look like one from a specific time period, and then choose five different types of small projectiles to shoot across a room and then find their projectile motion. This project is for one or two people. *The purpose of this project is to learn how to determine and explain projectile motion. Connects to outcomes 1, 2, and 5. You may want to choose this project if you enjoy doing lab experiments, building things, and math.*

Create a project: If you would prefer to develop your own project based on these standards, write a proposal and submit it to the instructor. He will determine if it is rigorous enough and aligned to the outcomes.

MY VISION-TO-ACTION PROJECT PLANNER

In the text of chapter 4, Allison's son used the Vision-to-Action Project Planner to share his ideas, plans, and challenges. Table AB.4 is a blank version of that template. Table AB.5 was generated by a staff member of Charlotte-Mecklenburg Schools to indicate what it might look like for a science project on the "Garbage Patch."

Table AB.4 Personalized Learning Vision-to-Action Project Planner

MY DESIGN PROBLEM OR CHALLENGE			
What is it? Why does it matter?			

MY DESIGN PROCESS			
Generate: *How do I approach it?* Focus: *How do I make sense of it?* Ideate: *How do I create?* Act: *Is it working?* Build (repeat cycle as needed): *How do I move it forward based on data and/or feedback?*			

MY PATHWAY TO ACTION			
What's my plan?			
WHAT *Task and Resources Needed*	**WHO** *Key Partners*	**WHEN** *Timeline*	**ACHIEVEMENT** *Evidence of Progress*

MY MINDSET	
Relevance *Why do I care? Why does the work matter? Is this the only way?*	
Growth Mindset *What are the criteria I am holding myself to? How am I doing right now? How do I feel right now?*	
Self-Efficacy *Where am I in my process? What are my next steps?*	
Sense of Belonging *How does this impact my connections with others?*	

Cocreated by Allison Zmuda and Jill Thompson

Table AB.5   Sample Personalized Learning Vision and Action Project Planner

MY DESIGN PROBLEM OR CHALLENGE *What is it? Why does it matter?*
What can we do about the garbage patch building up in our ocean? This matters because it effects our environment and the ocean's ecosystem.

MY DESIGN PROCESS Generate (1st cycle): *How do I approach it?* Focus: *How do I make sense of it?* Ideate: *How do I create?* Act: *Is it working?* Build (repeat cycle as needed): *How do I move it forward based on data and/or feedback?*
• We will research how massive of a problem it is. • How do we, as students, make people aware of this situation? • We will create and analyze a survey to gather an understanding of people's knowledge about the Great Pacific Garbage Patch. • We will use the survey data to create our public service announcement and awareness website. • We will see what our audience learns from the experience based on a feedback form and consider next steps and/or revisions.

MY PATHWAY TO ACTION *What's my plan?*			
WHAT *Task and Resources Needed*	**WHO** *Key Partners*	**WHEN** *Timeline*	**ACHIEVEMENT** *Evidence of Progress*
Research and discuss information	Our group: Researcher 1: Find video clips Researcher 2: Find visuals showing the location of the garbage patch Researcher 3: Find information about the history of the garbage patch Researcher 4: Find information about what is being done about the problem. Researcher 5: Find general information about the garbage patch.	We will each take a few days and teach each other the information we learned.	We will curate a work-cited list.
Create survey	Each group member will come up with two questions	1 day	We will review questions and analyze them together to make sure we like our survey.
Distribute and analyze survey results	Group	1 day	Completed survey results
Discuss viable solutions	Group	1 day	Delta/Plus chart of solutions

Table AB.5 *(continued)*

WHAT *Task and Resources Needed*	WHO *Key Partners*	WHEN *Timeline*	ACHIEVEMENT *Evidence of Progress*
Create public service announcement	Group members 1, 2 and 3	2–3 days	Public service video
Create survey and gather feedback from experts and nonexperts	Group members 4 and 5	2–3 days	Completed survey results

MY MINDSET [*Note: This is what one student might say*]	
Relevance *Why do I care? Why does the work matter? Is this the only way?*	• If the garbage patch continues to grow, soon we will not have clean water for the dolphins and whales. • This matters because it affects our environment and the ocean's ecosystem. • There are many ways to help the environment, such as recycling.
Growth Mindset *What are the criteria I am holding myself to? How am I doing right now? How do I feel right now?*	• I want to make a positive impact on the environment. • The more people who are aware of the garbage patch problem, the more I am helping. • I feel that our website and video will help others understand, but I still think we could do more. Maybe we could tweet out the website so we are spreading the word past our school.
Self-Efficacy *Where am I in my process? What are my next steps?*	• My team is working well together because we all care about the environment. • I am going to work on the public service announcement, but I like working with iMovie.
Sense of Belonging *How does this impact my connections with others?*	• While my team is working well together, sometimes I get frustrated because I don't think my ideas are as valued as another kid on the team. I am going to write this on the project reflection for today, but not really sure how I can make it better.

Developed by Jill Thompson of Charlotte-Mecklenburg Schools

Appendix C

Additional Resources for Chapters 5 and 6

SAMPLE OF DEVELOPING UNIT OR PROJECT IDEAS FROM AN INTERSECTION OF THEME AND TOPIC

Figure AC.1 represents a more detailed look at how to use themes and topics together to "open up" learning for students in a more personalized environment. This simple example is derived from program planning at the Futures Academy of International School of Beijing. It shows that a *theme* (in this case, change) can take on many forms when viewed through the lens of various *topics* (in this case, health, environment, economics, and community). The result is different contexts for exploring both the theme and the topics with a focus on appropriate disciplinary and cross-disciplinary outcomes. These contexts can become either units of study or projects. The framework also allows students to compare themes and topics as a way to target personalized learning opportunities.

DAY-IN-THE-LIFE EXAMPLES FOR MIDDLE SCHOOL AND HIGH SCHOOL

Here are two additional narratives to illustrate the process and environmental shifts described in chapter 5. These examples may be idealized or unrealistic right now given your conditions and resources, but they challenge you to see what could be, to craft

Figure AC.1 How to Use a Theme to Reimagine a Course or Unit

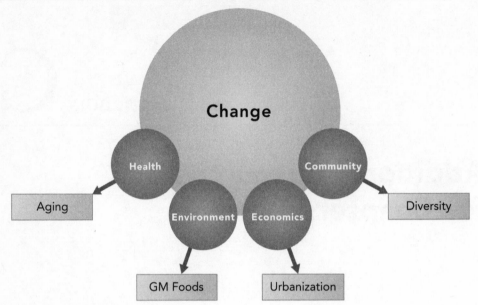

Developed by Greg Curtis

a collective personalized learning vision, and to pose questions about "how" rather than "why." Table AC.1 may be helpful to support the connections to the Personalized Learning Evolution.

Middle School Day-in-the-Life Narrative

Mateo and Kyle spoke together as they walked through the door of the school. "Man, I spent most of last night on science," said Mateo. "I was having a hard time with the cell structure stuff, so the system kept redirecting me back to things I missed. I got it in the end, but I'm glad I moved through the math simulations pretty quickly."

Kyle laughed. "I did that stuff the night before. I spent last night getting the draft of my opinion piece for the school's blog ready. Every time I thought I fixed something, the writing coach system kept finding something else … but I think it's good now." The two boys said hi to friends as they walked into their classroom.

"Now don't forget," said their teacher, Mr. Gwyn, above the noise, "you need to get stage 2 of your individual project plan ready to share with me before lunch."

"Stage 2? What's that one again?" asked Kyle.

Table AC.1   Decoding a Day-in-the-Life Example (Template)

Elements	
Disciplinary Outcomes	
Cross-Disciplinary Outcomes	
Feedback	
Environment	
Mindsets	*Relevance:* *Growth Mindset:* *Self-Efficacy:* *Sense of Belonging:*

"That's the learning plan part...how you're going to learn what you need to complete the project," answered Mateo.

"Oh, yeah. I think I know what I need to do."

"Just use the template and attach it to your project planner online." The students gradually took their seats as Mr. Gwyn asked for their attention.

"OK," he began. "Last night I finished going through your recent progress in the math, science, and English learning system. I can see that many of you have made some good progress, but many of you are also getting a little unbalanced as to where you are spending your time.

"The first thing I want you to do this morning is go into the system and get your progress summary for the past seven days. Then go to your goal setting page and compare where you've been spending your time with the goals you set for yourself a couple of months ago. Then I'd like you to enter a reflection around this sentence: 'Given the goals that I have set, I should spend more time doing X, Y, and Z in the adaptive learning system.' Obviously, I want you to contribute more than this, but this is your focus for this reflection. I'll give you twenty minutes for that, and I'll give feedback to you as your reflections come into my inbox."

After about twenty minutes, Mr. Gwyn said, "OK … I have sent you all an appointment request to take the next math challenge assessment in your list. Tonight, please try the practice scenarios for the assessment to see how prepared you are, and set a date this week to take your assessment. Now it's time to get together in your teams to work on your exhibition projects. You should check in with your project plan together and decide on your areas of focus for today."

There was a scraping of chairs as students rose to join their team members. Most of the small groups of three and four people gathered in a semicircle around a single tablet screen to look at their project planner to see where they were and what they needed to do next. Everyone was doing a project on something he or she thought was important to address in their town. Mateo's team had chosen the topic of public spaces in town and the difficulties in keeping them maintained and supervised in a time of budget cuts. They were proposing that residents would volunteer their time to maintain a few central spaces if the local government would maintain the equipment and pay for insurance. It would be presented to town council for approval.

"OK, where are we at?" asked Francesca, this week's team leader. "We only have two weeks until the exhibition at the town hall." They went through the list of contributions: Mateo had just about completed the blog with their research and proposal. He was ready to open that up to the public at any time. Ethan and Francesca had completed gathering data through the survey and were working on infographics to display the data. Ethan was good at the graphics, and Francesca was good with the data. Salena, always good with laying out a plan, was working on scenarios for cost-saving recommendations.

"Great," said Francesca. "Mateo, it looks like you can open up the blog with the survey. We need the survey numbers on how many people are in favor of this idea and a few good sample quotes. We need to combine this with what Ethan and I have … If we give you our stuff, can you do that? Remember, we're hoping to show support for the idea from different places. Salena, if you could get your stuff together by the end of the week, I could start getting things lined up for the presentation on the weekend. Ethan, maybe you could put the pamphlet together? That would give us a week to tune this up and practice for the exhibition. Sound good?"

Mateo said, "Yeah, great! I'll update the project plan with this stuff so that Mr. Gwyn can see the progress." After he finished this, Mateo finished up stage 2 of his learning plan for his individual project. He had already identified the things he needed to learn to complete the project and how he might learn them. He just needed to finish up the "Strengths" piece to identify how he was going to use strengths in his learning profile to effectively accomplish what needed to be done. He noted that his strength at sifting through information quickly and organizing it efficiently was something he really needed to use in order to learn all of the things he needed to learn for the project.

When Mateo met with Mr. Gwyn before lunch, Mr. Gwyn agreed with him that this was a reasonable learning plan and that his identification of the strength he would use was accurate. "Now," Mr. Gwyn said, "I want you to keep track of your use of this strength in your project blog. I'd like to see what learning approaches and skills you bring to that learning task. Just put everything down as you do it, and you can trim up the blog later. I'd like to know which strategies worked, which ones didn't, and what changes you made along the way. This will be a part of your evaluation on this project, as usual."

"Got it," said Mateo as he packed up for lunch.

After lunch, Mateo and his classmates broke up for their enrichments and options. Right now, he was enjoying his current selection of team sports and fitness, early engineering, music studio, and graphic design. He was able to take extra-long periods of two of the four on alternating days. This schedule gave him time to be more involved, get more done, and figure out if he wanted to pursue these areas further in the next semester.

As Mateo and Kyle left the school, they both laughed at things that had happened in their different afternoon experiences. They also shared what was on their to-do lists for the evening.

"I've got to check to see if I'm ready for my math assessment. I think I am 'cause all the practice I did on the weekend showed that I was really close. I've also got to do some research for my independent project and update my blog for that."

"Yeah," said Kyle. "Same for me with math, but I've got to run some more writing through the writing coach system. I keep having trouble with my sentences, but I think I've just about figured it out."

"All right. See you tomorrow," said Mateo.

High School Day-in-the-Life Narrative

Jing spent the first part of the morning at home working on her writing modules. She knew she had to get her research paper ready by the beginning of next week and wanted to finish her draft before she met with her writing coach. She liked to do this in the morning when she felt fresh. When Jing got to school, she met with her disciplinary standards advisor to go over her progress toward her diploma requirements. Jing was in the middle of grade 11 and had to map out how and when she would show that she had achieved the necessary standards for the diploma level she hoped to achieve.

"Come on in, Jing," said Mrs. Gonzales as she walked into the workroom. "So, where are we?"

"We were trying to see how I can design my capstone project to bring together standards from across different subject areas," said Jing.

"Right. We have to get your proposal ready by the end of the month. First, we need to see what we can tie together for your capstone and then we can start planning for how you might demonstrate other standards through smaller projects or stand-alone assignments. Remember, if we can bring things together from different subject areas, you can account for a number of standards and make your capstone stronger."

Jing said, "I started looking at standards based on our last meeting. Since my capstone is about the importance of 'play' in the twenty-first century, I've been able to look across the standards and choose some obvious ones. See, I have a bunch I think might work from science, social sciences, history, and psychology." They looked over Jing's list and talked about how she might demonstrate mastery of the standards in her project and broke some of these down into smaller areas of skills and knowledge to make a stronger connection with her capstone focus.

"These look pretty good, and I'm sure we can come up with more connections as we move along," said Mrs. Gonzales. "These will help with the research and theory behind your work. How about the design and action component?"

"I thought I could design a play-based program for Alzheimer's patients at the home down the road to help stimulate them and maybe even slow down the loss of brain function," said Jing. She went on to explain to Mrs. Gonzales how she hoped she could propose a program to the home's administration and make it into a service project for kids at her school.

"That's great," Mrs. Gonzales said, smiling. "Let's just make sure you also do this in a way that demonstrates achievement based on the disciplinary and growth outcomes."

Jing replied, "I was thinking for metacognition of doing a research trail where I can show how what I discovered through my research influenced my thinking and my design for the action piece. For problem solving, I have my problem already with the degenerative brain disease. And, for critical thinking … " Jing went on to list the ways in which she would use these skills and how she would also develop them through the long capstone project. She and Mrs. Gonzales put these ideas into the system as part of their proposal log.

"Well, Jing, I think you're getting pretty close. We'll just need to fine-tune this a bit to present it to a sponsor at the home and a capstone advisor here at the school. In the meantime, I suggest you research some other standards you might be able to bring into your project. I think there would be some good stuff you could do in statistics and science to plan a way for the home to test whether your program is achieving what you hope it will. I'll send you some starting points for this."

"That would be great, thanks," said Jing. "I'll be so happy to get this part done."

"Yes, the planning and alignment with the standards is always the hard part. Now, remember," said Mrs. Gonzales, "once this is done, we can look at the other standards you'll need to demonstrate for your diploma. Then we can look at smaller projects, individual and group, that can incorporate these, or stand-alone pieces for the ones we need to deal with that way. Then we'll have your plan for next year pretty much figured out, OK?"

"Yup, got it. I'll see you in a couple of days and show you what other standards I've found that might help with the big project," Jing said as she gathered her things.

Jing made her way to the science center. She had worked last night to prepare for one of her independent labs, and she felt that she was ready to do the lab. She went to the kiosk in the middle of the science center and asked to check out the materials for her lab. The lab technician asked her to review the procedures and safety elements of the lab and scanned the lab kit out for her.

Jing went to an open station and proceeded with the lab. She decided that she wanted to run through the experiment twice to make sure that the probes were logging the data properly. When she was done, she downloaded the data, went to the work area, and completed her lab through the online tool. When she was done, she submitted the lab, heaved a big sigh, and got up to leave. She liked the science labs because she could choose much of what she did, and the lab assistants always got her performance marks back to her quickly.

After a quick lunch with her friends, Jing met with her writing coach. They reviewed her progress in the "Writing Machine." Her coach talked to her about some of the mistakes that had been common in her early drafts and how she had corrected these. They also spoke about the sequencing of her paper and the flow from opening paragraph through to concluding paragraph. Jing decided to move a couple of pieces around to make things fit together properly. Her coach asked her to send him her next draft after she had made some changes and said that they would meet again in a few days.

Jing had some time to go to the Learning Center to check in on her MOOC. She was taking a course in media design from a college on the East Coast. It really helped her with her work placement at the advertising agency. There were also people in the course from all over the world, and she often got to work with them in smaller groups. She checked in with her group in their project space. They were doing a cool project on cultural icons in a globalized world. There were people in her group from three different countries; they got to share their cultural images and were trying to mash these up to show cultural fusion. It was pretty cool, and it counted toward the collaboration portion of her diploma.

Toward the end of the day, Jing met with her group to work on their engineering project. This was a math-science project, and she was in the math subgroup. The project itself wasn't hard (a materials and construction focus), but the math behind it was. She and her two math partners were working through some of the data, and Jing struggled a bit with the data tables, probabilities, and so on. One of her partners, Max, said, "I had a really tough time with that too. But there was a simulation module online that really helped me out. I'll send you the link … It's on the blended learning site."

"Thanks, that would help me out. I have to know how to explain this stuff better," Jing laughed.

Before she left to join her dance group, Jing logged her day's sessions for her advisor and tuned up her work schedule for the night.

- Probability module
- Math simulation for tomorrow's assessment
- Remix my research paper a bit
- Check in with my MOOC

Then she put aside her tablet and books and got ready to dance.

STUDENT-DRIVEN PROJECT MODEL

This last illustrative example highlights how a high school in New Zealand described four principles and related questions to generate student ideas. Table AC.2 inspires students to think about what difference they want to make in the world and how to grow the project.

Table AC.2 The Four Principles of Impact Projects at Albany Senior High School

	STUDENT OWNERSHIP AND AGENCY *Student ownership leads your project, how is it your interest/ passion?*	SUBSTANTIAL LEARNING BEYOND THE CLASSROOM *Why is this worth learning to you? What new learning is there for you?*	A QUALITY PRODUCT *How is it amazing?*	PARTICIPATING AND CONTRIBUTING WITH THE COMMUNITY *How can you grow your project to impact beyond you as an individual?*
Possible Questions	• How does this link to the "ideas generation" that you completed with your tutor? • So what are each of you particularly interested in with this project? • What appeals to you about the project? • What do you expect of the other members of the group? • How will you take the passion beyond yourself? • What is it about X that interests you? • What makes this a good idea to investigate further? • So far, what is in this project that will keep you interested and learning across the whole semester?	• How can you build upon the learning you have done in the relevant specialist subject(s)? • Who outside the school might have expertise in this field? • Who else in the school might be able to support you with this project? • How will the skills you are learning help you once the project is complete? • What might the different skills be that you need [to] make your product quality? • What types of skills do you want to develop? • How will you seek feedback to further develop and refine your ideas on what learning there is in this project? • What are you learning about yourself or projects or working with people etc. that will be useful later and how do you think it might be useful?	• What are the deliverables you are working on today? • How do these (deliverables) help you get quality at the end? • How will you decide who in your group is the best person for each deliverable? • How are you researching what will make your product the most effective/best quality? • What similar products that others have made could you look at? What can you learn from their experience? • What other solutions (products) can you think of that might solve your original question/problem? • What is the purpose of making X? • What are the key steps you have identified to make your product? • What will be particularly amazing about it?	• Who might be/is interested in your product? • Who outside your group might your product help or be used by? • Which people outside of school working in this field have you communicated with? • In what ways is your project relevant to your life/society? • What connections can you make to people or organizations outside of school? • How is this an extension of your day-to-day life? • How can you make an approach to … (relevant business, company, person)? • Who is going to help you progress your project? Why will they be able to help? Is there anyone else who could help? • Are there other skills apart from X that you will need an expert to help you with?

(continued)

Table AC.2 (*continued*)

	STUDENT OWNERSHIP AND AGENCY *Student ownership leads your project, how is it your interest/ passion?*	SUBSTANTIAL LEARNING BEYOND THE CLASSROOM *Why is this worth learning to you? What new learning is there for you?*	A QUALITY PRODUCT *How is it amazing?*	PARTICIPATING AND CONTRIBUTING WITH THE COMMUNITY *How can you grow your project to impact beyond you as an individual?*
Possible Questions		• How do we know it is time to stop and reflect on the learning in relation to our original idea? And, who can we talk to for feedback on this? • How do your ideas/work/learning so far support you to produce your final product? • In what areas do you need to extend your understanding? • What processes do you need to learn more about?	• From the feedback provided, what will you do to improve your final outcome? • How have your success criteria changed as your project has progressed? • Do you think you have developed your ideas of what quality looks like enough to revisit and change your success criteria? • How do we know it is time to stop and reflect on the product in relation to our original idea? • And, who can we talk to for feedback on this?	• What feedback has your stakeholder(s) (mentors and experts etc.) given you so far and how have you acted on it? • What feedback on your product so far has been useful and in what way has it been useful feedback? • What can you do to make sure communication with your stakeholder(s) works really well?

Used with permission from Albany Senior High School Auckland, New Zealand

Appendix D

Additional Resources
for Chapter 7

The Personalized Learning Vision-to-Action Plan deliberately resembles the student planning tool but is geared toward the personalized learning model. Table AD.1 is a blank template for your use. Table AD.2 is an illustrative example of how balanced literacy can be used as part of an elementary school personalized learning model.

Table AD.1 Personalized Learning Vision-to-Action Plan

OUTCOMES *What is your vision for personalized learning?*		
Design • How will we design a personalized learning pathway toward academic and growth outcomes? • How will we know if our design is viable?	**Implement** • How will we ensure quality control? • How does the plan evolve over time?	**Institutionalize** • How will we ensure sustainability?

INDICATORS *What is evidence of success at each stage?*

PATHWAYS TO ACTION
WHAT: What actions will we take? What is the optimal sequence?
WHO: Who should be involved, in what role/capacity? How will we build ownership?
WHEN: How much time is needed? When will this occur? What timing is optimal?

INDICATORS *Connection to Evidence of Success (listed above)*	WHAT *Task and Resources Needed*	WHO *Key Partners*	WHEN *Timeline*

Table AD.1 *(continued)*

CULTURE AND MINDSET
In what ways will current values, beliefs, and behaviors support attainment of our vision?
In what ways will current values, beliefs, and behaviors challenge attainment of our vision? What changes may be needed?

CHALLENGES AND OPPORTUNITIES		
What are potential challenges? Immediate? Long term?		
Personnel	Job descriptions (What's my job?)	
	Staff development	
	Staff appraisal	
Financial	Priority budgeting	
	Support (e.g., substitute, stipends, instructional coaches)	
	Incentives (e.g., conference attendance, iPads)	
Structures	Schedule for students	
	Schedule for staff	
	Grading and reporting	
External Factors	State/national accountability tests	
	College tests (SAT, AP, ACT)	
	Graduation requirements	
	GPA/college admissions	

Cocreated by Allison Zmuda and Jay McTighe

Table AD.2 Sample Personalized Learning Vision-to-Action Plan

OUTCOMES *What is your vision for personalized learning?*		
We want to create a balanced-literacy personalized learning environment. The goal is to create students who *want* to read and want to *think* about their reading by themselves and with others.		
Design • How will we design a personalized learning pathway toward academic and growth outcomes? • How will we know if our design is viable?	**Implement** • How will we ensure quality control? • How does the plan evolve over time?	**Institutionalize** • How will we ensure sustainability?
• Draft essential components of a balanced literacy program based on research and best practice • Create a "toolkit" for each component: a place where teachers can find playlists, tools, strategies, and prompts • Create "look-fors" in teacher-friendly language as a self-reflection and peer feedback tool • Create student self-reflection tools to monitor progress as a reader and a writer • Create personalized learning task frames based on a student-driven problem, challenge, or idea • Develop a structure for student-led conferences/conferring	• Test-drive "look-fors" and revise language to make it clear • Hold team meetings to analyze student work and determine additional (or revised) resources for the toolkit • Submit PD requests based on specific problems or challenges • Hold student-led conferences/confer on progress as a reader (both strengths and weaknesses) and identify next steps	• Feature student work via multimedia publications, rotating hallway displays, classroom visits, and digital portfolios

Table AD.2 *(continued)*

INDICATORS
What is evidence of success?

- Every toolkit resource has been both vetted on a rubric and "teacher tested."
- Featured student work demonstrates key components of balanced literacy.
- Student drafts demonstrate how they used the design process to guide them through a problem, challenge, or idea.
- Teachers analyze their own balanced literacy practice (self and peer) by using "look-fors."
- Student-led conferences are developmentally appropriate, but regardless of age or skill level, the student owns the experience.
- All PD requests on balanced literacy from teams are followed up on—the teachers' needs are used to design and deliver quality content.

PATHWAYS TO ACTION
WHAT: What actions will we take? What is the optimal sequence?
WHO: Who should be involved, in what role/capacity? How will we build ownership?
WHEN: How much time is needed? When will this occur? What timing is optimal?

INDICATORS *Connection to Evidence of Success*	WHAT *Task and Resources Needed*	WHO *Key Partners*	WHEN *Timeline*
Every toolkit resource has been both vetted on a rubric and "teacher tested."	Create a rubric	Literacy team Learning and teaching literacy specialist	By the opening of school 2015
	Test-drive each resource	Teachers (more than one)	First quarter (end of October) As needed based on continued development

CULTURE AND MINDSET
In what ways will current values, beliefs, and behaviors support attainment of our vision?
In what ways will current values, beliefs, and behaviors challenge attainment of our vision? What changes may be needed?

- Some educators believe that students need to learn one reading comprehension strategy at a time.
- Some educators believe that spelling and vocabulary/word study should be a stand-alone set of activities and assessments.
- Some educators believe that writer's workshop is too cumbersome to use regularly.
- Some educators separate out "reading" from "writing"—both in terms of time blocks as well as genre or structure.

Cocreated by Allison Zmuda with Charlotte-Mecklenburg Schools

Index

Page numbers followed by *f* or *t* refer to figures and tables, respectively.

A

Access technologies, 121, 122*t*
Adaptive technologies, 122, 123*t*, 124
Advancement (Element 12), 18*t*, 145, 145*t*, 146
Advisor, teacher as, 20
Aguilar, Elena, 64–65
A la carte model, 11
Albany Senior High School (Auckland, New Zealand), 136, 200, 201*t*–202*t*
Arizona, 168
Art installations, 88
ASCD, 8
A+ Schools, 166
Asia Society, 90
Asperger's syndrome, 44
Assessment(s):
    of cross-disciplinary outcomes, 24–25
    of mindset outcomes, 24–25
    summative, 133, 136
Assessor, teacher as, 20
At-risk students, 13
Audience (Element 5), 16*t*, 63–67, 63*t*
Aveson Charter School (California), 113–115, 120, 153, 155
Avon Public Schools (Avon, Connecticut), 27–28

B

Balcony thinking, 150
Bean, Kate, 153, 155
Beijing, China, 43
Belonging, sense of, *see* Sense of belonging
Berger, Ron, 29, 53, 65
Bill of rights, student's, 55
Blended learning, 11–12
Bolton, England, 64
Boss, Suzie, 64
Brain Pop, 122*t*
Briceño, Eduardo, 47
Brick, Peyton, 84
British Columbia, 29, 165–166
Business operations, 88
"Butterfly Story," 184, 186

C

California, 113–115, 120, 133, 153, 155
CCSSO, 8
Center for Collaborative Education, 138
Change, management of, 155–158, 159*t*–160*t*
Charlotte-Mecklenburg Schools (North Carolina), 61
Chicago, Illinois, 47
Children, personalized learning and growth of, 7

China, 43

Clarke, John, 37, 66, 137

Classroom facilitator, teacher as, 20

Clayton Christensen Institute for Disruptive Education, 11

Coach, teacher as, 20

Coalition of Essential Schools, 8

Collaboration, 32*t*, 41–43, 169*t*

Colorado, 34, 112

Common Sense Media, 35

Communication (as cross-disciplinary outcome), 32*t*, 39–41, 169*t*

Communicator, teacher as, 20

Concerns-Based Adoption Model, 154

Connecticut Association of Public School Superintendents, 20

Connector, teacher as, 20

Consortium for Public Education in Pittsburgh, 84

Consortium on the Chicago Schools (University of Chicago), 47

Contemporary literacies, 6

Content, in Instructional Core, 157

Content standards, 25

Control of learning experience, 12–15, 12*f*, 14*f*

Cornally, Shawn, 63, 64

Costa, Art, 32

Council of Chief State School Officers, 31

Creative Problem Solving, 61–62

Creative thinking, 32*t*, 33–35, 169*t*

Critical thinking, 32*t*, 35–37, 169*t*

Cross-Disciplinary Outcomes (Element 2), 16*t*, 30–46, 30*t*

    acquisition of, 24

    aims of, vs. disciplinary aims, 24–25

    assessment of, 24–25

    collaboration, 41–43

    communication, 39–41

    creative thinking, 33–35

    critical thinking, 35–37

    demonstration of, 24

    development of, 24

    disciplinary outcomes vs., 23

    illustrative examples of, 32*t*

    with LearningBoard, 141

    metacognition, 43–46

    problem solving, 37–39

    recommendations, 46

    resources, 168–179

Csikszentmihalyi, Mihalyi, 51, 60

Culture, school, 154

Curriculum, standards vs., 25

Curriculum planner, teacher as, 20

Cushman, Kathleen, 47, 49, 50, 54

Customized learning experiences, 6

D

Dalton Plan, 7–8

Dalton School, 8

Daniel, David, 14

Darling-Hammond, Linda, 44

Day-in-the-life narratives, 193–200

    high school, 197–200

    middle school, 194–197

Deci, E. L., 60, 69

Demonstration of Learning (Element 10), 18*t*, 132, 132*t*, 133, 136–143

    authentic assessment tasks, 134*t*–135*t*

    with LearningBoard, 140–141, 142*t*

    recommendations, 142–143

Denver Montessori School, 34

Dewey, John, 7

Digital portfolios, 136–137

Disciplinary Outcomes (Element 1), 16*t*, 25–30, 25*t*

    cross-disciplinary outcomes vs., 23

    for English Language Learners, 28

    with LearningBoard, 141

    for mathematics, 27

    recommendations, 30

    resources, 166–168

    for science, 28

Dopamine, 50–51

d.school (Stanford University), 86

Duckworth, Eleanor, 60

Dweck, Carol, 49

E

Educational equity, 9

Education Commission of the States, 146

Education Leadership, 8
Education on the Dalton Plan (Parkhurst), 7–8
EduTect, 140
eMAPS, 84
Enabling Innovation: Transforming Curriculum and Assessment (British Columbia Ministry of Education), 29
England, 64
English Language Learners, Disciplinary Outcomes for, 28
Enriched virtual model, 11
Environment (Element 9), 17*t*, 119–122, 119*t*, 124
    and access technologies, 122*t*
    and adaptive technologies, 123*t*
    and facilitative technologies, 123*t*
    narrative example, 124, 125*t*, 126–128
ePALS projects, 95
Equity, educational, 9
"Ethic of excellence," 29
An Ethic of Excellence (Berger), 29
Evaluation (Element 7), 17*t*, 70–72, 70*t*
Exhibitions, 136–137

F

Facebook, 66, 170
Facilitative technologies, 121, 122, 123*t*
Feedback (Element 6), 17*t*, 67–70, 68*t*
Ferlazzo, Larry, 81
First impressions, 81
Fisher, Michael, 181, 184
Five Levers to Improve Student Learning (Frontier and Rickabaugh), 19
Fixed mindset, 49, 50*t*
Flex model, 11
Florida, Richard, 30–31
"Flow," 51
Ford, Henry, 34
Freelancing, 31
Frontier, Tony, 19
Fullan, Michael, 32, 73

G

Games for Change, 97–98
Gateways, 136–137

Gerjoy, Herbert, 31
Girls on the Run, 84
Global literacy, and task design, 90, 91*t*–94*t*, 92, 94–95, 96*t*–98*t*
Glossary of Education Reform, 166
Gloyd, Jesse, 113–114
"Golden Circle," 150, 151*f*
Goodenow, C., 53
Growth mindset, 48*t*, 49, 50*t*, 152

H

Hampshire College, 65
Harms, Bryan, 45
Harvard Graduate School of Education, 156
Harvard University, 39–40
Hattie, John, 67, 68
Heathfield Community Primary School (Bolton, England), 64
Heifetz, Ronald, 149, 150, 155–156
Henry County Public Schools (Virginia), 168
Henry Street School for International Studies, 55
Hernandez, Andrea, 66, 67
High school day-in-the-life narrative, 197–200
High Tech High School, 45, 137
Houston, Scott, 181
HydroPod, 94

I

Illinois, 47
Independent Project, 13
India, 95
Instructional Core, 156, 156*f*, 157
Instructional level, personalized learning at, 109–129
    Environment (Element 9), 119–122, 119*t*, 122*t*–123*t*, 124, 125*t*, 126–128
    Process (Element 8), 110–117, 110*t*, 112*t*, 114*t*, 117*f*, 118*f*, 119
Instructional Rounds in Education (City et al.), 158
International Baccalaureate Diploma Program, 137–138
International School (Beijing, China), 43

International Studies School Network (Asia Society), 90

Interviews, 88

J

Jacobs, Heidi Hayes, 6

Jobs, Steve, 34

Jones, Makeba, 7

Jordan, 95

Journal of Emerging Investigators, 39–40, 75

Joyce, Bruce, 153

K

Kallick, Bena, 32

Katy Independent School District (Texas), 168

Khan Academy, 12, 122*t*, 139

Knewton, 123*t*

L

Labor market, 30–31

Lake Havasu Public Schools (Arizona), 168

Langworthy, M., 73

Laurie, Donald, 149

Leading the New Literacies (Jacobs), 6

Learn4Life, 27

Learn4Life Charter Schools (California), 133

Learning:
 blended, 11–12
 reconceptualizing, 6

LearningBoard, 140–141, 142*t*

Learning experience, control over, 12–15, 12*f*, 14*f*

Learning management systems (LMSs), 139, 140, 155

Learning outcomes, personalized learning and attainment of, 7

Learning process, ownership of, 6

Levin, Sam, 13

Linsky, M., 150, 155–156

Literacies, contemporary, 6

Liu, M., 23

Local challenges, and task design, 86, 87*t*, 88, 89*t*–90*t*

Local enterprises, 88

Local experts, seeking out, 66

Long-term transfer goals, 26

M

Macedonia, 95

Maine Department of Education, 142, 145

March, Tom, 60, 67

Massive open online courses (MOOCs), 12

Mathematics, Disciplinary Outcomes for, 27–28

McClure, Larry, 7

McCusker, Shawn, 110

McTighe, Jay, 26, 151

Metacognition, 32*t*, 43–46, 169*t*

Meyer, Dan, 13

Middle school day-in-the-life narrative, 194–197

Miller, Mark, 65

MindMeister, 123*t*

Mindset (Dweck), 49

Mindsets (Element 3), 16*t*, 23, 47–55, 47*t*–48*t*
 acquisition of, 24
 aims of, vs. disciplinary aims, 24–25
 assessment of, 24–25
 demonstration of, 24
 development of, 24
 and giving back the work to teachers, 152
 growth mindset, 49, 50*t*
 recommendations, 54–55
 relevance, 47, 49
 resources, 179–180
 self-efficacy, 50–51, 52*t*, 53
 sense of belonging, 53

Mindset Works, 47, 83–84

MindShift (blog), 110

Mitchell, David, 64

Montessori, Maria, 7

Montessori schools, 8, 34

MOOCs (massive open online courses), 12

The Motivation Equation (Cushman), 49

Moulton, Jim, 66

Mt. Abraham High School (Vermont), 66

MY HERO, 96

N

Narrative, 40, 124, 125*t*, 126–128
 high school day-in-the-life narrative, 197–200

middle school day-in-the-life narrative, 194–197
National Academy of Engineering, 90
National SAFE KIDS Campaign, 38
New Hampshire State Department of Education, 138, 146
Newport News, Virginia, 28
Newport News School Division (Virginia), 171
New York State, 168
New Zealand, 136, 200, 201t–202t
Northgate High School, 41

O

Obstacles, 6
100 People Foundation, 94–95
Oneida-Herkimer-Madison Board of Cooperative Educational Services (New York), 168
One-sentence project, 81
"One-size-fits-all schooling," end of, 163–164
One Young World Summit, 40
Online learning model, 11
Osborne, Alex, 61
"'Our' Curriculum vs. 'Their' Curriculum" (Richardson), 13
Owning the learning process, 6

P

PACE (Performance Assessment for Competency Education), 138
Parker, Clay, 31
Parkhurst, Helen, 7–8, 14
Parnes, Sydney, 61
Pederson, S., 23
Pennsylvania, 37, 40–41, 84
Performance Assessment for Competency Education (PACE), 138
Personalized Learning (Clarke), 37
Personalized learning (PL):
    articulating and creating urgency for, 150–152
    and attainment of learning outcomes, 7
    and children's growth, 7
    definitions of, 7, 165–166
    differentiation vs., 9, 11, 11t
    and giving back the work to teachers, 152–155
    historical roots of, 7–8
    individualization vs., 9, 10t
    and managing change as it occurs, 155–158, 159t–160t
    power of, 1–2
    recent popularization of, 8–9
Personalized Learning: Student-Designed Pathways to High School Graduation (Clarke), 137
Personalized Learning Evolution, 15–20, 16t–18t. *See also individual elements*
Personalized Learning Foundation, 165
Personalized Learning Plan platform, 139–140
Personalized Vision-to-Action Plan, 203, 204f–207f
Phi Delta Kappan, 133
Philadelphia, Pennsylvania, 37
Physics, 187–188
Pink, Dan, 81
Pirsig, Robert M., 60
Pittsburgh, Pennsylvania, 40–41, 84
PL, *see* Personalized learning
Problem solving, 32t, 37–39, 169t
Process (Element 8), 17t, 110–117, 110t, 112t, 114t, 117f, 118f, 119
Prosper Independent School District (Texas), 167
Public Education Leadership Project (Harvard Graduate School of Education), 156

R

Reilly, Erin, 34
Relevance, 47, 48t, 49, 152
Remix Culture (Reilly), 34
Remixing, 34–35
Richardson, Will, 13, 131
Rickabaugh, James, 19
Riley, Benjamin, 13
Rosin, Carl, 35
Rousseau, Jean-Jacques, 7
Ryan, R. M., 60, 69

S

School culture, 154
Schoology, 140

Science, Disciplinary Outcomes for, 28
ScootPad, 123*t*
Self-efficacy, 48*t*, 50–51, 52*t*, 53, 152
Seligman, Martin, 60
Senge, Peter, 163
Sense of belonging, 48*t*, 53, 152
    and task design, 76, 79, 80*t*–83*t*, 81, 83–84,
      85*t*–86*t*
Service projects, 88
Showers, Beverly, 153
Siemens, 92
Sinek, Simon, 150, 151
Six-word memoir, 76, 79
Sizer, Thodore, 8
Skyline High School (Michigan), 92
SMART goals, 51, 52*t*, 53, 54
Smart Sparrow, 123*t*
Social media, 41, 67, 93*t*, 135*t*
"Social-Psychological Interventions in
    Education" (Yeager and Walton), 47
Social studies, 167–168
Software & Information Industry Association, 8
South Korea, 95
Special education, 167
Stafford, Shauna, 115
Stakeholders, engagement of, 152
Standards, content, 25
Stanford University, 86
Starbucks, 36
Stories, 152
Strauss, Valerie, 13
Student(s):
    changing role of, in task design, 103–104,
      105*t*–106*t*
    role of, in Instructional Core, 157
Student-driven model, power of, 7–12
Student's bill of rights, 55
Summative assessments, 133, 136
Summit Public Schools, 139, 140
Surveys, 91*t*, 170, 190*t*–191*t*, 196
Svitack, Adora, 1
Systems level, personalized learning at, 131–147
    Advancement (Element 12), 18*t*, 145, 145*t*,
      146

Demonstration of Learning (Element 10), 18*t*,
    132, 132*t*, 133, 134*t*–135*t*, 136–143, 142*t*
Time (Element 11), 18*t*, 143, 143*t*, 144

T

Task (Element 4), 16*t*, 60–63. *See also* Task
    design(s)
    design process, 61*f*
    recommendations, 60*t*, 62–63
Task design(s), 75–108
    changing role of student in, 103–104,
      105*t*–106*t*
    changing role of teacher in, 95, 98, 99*t*–102*t*,
      102–103
    and going global, 90, 91*t*–94*t*, 92, 94–95,
      96*t*–98*t*
    and going local, 86, 87*t*, 88, 89*t*–90*t*
    and going personal, 76, 79, 80*t*–83*t*, 81,
      83–84, 85*t*–86*t*
    process of, 61*f*
    transdisciplinary tasks, 104, 106–107
Task frames, 181
    illustrative examples for generating,
      183*t*–186*t*, 184, 186–187
    template for, 182*t*
Teacher(s):
    changing role of, in task design, 95, 98,
      99*t*–102*t*, 102–103
    personalized learning and giving back the
      work to, 152–155
    role of, in Instructional Core, 156, 157
"Teaching to What Students Have in Common"
    (Willingham), 13–14
Technology(-ies):
    and blended learning, 12
    leveraging of, 9
Texas, 167, 168
This I Believe, 81, 83
ThunderRidge High School (Colorado), 112
Time (Element 11), 18*t*, 143, 143*t*, 144
Timperley, Helen, 67, 68
Traditional classroom walls, breaking down, 6
Traditional school model, disconnect of, with
    today's world, 6
Transdisciplinary tasks, 104, 106–107

Trello, 123*t*
Twitter, 170

U

Ullman, Diane, 20
US Consumer Product Safety Commission, 38
US Department of Education, 146
University of Chicago Consortium on the
    Chicago Schools, 47

V

Virginia, 28, 168, 171
Vision-to-Action Plan, 158, 159*t*–160*t*
    Personalized learning, 203, 204*f*–207*f*
Vision-to-Action Project Planner, 188, 189*f*–191*f*
Visual and performing arts, 167

W

Wagner, Tony, 31, 32
Walton, Gregory, 47
Washington Post, 13

Wesley College (Australia), 42
Why School? (Richardson), 131
Wiggins, Grant, 25, 26, 67, 69–70, 133, 151
Wiley, Brandon, 90
Wiliam, Dylan, 69
Willingham, Daniel, 13–14
Willis, Judy, 50–51, 54
WordPress, 123*t*
World Digital Library, 122*t*
Wright, Paul, 35
WriteItNow, 123*t*

Y

Yeager, David, 47
Yonezawa, Susan, 7
Young, Ethan, 131

Z

Zambia, 34
Zmuda, Allison, 27, 67, 84, 155, 171, 188
Zmuda, Zoe, 84